Open the Gates!

EHUD AVRIEL

Open the Gates!

*A Personal Story of
'Illegal' Immigration to
Israel*

Preface by Golda Meir

Atheneum *New York*
1975

Preface

SOMEHOW, a full generation after the fact, it is still easy to remember those awesome ten years before the establishment of the State of Israel, but it is far more difficult to recapture the atmosphere of those times in words. It is easy enough to say that those were terrible times, but that is neither an effective description nor an accurate statement about the full picture of that decade. For the cliché that hard times bring out both the worst and the best in people was never truer for the Jewish people than during the most tragic and brutal experience of its long and difficult history: the Nazi Holocaust.

We did not yet have a state of our own then, and there were no formal institutions – no army, no diplomatic corps, no treasury (and only very meagre funds). Yet the overpowering sense of responsibility to one's brethren was never felt more keenly by the Jews of Palestine than in the years when our small and all but penniless community witnessed the Jewish people facing one of the most powerful and vicious enemies of all time and finding itself without an ally in the world. After the conference at Evian-les-Bains, when it became chillingly clear that the Jewish people were entirely 'on their own', the necessity to take the initiative and scoff at all the odds in the struggle to save the Jews of Europe became a password in Palestine.

It was out of this sense of 'If I am not for myself, who will be for me?' that the Mossad was born. And the men and women (many of whom were still boys and girls) who joined its ranks to save as many as they could did so not out of a sense of adventurism, not as a way to prove their 'manhood' in a world where others went off to war and they were not allowed to join in the fight. While many clung to the security of their homes and found preoccupations to distract their thoughts from the grim truth about events in Europe, these young people volunteered to risk their lives in order to preserve their personal sense of integrity, so that when it would all be over they could live with themselves and honestly say to themselves 'I truly did everything I could.' Integrity is bought at a high price, and there were many dangers involved, many frustrations and disappointments, many fears. But the longer the war went on and the more we learned about the black events inside Europe, the stronger became the need to do one's share – small as it might be compared to the scope of the tragedy – to counteract the power of the Nazi demon. This is why the Mossad grew; and this sense of unswerving dedication, oblivious to such considerations as 'odds' and personal danger, is why it succeeded.

When the war ended, when Jewish lives were no longer threatened with annihilation, the Mossad continued to operate and grow not because of the rules of inertia, but because the opportunity to fulfil its ultimate task was finally at hand. From 1945 to 1948 (when the State of Israel was established and its gates were opened to unlimited immigration), the Mossad continued to display the same determination that had characterized it during the war, and it exploited every device, every trick of wit, every possible channel to defy the British blockade against Jewish immigration to Palestine and bring the Jews out of the wreck of Europe to their own land. On the surface, their escapades are the stuff of a dramatic adventure story – a fact which has not escaped some writers. But those who see the story of the Mossad's activities only in terms of 'exploits' and 'escapades' miss the heart of the matter. For after the war the Mossad became one branch of an integrated struggle to create a Jewish State – not for its own sake, but as a framework in which the Jewish people could be rebuilt and flourish.

Survival was no longer sufficient as an aim. The struggle now was not for Jewish lives, but for Jewish souls – for the entire personality of the Jewish people in the decades and centuries to come. It may have been a more subtle goal than snatching innocent people from the jaws of death, but from the moment the war ended it became the sole preoccupation of the entire Jewish community of Palestine. Together with the military struggle of the Haganah, the Palmach, the Palyam and other organizations, the efforts of those who travelled abroad to acquire arms and the funds to buy them, the diplomatic activities in all the major capitals of the world and at the newly formed United Nations, the task of bringing the Jews of Europe to the place they claimed as home was a function of the fight to establish the Jewish State. Perhaps there was an element of adventure in it, but if so it was part of a much larger drama that was essentially an adventure of the spirit. This is what the story of the Mossad is really about, and this is why it deserves to be told. And Ehud Avriel, who was one of this group, and participated in so many of its actions, can tell the story as one of those who created the Mossad.

Ramat Aviv GOLDA MEIR
October 1974

Foreword

THIS BOOK IS NOT intended as the definitive history of the exploits of the Mossad. It is a personal memoir of one who was privileged to participate in the rescue work organized by the Haganah underground during ten crucial years. As such, it can at best offer a fragmentary account of the mammoth disaster that befell Europe's Jews as a consequence of Hitler's ascendancy and the constricted but dogged efforts to save the doomed. I have not aspired to academic objectivity or to a comprehensive analysis of the historical background on which the Mossad functioned. Rather, I have attempted to present candid insights into the clandestine operations of an organism that earned the respect and begrudging praise of at least two of its most cunning adversaries as 'one of the finest [underground organizations] in the field', and I have tried to be equally frank about the limitations of our capabilities. During the ten years covered in this work, the Jewish people – perhaps more than ever before – were opposed by powerful hostile forces. We of the Mossad worked to the absolute limits of our capabilities under adverse conditions in order to save as many lives as possible and to minimize both superfluous risks and hardships for those who had already undergone a cataclysmic trauma.

Our work was, by its very nature, teamwork, and there were very few exceptions to the requirement of anonymity and self-effacement of the members of the team. The Mossad was a large unit of fighting men and women whose basic tenet was the vow our forefathers took in the desert of Sinai when Moses presented the Ten Commandments to them: 'We shall act first and question thereafter.'

In the course of my research prior to the writing of this book, I read most of what has been published about the Mossad and talked to many of my former colleagues. If I have overlooked anyone or have omitted details deemed of primary importance to those directly involved, I can only explain that my intention has been to present an account of the work in which I participated personally or was able to observe from close quarters. In many cases, while renewing delightful friendships with old comrades in the course of gathering material for this book, I also found that memory can play strange tricks. Responsibility for the result of my research is, naturally, wholly and entirely my own; and I apologise to all those who, for one reason or another, do not find themselves reflected in these pages as they remember their story.

I wish to express my profound gratitude to my colleagues and to all those who gave of their time and their generous aid in various ways: the Archives of the Zionist Organization in Jerusalem; the Archives of Mezudat Ze'ev in Tel Aviv; the patient gentleman in a Foreign Office department in London, where I was allowed to delve into classified material only recently made accessible to the public; the Institute for the Study of Zionism at Tel Aviv University; the Institute of Contemporary Jewry at the Hebrew University of Jerusalem; the Archives of the Haganah in Tel Aviv and many others. My family and my kibbutz know how grateful I am to them not only for making it possible for me to write this book but for enabling me to participate in the activities described therein.

My final tribute is reserved for Helga Dudman, who with the strength of her admirable personality helped me turn disjointed episodes into what I believe has become a coherent account and who encouraged me untiringly, to the last word of this book, whenever I was on the point of abandoning the task of describing what I have lived through and beheld with my inner eye. Without Miss Dudman, this book would never have been.

E.A.

Neot Mordechai
Hagalil Ha'elyon

Contents

PART THREE: THE SEINE

PART ONE

THE DANUBE

(I)

Recruitment

IT WAS MEANT TO BE a glorious day. On a spring morning early in April 1938, my turn came to be called up for service in the German Army. It was barely a month since the annexation of Austria by Nazi Germany, on 13 March, and the integration of Austria's armed forces into the German Army had not yet reached the stage whereby Jews were weeded out of the lists of eligible recruits (this came soon afterwards). I turned in from the sunny street and walked up the wide stone stairs of the medieval building which looked like a monastery but served as a recruiting office. In the hall upstairs I found a group of boys my age – I was six months short of twenty-one – including several friends from high school.

For the first time since the Germans entered Austria, I felt like a citizen again. In that early period of Nazi domination, the relationship between Aryans and 'sub-humans' was not yet strictly regulated. In the leveling atmosphere of the huge recruiting hall, even the picture of Hitler on the wall which had replaced the former Austrian emblem of sovereignty, did not affect the *camaraderie* among boys facing, as it appeared during that brief moment, the same destiny.

The banter stopped as soon as the sergeant entered. We listened attentively as he read out the list of those who had passed their medical tests and had been accepted for military service. As each name was called out, a young man stepped forward and crossed to the far side of the hall. When my name was called, I, too, joined the 'lucky ones'. But now the moment arrived for the question which would bring me back to reality.

'Since I am a Jew, sir,' I asked, 'what is my status in the army?'

Embarrassed silence and some uneasy stirrings followed. Suddenly we had become two camps. They – all of them – and I. Uncomfortable in his new German uniform, the sergeant shifted the list from one hand to the other and took out a handkerchief to wipe his neck.

'The army has found you fit for service physically. As to your ideological fitness, the Party and the State will decide.'

Then we all walked down the stairs and back out into the sunshine. My momentary feeling of being a regular citizen had vanished. The greatness of the day belonged to the Aryan members of my class. Gone, too, was my chance for military training before I joined a kibbutz in Palestine and entered the ranks of the Haganah (the underground defence organization in Palestine), whose policy was to encourage Jews in Europe to join the armies of their native countries in order to acquire military experience.

Outside on the busy street we were immediately surrounded by a cluster of young girls in dirndls, the traditional Austrian peasant dress. It was an old custom that girls waited to greet new recruits and, for luck, pinned on the lapel of each boy's coat a bunch of clover-leaves with the inscription 'Hooray! They took me on!' Then they would go off with the proud, fresh soldiers for a celebration of beer and kisses.

I walked away in the opposite direction, towards Marc Aurel Strasse and the office of the Zionist youth organization in which I had been working as a volunteer for three years.

In quieter times we had functioned in smaller premises; now, with conditions suddenly so changed, the Palestine Office and all other local Zionist organizations had moved to this busy neighbourhood in the First District of Vienna, a section of large office buildings and warehouses. It was a short walk through crowded streets I had always known. But the distance between the army recruiting station in the medieval hall and our offices in Marc Aurel Strasse was a distance that separated two worlds; and on the same morning that I was, in effect, rejected by the German Army, I was to meet the man who enlisted me in a diametrically opposed service.

The pressures building up in Europe during that spring were, as usual, determined by government leaders, and the effects of their decisions – and frequently of their miscalculations – were to destroy the lives of millions of individuals in the next few years and to re-shape the experiences of many millions more. In my case – and I was extremely lucky – the tasks that were to absorb my friends and myself were in direct response to what was happening in distant and unknown corridors of power. And as it happened, we were even sometimes to approach and enter those corridors.

I was lucky for many other reasons as well. One of them was the fact that as a young man I became a member of a group engaged in active attempts to rescue the victims of what was about to happen. The events in the history books filtered down to shape the nature of our work, and newspaper headlines and government documents became – at the operative level of a long chain of circumstances – the raw material of telephone conversations and meetings in cafés or offices.

Our resources against those headlines were pathetically limited, and others sometimes felt that our aim was hopeless. But the fact was that we decided not to become simply the pawns of history. The first firm guidance from Palestine toward this aim became real for me when I reached our office that day.

That spring, when I was twenty, I was in many ways a

typical product of a pleasant, middle-class Viennese home. My father was the head of an import-export firm, and both my parents were liberal, tolerant people who valued stability and comfort. The atmosphere in which they and their friends moved – at least until a year or so before 1938 – had been one of optimism and security: the future seemed safe, children and careers assured. The comfortable house in which I was born and grew up was a model of Austrian cosiness. I remember the long summer afternoons when my parents' friends – lawyers, engineers, doctors, officers who served with my father in the First World War – gathered in our large garden under the trees to discuss music, the theatre and the topics of the Viennese times. My father, an unusually good linguist, knew Turkish well. He had been an interpreter in the Austrian Army and was present when the Turks surrendered to the British in 1918. He was fond of reading the Koran in Turkish and telling us stories from it – as well as episodes from the lives of Talleyrand, Metternich and the Medici. Our library was a key to the whole world of European culture: Goethe was a favourite of my father's, as was Rabelais, and we had a wide collections of books in French, which I learned as a child.

Yet perhaps the strongest early memory I have is one that evoked a distant land I had never seen but had heard about ever since I could remember – an unknown place which, even as a child, I knew would one day be my home. This was the pungent scent of the *etrog,* the yellow citrus fruit used by Jews to celebrate the autumn harvest holiday of Sukkot. Each year there was an *etrog* in our home near the Vienna woods. It was often brought by one of the students from Palestine who taught Hebrew to my older sister, younger brother and me, and occasionally lived at our house. That scent, a sweet and mysterious mixture of jasmine and lemon, was a powerful and lasting evocation of somewhere else: a place in the Middle East, completely strange, yet completely a part of me.

I have always been grateful to my parents for the courage, long before the Nazi threat, to raise their children to know that their real home was elsewhere. My mother for many years directed a Hebrew school in Vienna, and our house was a centre for Palestinian students. My parents were not religious in any orthodox sense, yet they were not trying to assimilate and be 'more Austrian than the Austrians'. They were not 'organized Zionists', whom they regarded as given to speech-making and travelling to and from Palestine while not necessarily planning to live there; but my parents always knew that we would indeed go to Palestine one day.

Couched in this attitude towards Palestine as the Jewish National Home, it was natural that at the age of nine I joined the Zionist youth organization Blau-Weiss (Tchelet-Lavan in Hebrew), named after the colours of the Zionist flag (now the flag of Israel). As I grew older I gave more and more of my time to the movement, eventually becoming a youth leader and volunteer at the central office. Tchelet-Lavan was the largest Zionist youth organization in Vienna and was linked to Palestine's dominant Labour Party. It was moderate socialist and democratic in outlook. In Vienna we added a rather bourgeois flavour and occasionally cooperated with the local non-Jewish trade-union movements.

Ideologically to the left of our group was Hashomer Hatzair ('The Young Watchman'), whose Palestinian counterpart incorporated the more radical socialist movement. To our right came the General Zionists, which was divided into two wings, again reflecting the political situation in Palestine. Further still to the right were the Revisionists, committed to nationalism and activism at all costs and opposed to any level of cooperation with the Arabs of Palestine until the British (who held a Mandate over Palestine) had been driven out. In addition to these groups were the religious parties of varying degrees of orthodoxy.

The framework for cooperation between the various youth movements of these parties was Hehalutz ('The Pioneer'), a roof organization of those movements affiliated with the Histadrut (National Federation of Labour) in Palestine. In Vienna, these included Tchelet-Lavan, Hashomer Hatzair, one branch of the General Zionists and one of the religious groups.

Yet for all this wealth of parties, those Jews of Vienna who were actually affiliated in any active sense were an infinitesimal one-half of one per cent of the city's total Jewish population. Before the *Anschluss* the situation was perhaps only faintly ridiculous: an impressive number of organizations were fighting for the souls of, say, the six Jewish children in my school. Later, as we moved into the period of terror and the fight to save human lives, this pattern of conflict sometimes resulted in tragedies. Had we been able to surmount our differences and cooperate, our pitifully meagre resources might have accomplished more. It seems to be a recurring tragedy of history that revolutionary movements are beset by internecine splits and conflicts and that the most dedicated of fighters spend their limited resources in opposing alignments among their own comrades, rather than in coming to a workable agreement against the common enemy.

When I finished high school in 1936, my parents wanted me to enter the university and study classical languages, a subject in which I had shown interest and ability in high school. I, on the other hand, wanted to study something 'useful', to prepare myself for life on the kibbutz in Palestine, for I believed that the Jews must be a nation like any other nation, that we must establish, in our own land, a new and free way of life in which we would be not only businessmen and intellectuals, but farmers and craftsmen. I wanted to spend the time while waiting for my immigration certificate either learning a manual skill or, better yet, joining a group of other young people undergoing agricultural training in Austria or receiving military training in the Austrian Army.

Before I decided definitely on which course to pursue – for

we still believed that the future was entirely in our own hands – my father suggested that I take a trip to England, where he had friends, to see the world, to learn about new people and different ideas and to get to know London – at that time still the undisputed capital of the world. This was a normal course for a young man from a comfortable family, even though 1936 was a year in which the political events anticipated the future: the Spanish Civil War began; German troops occupied the demilitarized Rhineland; Japan and Germany entered into the 'Anti-Comintern' pact; Hitler signed a treaty with Austria and promised to recognize the Austrian frontier.

After having spent the first few days in London with my parents' British friends, I discovered Palestinian emissaries who, in turn, were interested in a newcomer from the Zionist youth movement in Austria who spoke Hebrew and was at a turning-point in his life. After the civil unrest of 1934 and the fascist take-over, Austria was much on the minds of Zionist-Socialists from Palestine. The specifically Austrian brand of anti-Semitism – competing with that of Hitler, who had taken power in Germany just eighteen months before – worried the people in Palestine. Austria was the birth-place of Herzl's Zionist Organization, a centre of Jewish learning and traditions and a democracy that had for years staunchly defended the rights of its Jewish minority against repeated attacks. It was a bridge between Palestine and Eastern Europe, for the Jewish community there was less assimilated than those in most Western countries. The loss of Austria to Fascism would endanger the Jewish community and sever an important and long-standing link between the Palestine Zionist Labour movement and like-minded comrades in the Austrian socialist movement. Their cosmopolitan view of the parochial affairs of the relatively small community in Vienna, in terms beyond the immediate importance of the Jewish community of Austria, was completely new and fascinating to me. So, too, was my first personal contact with leaders from Palestine in the fortress of Britain, where the diplomatic battles for the Jewish National Home were fought.

Shortly after my arrival on what was supposed to be my 'grand tour', I was introduced to Shaul Avigur, one of the leaders of the Haganah. Laconic, drab and humourless in expression, stern and penetrating in manner, Shaul interrogated me closely about every aspect of Jewish life under Dollfuss' Christian-Social Fascism, the civil unrest, the reliability of the Zionist movement and the urgency of emigration from Vienna in face of rising anti-Semitism. I was astonished by the degree of intimate knowledge that the commanders of the Haganah had about our life in remote Vienna. As I described every stage of our work and our attempt to broaden the base of the movement in Austria, it all became more significant and universally important to me, for I realized that we were not isolated, but part of the world-wide effort.

My involvement was deepened when I met Berl Katznelson, who, together with David Ben Gurion, was considered the spiritual father of Zionist activism and of the Palestinian Labour movement. The soul of kindness and humility, Katznelson earnestly fixed his warm eyes on mine as he listened to my accounts, and the feeling that he was deeply interested in every thought prompted me to eloquence.

If I had briefly considered going to the university rather than continuing in the Zionist youth movement, I now abandoned such thoughts under the spell of these meetings with the central figures of the real pioneering movement. Now more than ever, I knew that our work was of significance for the Jewish people as a whole; that we were not alone but part of a great effort. We had a real chance to establish our own identity in Palestine through the physical labour of Jews dedicated to the community rather than their own individual interests, and every trifling activity in the framework of

Hehalutz was part of a force encompassing the entire Jewish world.

On my return to Vienna from London, my parents realized that I was more determined than ever to be an active Zionist. This was, after all, the direct result of the education they had given their children. So they readily accepted my decision to prepare myself for pioneering in Palestine and found me a job as an apprentice in a large carpentry shop owned by friends. At the same time, I attended lectures in classical languages and political science at the University of Vienna and worked after hours at the Zionist office.

Nineteen thirty-seven was a year in which the Zionist movement was engaged in a deep crisis brought about by the proposals of the Royal Commission under Lord Peel. The commission had proposed the partition of Palestine as a lasting solution to the hostility that had existed between Arabs and Jews ever since Britain had become the mandatory trustee of Palestine on behalf of the League of Nations in 1921.

Immediately after assuming responsibility for the government of Palestine, the British proceeded to partition the country for the first time. In search of a throne for Britain's staunchest ally in the First World War, Winston Churchill, then Colonial Secretary, established the Emirate of Transjordan (today the Hashemite Kingdom of Jordan). The Zionist leadership had been given to understand that the Balfour Declaration, which provided for a 'Jewish National Home', would henceforth be implemented in western Palestine. But no sooner had Transjordan been created than extremist leaders among the Palestinian Arabs began to clamour for the destruction of the Jewish National Home.

During the 1920s and early 1930s, the Arab-Jewish conflict within Palestine intensified. By 1937 a majority of Zionist leaders, Chaim Weizmann and Ben Gurion foremost among them, were ready to accept the partition proposal of the Peel

Commission in the hope that concessions on the part of the Jews – although the portion of Palestine adjudicated to them did not include many historically significant sites – would finally induce the Arabs to a conciliatory line. Time would heal the wounds inflicted by the new partition, its supporters argued. Coexistence between Jews and Arabs would gradually become possible; no strict delineation would persist between a small Jewish state with a considerable Arab minority and an adjacent small Arab state with a sizable Jewish minority. Sooner or later, the two entities would form some sort of federation. These supporters of partition in 1937 – four years after Hitler's declaration of war on the Jews – had a further consideration in mind. They believed that sovereignty over even a small area was preferable to the existing state of affairs, for it was the only way to save Jews from certain doom. A Jewish government would decide on immigration according to its own considerations, instead of having to fight with hostile Arabs and Britons for certificates. Furthermore, they would have a chance to participate in the war against Hitler that was clearly becoming inevitable.

The Jewish Agency for Palestine was the publicly acknowledged spokesman of the Jewish people regarding Palestine. The main subject of negotiations between the Jewish Agency and the British was immigration certificates. Twice yearly, certificates were scheduled for distribution through the Palestine Offices of the Jewish Agency in every major European city. The number of certificates was a constant issue of disagreement, and the outcome of the haggling between the two sides was an indication of the trend that British policy was taking towards Zionism.

In 1931, the year before Hitler assumed power, the Jewish Agency received a total quota of 4,074 certificates. In 1935, the year in which the Nuremberg race-laws were enacted by the Nazis, the British allotted 61,854 certificates, an all-time high. But there were never enough certificates for all the Jews demanding entry into Palestine, not only from Nazi Germany but also from the Jewish communities in Poland and Rumania, countries which had known anti-Semitism long before it became the official policy of the German Reich. After the record year of 1935, however, the number of certificates decreased, while the need for them was desperately on the rise.

The Nazis occupied Vienna on 13 March 1938, and, as the Germans entered, members of the illegal local Nazi movement proudly displayed their hidden armbands. Most Austrians rejoiced in the 'liberation' of their little rumpland by the powerful neighbour who, to their infinite pride, was led by a genius of Austrian descent. Less than one month after the *Anschluss,* a plebiscite was held. The result was a vote of 99.75 per cent in favour of the 'union' with Germany, though this was far from a free election. Entire groups of socialist underground workers had brought out their red flags and 'reconsecrated' them to German Socialism – which was National Socialism. The fascist predecessors of the Nazis in Austria, who had held power in their dark grey uniforms for four years, had an even less complicated metamorphosis to go through in order to become brown. The joy in the streets, the celebration of the 'Homecoming into the Greater Reich', the new slogan 'One People, One Country, One *Fuehrer'* resounded everywhere from merry lips. A number of Christians and faithful socialists, and all Jews without exception, found themselves excluded from the hilarious mood. Later, this period became known as the 'Rape of Austria', and much was made of Austria having been the first victim of Hitler's expansion. To a large extent, she was a willing victim.

From the outset it was evident that the process of extruding the Jews in Austria was going to be infinitely faster and even more cruel than in Germany itself. The Gestapo arrived with the invading army and their newly established headquarters included a Central Department for Jewish Affairs. Jews were almost the only ones in the early days of the 'Rape of Austria' who did not brandish the Nazi Party emblem on their lapels. Jewish men, and especially women, were arrested in the streets and, under the scornful laughter of the Viennese, were forced to wash away the slogans painted during the desperate few weeks while Austria's fate lay in the balance. Jewish shops were broken into and plundered by the mob while Jews specially apprehended for the purpose stood in front (guarded by SA men, armed to the teeth) holding signs saying 'Aryans, don't buy at the Jews'.' When dusk fell the emptied shops were abandoned by the looters. The SA then would collect the Jews who had been posted before the shops in one street, force them into a procession surrounded by Viennese of all ages and, while their Austrian neighbours shrieked and spat into the Jews' faces, led them down the road into some dark alleyway where the Austrians were allowed to beat them viciously. Jews were evicted from their flats by their own landlords or by jealous neighbours. Jewish students were turned out of their schools. The prisons became full of innocent people jailed simply because they were Jews. Many other 'subtle' hints were given to the 220,000 Austrian Jews that their time was up, that it *had* happened here, that German pedantry had joined up with Austrian malice to make their life unbearable.

Austria's Jewish community was unprepared for its fate. Each year before the *Anschluss* a few Jews had emigrated to Palestine. A few dozen youngsters, members of Zionist youth movements, had left the towns and gone to farms especially established to train them in agriculture in preparation for their lives in Palestine. But hardly any native Viennese Jews left. My elder sister, for example, was the first of our family to go to Palestine. In 1937 she left Vienna to marry the son of a Jerusalem writer who had several times been a guest at our house. The plan was that as soon as she married she would apply for immigration permits for my parents and brother, as was permitted under the family reunion clause. (I was instructed by Hehalutz to remain in Vienna and continue working for our cause.) But procedures did not move quickly enough, and my parents were still in Vienna when the Nazis took over. They, at least, had foreseen this event; though, as it happened, when they did leave for Palestine soon after, they did so together with the 'optimists' – those who had never believed the catastrophe could occur but who now, too, were refugees.

The sudden breakdown of Jewish life in Vienna propelled the existing Jewish institutions into positions of great importance, for all were suddenly overrun by endless numbers of people who overnight had lost all security – and in many cases also all their property. Turned down by one foreign consulate after the other, they realized that no country would take them in. This is how the Palestine Office became the focal point in the search for emigration possibilities and the local branch of the Jewish Agency for Palestine. But Palestine was a British Mandate, the Jewish Agency operated on sufferance of the British, and the local offices had no official legal standing in matters of visas, emigration and diplomatic representation. At most, the Palestine Office could recommend candidates for immigration to the local British Consul who then had to apply to the Mandate authorities in Jerusalem for approval of each case. Each request for an immigration visa was checked against the current schedule of immigration certificates issued semi-annually by the mandatory government on the basis of decisions handed down by the Colonial Office in London. On the day Hitler took over Austria, there was a total of sixteen immigration certificates at the disposal of the entire Austrian Jewish community.

As an immediate response to this situation the Palestine Office and the Zionist Organization tried to obtain transit arrangements in other countries. Jewish organizations, com-

munities and charitable associations, as well as influential individuals, were approached in European and Latin American
countries with a view towards obtaining temporary residence
for Austrian refugees. In this way a few hundred places
for agricultural workers were found in England, Holland and
Denmark. These three countries were most helpful, but of
course there were two very serious drawbacks: limited numbers (hundreds in view of the desperate needs of tens of
thousands) and restrictions as to age and physical condition.
The beneficiaries, in almost all cases, had to be young and
ready to do hard – and unfamiliar – work. Nonetheless
'Agricultural Training Abroad' became a channel of salvation for many who could not obtain regular visas to Palestine
or elsewhere.

This, then, was the general situation when I arrived at our
building in Marc Aurel Strasse after the episode at the recruiting office. Just across the street from our new office
another organization had recently moved: the Gestapo had
requisitioned the Hotel Metropol. Here, a stone's throw from
our building, was the dreaded Department for Jewish Affairs,
under a certain Herr Kuchmann, which dealt with exactly the
same matters we did – but from a diametrically opposed
position.

I passed the Hotel Metropol and worked my way through
the entrance of our building, where, as always, crowds of
Jews were milling about, waiting their turn for interviews
about chances for emigration. Just then a horse-drawn fiacre
drew up in front of the building – an unusual vehicle at that
time of day and in these unromantic surroundings. The man
who alighted from it seemed familiar to me, though I had
never seen him before in my life. He looked under forty,
sturdy, with a shock of blond hair and sadly smiling grey
eyes. He wore an open shirt under his brown raincoat. As he,
too, made his way through the crowd, I turned to ask him
who he was.

'I am Moshe Agami,' he said to me in Hebrew, 'from Palestine.'

We had been expecting our new chief, and now he was here. From then on we would have the leadership so desperately needed in our desolate situation. The scene in the recruiting office now disappeared far into the past. My meeting with Agami was in a sense the act of my recruitment into a network of operations whose far-flung implications I could not possibly have imagined on that sunny day in the tragic spring of 1938.

(2)

The Baths of Evian

BARELY TEN DAYS after the first German troops had marched into Austria, a rumour spread through the Jewish community of Vienna: President Roosevelt, the champion of human rights, the leader of the country of 'unlimited possibilities', had called together an international conference on the fate of Hitler's Jewish victims. People who had spoken to relatives abroad claimed they had heard that an announcement had been made. Viennese Jews who knew foreign correspondents whispered to their friends that something tremendous was going to happen soon. For a few days it seemed there might be a real remedy for our terrible predicament and that everything was going to end well.

In actual fact, President Roosevelt had called a press conference at Warm Springs, Georgia, on 22 March 1938 and had launched 'a bold plan of action': he invited the governments of thirty-three states to join in an effort to aid the emigration of political refugees from Germany and Austria. These governments included twenty Latin American republics, Great Britain, France, Italy, Belgium, Switzerland, Norway, the Netherlands, Denmark, Canada, New Zealand,

Australia and South Africa. The American invitation to the conference specified that no country 'would be expected or asked to receive a greater number of immigrants than is permitted by existing legislation'. But it called upon the freedom-loving nations to work together to solve the tragic problem.

This point was specifically stressed by the President. America was, traditionally, a haven for the politically oppressed of all nations. But, he assured his listeners, the proposed conference would not result in an increase or revision of United States immigration quotas. It would be up to private groups, rather than the United States Government, to finance any movement of refugees. Replying to a question, the President said that the Jews would not be 'the only beneficiaries of American generosity'.

The immediate reaction of the American public to their President's announcement was one of delighted exuberance. Church bodies, women's organizations and civic groups announced their readiness to help with generous offers of funds, assistance and encouragement. The Federal Council of Churches of Christ 'hailed with appreciation the United States proposal'. Jewish organizations, naturally, announced their fervent support and their deep gratitude. Even the American Federation of Labor – not always in favour of new jobseekers entering the country – responded warmly. William Green, its president, stressed, however, that the United States should admit no more than the number of immigrants provided by law because of the competition for jobs.

None of these details were known to us in Vienna at the time. Dr Alois Rothenberg, the head of the Palestine Office, received a telegram from the Jewish Agency Executive in Jerusalem stating the bare facts of President Roosevelt's announcement. He called the representatives of the various Zionist organizations in Vienna to his office so that they would be able to respond to the growing volume of optimism based on rumours of an impending conference that was to heal all our ills.

'Whatever may result from this messianic conference, it is important that we do not let ourselves be swept away by facile optimism,' said Willi Ritter, General Secretary of Hehalutz in Vienna. 'We must continue to work as if there was no announcement from Roosevelt. Personally I doubt whether the results will in any way correspond to the wild expectations the public holds with regard to this conference.'

One of the older, more mature and more refined Zionists present murmured something about the constant pessimism of the younger generation. President Roosevelt ought to be given a chance to show that he meant what he had announced. We agreed that the American President must be given a chance, but the meeting broke up with the feeling that we could not permit ourselves to be seduced by rosy hopes. We had to work harder than ever to save people, rather than passively waiting for results of the great international meeting.

The Division of European Affairs in the American State Department analysed the motives for the proposed conference with detachment. The *Anschluss,* said its memorandum, had brought about a public outcry for greater State Department action in favour of refugees. Outstanding journalists – notably Dorothy Thompson – as well as certain Congressmen with metropolitan constituencies were the principal sources of these pressures on the administration. The Secretary of State, Cordell Hull, had decided that it was opportune for the State Department 'to get out in front and attempt to guide the pressure, primarily with a view toward forestalling attempts to have the immigration laws liberalized'.

The Undersecretary of State, Sumner Welles, had devised the idea of an international conference. He believed that the very announcement of a conference, the preparations for it, and the commotion created by contacts between the many

governments involved would in themselves act as an indication of the American Government's stand and perhaps influence the Nazis. The President, acquainted with his Secretary's
thinking, approved of the idea.

The German response to Roosevelt's proposal came at
once. In a speech delivered in Königsberg at the beginning of
April, Hitler said: 'I can only hope and expect that the other
world, which has such deep sympathy for these criminals,
will at least be generous enough to convert this sympathy
into practical aid. We, on our part, are ready to put all these
criminals at the disposal of these countries, for all I care,
even on luxury ships.' 'The criminals' drew hope from this
speech. There could be no doubt; the 'other world' was to
convert its sympathy into practical aid. And Hitler had promised to let us go – never mind the hateful wording of his
statement.

The need for any kind of encouragement grew from day to
day. The brutality of the Nazis increased and took forms that
had never been experienced before, even in Germany. Jews
were indiscriminately arrested in the streets, crammed into
jails and, when no more cells were available, transported to
newly established concentration camps. Families rarely received word of their relatives' whereabouts. Some disappeared
never to return. Others were released as suddenly as they had
been arrested. But before they were allowed to leave jail,
they were sternly warned that they had to leave Austria at
once. If they were apprehended again, they would be sent to
Dachau, or to one of the newer concentration camps, to
perish.

According to a *London Times* report from Vienna two
weeks before President Roosevelt's conference opened, thousands stood outside the consulates of the United States,
Great Britain and other countries waiting through the night
to register their names. The report continued, 'the segrega-
tion of Jewish from "Aryan" children is complete in ele-

mentary schools. Even the youngest are not spared. Infants of the kindergarten can no longer play in public parks, and on the doors of their schools is painted the slogan "Cursed be the Jew." '

In the middle of May, France approved Evian-les-Bains as the site of the conference on refugees. Located around a casino and famous for its health-inducing waters, Evian was a luxurious resort frequented by the wealthy. The Hotel Royal was rented by the organizers of the conference. It would provide comfortable accommodation for the representatives of thirty-two nations who had agreed to come. Only fascist Italy, Germany's ally, had declined. South Africa sent an observer.

One people had not been invited to attend the conference at all: the Jews. It was mainly their fate that was to be discussed, but having no government of their own, they could not be invited to send a representative, like the sovereign nations. The Jewish Agency was the widely recognized spokesman of the Jewish nation. On matters pertaining to Palestine, it was even acknowledged under the terms of the League of Nations Mandate for Palestine. American Jewish leaders, therefore, worked behind the scenes to obtain an invitation to the conference for Dr Chaim Weizmann, President of the World Zionist Organization and of the Jewish Agency for Palestine. They could not imagine that President Roosevelt, who had himself called the conference, would deny their spokesman the opportunity to present the case of the persecuted to the plenary that was convening to decide on ways to relieve their hopeless misery.

The chief American negotiator at the Evian Conference, Myron Taylor, met in secret with the British representative, Sir Michael Palairet. Realizing the strong British opposition to Dr Weizmann's appearance before the conference, Taylor suggested a compromise: Weizmann would be allowed to address the conference on immigration to Palestine only at a private meeting of the Evian gathering. Sir Michael turned down this strange compromise as well. Palestine had received more refugees than any other single country, but the Palestine issue was highly controversial. The conference, he said, could not be burdened with 'what was primarily a political issue'.

The two major powers therefore agreed that the one practical offer – that of the Jews of Palestine to take in unlimited numbers of their fellow Jews – should not even be presented to the conference. The Jewish Agency had not expected much from the preliminaries to a conference that it regarded as an abortive exercise in evasive diplomacy. But an international gathering of so many well-meaning countries could not be allowed to pass without any attention from the Zionist camp. As often before, refuge was taken in an effective subterfuge: where the Jewish Agency as such could not or would not appear under its own name, the Histadrut (the Palestinian Jewish Federation of Labour) would step in unofficially.

This is how two representatives of the Histadrut appeared in the glittering surroundings of the world-famous health resort. Secretly, they were both members of the Haganah. Dov Hos was the head of the Political Department of the Histadrut and an experienced diplomat and negotiator. He had established sensitive contacts with many labour leaders in various countries and with men of influence in all walks of life. (He died in a motor car accident before the establishment of the State of Israel.) With him came a young woman who had made a name for herself in the labour movement as an ardent advocate of the cause of Palestine's Jews. She had grown up in America, where she had been a teacher, and came to Palestine intending to live in a kibbutz. But the labour movement soon discovered her talents for leadership and the poignancy of her courageous style. Evian was her first encounter with the world's experienced diplomats and skilled negotiators. There Golda Meyerson (later Prime Minister Meir) made her *début* on the international political stage that was to remain her home from then on.

To the agitated surprise of the gentlemen who had planned the Evian Conference, another, quite different, group of people arrived at the health resort. They, too, had not been invited by the conveners of the conference. Unlike the participating governments, they did not represent a 'freedom-loving nation', the prerequisite for the invitation sent out by the American Chief of State. They looked like an army detachment in mufti, rather than a diplomatic delegation of experts. They were, in fact, observers from Nazi Germany. The conveners of the conference, hushed by this unexpected development, made the natural decision not to pass judgement on the status of their uninvited guests. The German observers took their seats and followed every word that was said in the plenary sessions, doing all they could 'to obtain a clear picture of the goings on behind the scenes'.

The conference opened officially on 6 July 1938. The first two days were devoted to a debate that had nothing at all to do with the fate of the Nazi victims who were anxiously looking to Evian: the three main powers – the United States, Britain and France – discussed which one should chair the conference. Each country insisted on honouring the other with this eminent position. Finally, since the United States had initiated the meeting, its representative was chosen.

What had been announced five months earlier as one of the great humanitarian acts of our time had been played down during the period of preparations to such an extent that the *New York Times* informed its keenly interested readership of the actual beginning of the long-awaited gathering only on page 13, and devoted less than half a column to the story. On the front page of that day's issue of the *New York Times,* however, there did appear a full-length column reporting in great detail the opening of an art exhibition in Munich by the *Fuehrer.*

As the conference proceeded, one country after another rose to make known its contribution to the refugee problem. The pronouncements were not heartening. Australia announced that 'since we have no racial problem, we are not desirous of importing one.' New Zealand saw no way of lifting existing restrictions. Great Britain informed the conference that the British Colonial Empire contained no territory suitable for the large-scale settlement of Jewish refugees. Their fate was duly deplored. Mention of Palestine was carefully omitted.

Some countries took an ostensibly positive stand: they declared that they would take in agricultural immigrants, but no others. Farmers were few and far between among the persecuted Jews of Nazi Germany. Certain other countries spelt out their reservations in more clearly negative terms: Peru was sternly opposed to the immigration of doctors and lawyers, whose admission would mean the creation of an intellectual proletariat that might upset the power of the ruling class in that country. The Peruvian delegate cited the 'wisdom and caution' shown by the United States as a 'shining example that guided the immigration policies of [his] own government'. A few other Latin American countries erected still higher barriers: they excluded not only intellectuals but also 'traders' from those eligible for admission.

Argentina and France were among those who proudly reported how many lives they had already saved and indicated that they seriously could not be expected to do more than some of the larger countries. Denmark and Holland gave expression to their traditional humanism. Holland had already accommodated nearly 30,000 refugees; the Dutch delegate nevertheless declared that his country was willing to accept more temporary residents. Denmark was so overpopulated that there was a constant trickle of emigration of Danes. Nevertheless, its delegate declared in clear and simple terms that his country would continue to receive refugees.

One miracle, however, stood out from all other statements

made by the participating countries: the Republic of Santo Domingo declared that it was willing to open its gates to 100,000 refugees. For a brief moment it seemed that this offer would present the conference with a challenge. But Santo Domingo remained alone. The only other practical result was that the American delegation announced that it was ready, for the first time, to accept its full legal quota of 27,370 refugees annually from Germany and Austria.

During the conference it dawned on many delegates that behind the grave problem of approximately half a million Jews already under Hitler's terror there loomed a far larger problem of four million Polish Jews under the anti-Semitic 'Government of the Colonels'. At this point the conference 'developed an unfriendly atmosphere of evasions and rationalizations'.

The many delegates and representatives of refugee organizations irritated the conference ('their conference') even further by asking to be heard individually by the plenary session. Each organization was convinced that it could best present the case and gain the most by speaking on its own behalf. These unwelcome presentations were all scheduled for one afternoon. The time allotted to each individual statement was ten minutes. As the depressing depositions droned on and on, a ruling was made that cut the time for each *exposé* to five minutes.

It is quite probable that the delegates from the different countries rationalized that the civilized world must constitute a united front of abhorrence and disgust towards the Nazis' treatment of the Jewish minority – and other minorities – inside the Third Reich. The free countries did not believe then that it was possible to absorb the Jews of Germany if the Nazis unilaterally decided to get rid of them all. Some conference tacticians might have thought that it was responsible, realistic and diplomatically shrewd to confront the Nazis with a limited absorption capacity for their prospective victims. They may have hoped that such an attitude would deter the Nazis from further expulsions. Other – not less naïve – beliefs were held at that time by the leaders of the world on issues no less fatal for mankind.

We in Vienna interpreted the decisions of Evian differently. On the last day of the conference, when a resolution was passed stating that 'the countries of asylum are not willing to undertake any obligation towards financing involuntary emigration,' we understood simply that our hopes had been in vain. The 'freedom-loving countries' were not going to accept us destitute and deprived – which was how the Nazis were willing to give us to them.

On the day after the Evian Conference ended, Golda Meyerson met with the press in the ornate private dining-room of the Hotel Royal. The *Basler National Zeitung* reported how a lonely woman sat opposite a large number of inquisitive journalists, parrying their questions with ease. When she was asked what was on her mind now that the conference was over, Israel's future Prime Minister replied: 'There is one ideal I have in my mind; one thing I want to see before I die – that my people should not need expressions of sympathy any more.'

The Nazi Government also informed the world of its evaluation of Evian. The Party declared that 'Evian had revealed the danger which World Jewry constitutes.' Propaganda Minister Goebbels' press – wholly controlled by his ministry, and the organ of official policy – was more eloquent: 'We see that one likes to pity the Jews as long as one can use this pity for wicked agitation against Germany, but that no state is prepared to fight the "cultural disgrace of Central Europe" by accepting a few thousand Jews. Thus the Evian Conference served to justify Germany's policy towards the Jews.'

The one country that felt it did not have enough Jews was Palestine. But for Jews to enter, British permission was required, and in spite of the radical deterioration of the situation in Germany, the British were adamant. A new pretext was added to the long list of excuses for the limitation of entry permits: war was imminent, and if there were mass immigration from Germany there was no guarantee that the Nazis would not infiltrate secret agents into the Middle East disguised as rescued Jews.

While the British procrastinated, illegal immigrants were arriving secretly in small ships. The break-away New Zionist Organization (the Revisionists), refusing to submit to the discipline of the Jewish Agency, organized illegal immigration at a time when the official Zionist bodies were strongly opposed to such operations. The official Zionist movement was convinced that illegal ships could never bring huge numbers of immigrants, and the clandestine character of the operation meant smaller numbers than even the most pessimistic forecasts for legal British entry permits. Furthermore, the British were subtracting a number of certificates from the agreed schedule on the assumption that illegal immigrants had arrived during any given period. Consequently, there was no net gain in the number of arrivals. An additional consideration was that the central position held by the Zionist organization among Diaspora Jewry and its hegemony over the Jewish community in Palestine would be seriously threatened if its one symbol of power – the coveted immigration certificate – should slip from its firm grip.

This policy was to undergo a gradual change during the months to come when it became clear to the leaders of the Jewish Agency that the only force in the entire world against whom the British remained forceful and unrelenting was the Jews of Palestine.

(3)

Agami Takes Over

FROM THE DAY Agami took charge of operations at the Palestine Office on Marc Aurel Strasse, we felt an all-round tightening of our activities: now we had a firm link with Palestine. Our work was a chaotic attempt, against overwhelming odds, to get Jews out of the Greater Reich. In pre-war Germany these operations were neither legal nor secret: the Gestapo office directly across the street from our own knew exactly where we were and what we were doing; the illegality began only at the shores of Palestine with the British blockade. But in Vienna, as elsewhere throughout Europe, our resources in manpower and money were a pathetic drop in a churning ocean.

Agami, who was born in Latvia and had gone to live in Palestine in 1926, was a hardened kibbutznik from the place in northern Galilee where Joseph Trumpeldor, a hero of the early labour movement in Palestine, had died defending his fledgling commune against an overwhelming number of Arabs. As such, Agami seemed to us, having grown up among the boulevards and cafés of Vienna, even more legendary than other emissaries from Palestine. 'The Wild Man from the Syrian Border' was the term we sometimes

used for him, yet his composure and powers of analysis were
remarkable. He taught us to be tough and purposeful; not to
waste time, money, or material; to think in terms of hard
facts and never of optimistic dreams; and above all, never to
rest.

Agami was one of a number of Haganah men already
operating in key spots throughout Europe on the mission of
rescuing Jews. Other Haganah men in Europe were Dani
Shind, Yulik Braginski and Zvi Yehieli. I was soon to meet
them all and, in the process, to become a kind of 'Man
Friday' to Agami.

By background and temperament, the men who made up
the personnel of our local Palestine Office were completely
different. Willi Ritter, the General Secretary of Hehalutz, was
a bespectacled intellectual with a keen, analytical mind. The
nerve-centre of our activities, the office from which our
network of training farms was directed, was run by Mirco
Rudich, a short, stocky agronomist and engineer who was all
energy and tireless good humour. In the placid days before
Hitler's rise to power, Rudich had helped with technical
advice on the training of young people going to Palestine,
and we had run several farms where boys and girls received
agricultural instruction before leaving for their new life on a
kibbutz.

Now our programme was suddenly expanded to meet an
entirely different challenge. We wanted to take as many
young Jews as possible off the streets of Vienna, where they
were in constant danger of being trapped by the Gestapo and
sent to concentration camps. We found that the training
camps were, in addition to their official function, a sanctuary
where young people were a bit safer than in town. And the
very fact that young people moved from their homes to a
place where they received instruction towards their emigration was a clear indication of their active wish to leave
Austria. Since our actual emigration opportunities were so

restricted, we had to resort to all sorts of subterfuge in order to show the Nazis that we were doing everything possible to leave the country and thereby invite their indulgence if it took a little longer than they demanded. And we prayed.

It was hard for Rudich to regard the farms as sanctuaries rather than as severe training centres, but Agami insisted that quantity was more important at this time than quality. And while Mirco was busy ordering saucepans, boots and tents for the farms, Agami was tormented by the thought of how to get the trainees out of them and on their way to Palestine as soon as possible.

Illegal immigration to Palestine was at that time organized by two types of people. The first can only be described as highway robbers who took advantage of the plight of Jews in Nazi-dominated countries and offered alluring trips to far-away places like Shanghai and the Caribbean Islands, but also to Palestine. Many would collect their money and then disappear. But in some cases, after having paid exorbitant prices, Jews were placed on a completely unseaworthy ship and tossed about the seas. As the British were watching out for ships carrying immigrants, in most cases these boats could not land and were sent back to their ports of departure.

The second group was a far more responsible element: the Revisionist Party. The activist extremists who had long ago lost patience with the 'prudent compromises' to which the Zionist Executive resorted in dealing with the British authorities had decided that the time for negotiations with the British about immigration quotas was over and that they had to take matters into their own hands. The Revisionists organized ships of their own, and they too accepted those who had money to pay for the trip – only because they themselves had to pay huge prices for chartering boats. Everyone in the market was taking advantage of the plight of the European Jews.

Up until the time of Agami's arrival in Vienna, the one

organization that had abstained from engaging in illegal transport of Jews, with one unsuccessful exception, was the Jewish Agency. The exception had been the affair of the *Velos,* a tiny ship that in 1934, under the auspices of the Polish Hehalutz, had attempted to land Polish Jews on the shores of Palestine and had been caught by the British on its second trip. At the time of the *Velos* episode, I knew nothing of the men who had been involved – Yulik Braginski and Dani Shind, who now (four years later) were Agami's colleagues in rescue work elsewhere in Europe. Partly as a result of the *Velos* venture, these two men were instrumental in changing the official Jewish Agency view on illegal immigration – a change which, as it were, put Agami and me into business.

The *Velos* had been a very small response to the plight of the Jews of Poland, where, paralleling Hitler's rise to power in 1933, anti-Semitism became overt government policy. Yulik Braginski, then a leader of the Polish Hehalutz, was one of the participants in the scheme to bring Jews from Poland to Greece and from there to Palestine in the little boat. He and his colleagues had high hopes when, with 340 on board, they landed undetected at night and disappeared into the neighbouring kibbutzim. The *Velos* returned immediately to Greece, and another group of 'tourists' was sent from Poland to board the boat. This time the British were tipped off; they intercepted the boat near the Palestine coast and forced it to return. Thus ended, in confusion and recrimination, the labour movement's first attempt to supplement the official schedule of entry certificates.

By 1935, with conditions in Poland steadily worsening, membership in the Polish Hehalutz swelled to about a quarter of a million, out of an overall Jewish population of three million. This was the record year for entry permits to Palestine, and a total of 60,000 Jews were allowed to immigrate into the country. But Hehalutz, like all other Zionist organizations in Poland, could do next to nothing to help its members reach their goal. There were hardly any certificates left for Poland's Jewry, as the certificates at the Jewish Agency's disposal were sent to Greater Germany, in view of the pressing political situation there. The Polish Post Office had to employ special vans in order to deliver the tons of applications for certificates to the Palestine Office in Warsaw. There they remained. There was no answer for the fervent appeals for rescue.

In 1936, to the shock of European Jewry, the British authorities cut the number of entry certificates by half, and of these 30,000 entry permits none could be spared for countries outside Hitler's direct rule. The permits were allotted to the Jewish Agency on account of the emergency in Germany. The hopeless misery of three million Polish Jews was not an emergency; it was their normal condition.

Demoralization became widespread as it became clear that, at the present rate, it would take something like 100 years for the Zionist movement to transport to Palestine all those who had followed its appeal.

Braginski, carrying on with the hopeless tasks of Poland's Hehalutz, was perfectly aware that the Jewish Agency and the responsible leadership of the Zionist movement objected to the renewal of clandestine departures. As long as there was a glimmer of hope to reach an acceptable minimum of certificates through negotiations, they did not want to jeopardize cooperation with the British and strain an already tense relationship. The British proceeded to deduct certificates from the official schedule against illegal arrivals, and the Jewish Agency realized in anguish how the traditional system of meticulous selection of immigrants had begun to disintegrate. Yet as long as the Jewish Agency could hope to reach an understanding with the British concerning the number of certificates, it saw no advantage in abandoning the position of strength that resulted from its insistence on straightforward dealings without recourse to underground practices.

In 1937 an emissary from the Palestine Labour movement arrived in Poland to strengthen the ranks of Hehalutz. A shepherd by training, he had a tycoon's business acumen and was a veteran fighter and educator in the pioneering movement. This was Dani Shind. He was overwhelmed by the plight of the Jews in Poland and by their determination to face any risk or hardship in order to get to Palestine. Soon after his arrival, Dani participated in an emergency meeting called by the leadership of one of the branch organizations of Hehalutz. It was at this meeting that Dani met Yulik Braginski, who had long wanted to discuss his private ideas about clandestine immigration. As the conversation developed, Dani understood that his own thoughts were identical with those of his companion.

Opinions inside the Palestine Labour movement were sharply divided, but the conspirators found understanding and support in important quarters. Since much preparation was needed for such clandestine transport operations and no one could foresee what changes might take place in the political situation before an illegal ship was ready to sail, it was tacitly understood that no formal decision was required at the moment. Braginski took it upon himself to go to Greece and scout for contacts with shipowners. He took with him Levi Schwartz, like himself a veteran of the *Velos* experiment and a member of the United Kibbutz movement, and the two proceeded to Athens.

Greece looked auspicious to them. The smuggling of arms to Spain had initially been handled by Greeks. But by the time our men arrived, the principal powers had begun supplying arms to their respective clients directly, and the Greek smugglers were looking for new opportunities. Braginski reasoned that only small craft could succeed in slipping through the British patrols along the coast. So Braginski and Levi Schwartz looked for 'honest crooks' who would make a reliable deal for small boats. 'What the hell,' Braginski used to say, 'Columbus discovered America in a 49-ton barge.'

Meanwhile, Dani Shind saw to the other end of the operation: landing on the Palestinian coast. He took into his confidence an old comrade, Davidka Nameri, another member of the United Kibbutz movement. With the tacit approval of Eliahu Golomb, the leading figure in the Haganah at the time, Davidka laid the foundation for what was to become an intricate, far-flung maritime organization that later became known by the name of Palyam, the naval wing of the Palmach (Haganah's shock-troops).

Dani put off the 'hardest nut to crack' for as long as possible: the dreaded interview with Ben Gurion. He knew that the chairman of the Jewish Agency Executive believed that the time had not yet come for the Haganah to organize clandestine immigration. Ben Gurion understood that he was being let in on a secret concerning an operation that was already in full swing. No properly appointed authority had ever discussed the matter thoroughly. Casual and sometimes unrelated talks had taken place, but no authorized body of the Zionist movement had dealt with this issue coherently; no binding decision had been arrived at unanimously.

'Of course,' Ben Gurion said, throwing his words brusquely at Dani, 'our right to immigration is not negotiable. Thank you for reminding me of this original notion . . . But where shall we get to if a bunch of self-appointed saviours make decisions of their own volition and then inform the responsible leadership when it is too late to undo the consequences of their acts?' Nonetheless, Dani got from Ben Gurion all he had expected. 'You can tell Davidka and your other friends that when the boat arrives I shall go down to the shore, take off my shoes, wade into the water and help the boys disembark the newcomers and bring them to shore on my own back. But then I shall go directly to a meeting to have you all disciplined for your utter irresponsibility.' Such

a meeting was never convened. On 12 June 1938 the first
boatload, a mere sixty-five people, arrived safety in Davidka's
bay.

While these decisions were being made in Palestine, Agami
was arriving at very similar conclusions about the need for
clandestine emigration from Austria.

'We can no longer be content with the slow, routine job we
are doing,' he reflected as we walked the streets of Vienna
one evening. 'It is still important to get youngsters into
agricultural training, and it is safer for them than staying in
the cities. But it's no longer enough. We must get them out of
Austria, not only out of the cities but across the borders.
Perhaps we can get a few into other countries in Europe
where they can train in agriculture and await their immigration certificates. But there is one other way. We must
organize illegal boats.'

Agami was aware of both the existence of clandestine
immigration on a very limited scale and the political debate
surrounding it in the inner policy circle. But decorum demanded that one ask no questions of the initiated. Much as he
felt he had to broach the subject of illegal immigration as a
means to increase the possibilities of departure from Austria,
he hesitated to take the initiative. Yet as we walked through
the beautiful park in front of the Imperial Hofburg, Agami
came to his decision. He was going to call the heads of the
Haganah in Europe first thing the next morning and propose
that Vienna become a point of departure for their illegal
transports. We stopped at one of the stalls on the Kärnthner-
strasse that served frankfurters and, in the incongruous company of several SA men, helped ourselves to some sausage
and beer. This was as near as we could come to celebrating
the fateful decision.

Next morning, when Agami sat down at the telephone
with a heavy sigh, he confessed that he had not been able to
work out how to reach any of the Haganah's operatives. He

knew that Braginski was in Paris, Dani in Rome, Zvi in Athens, but their addresses were probably known only to one another. They frequented inexpensive hotels and changed as often as they felt that their international phone calls and outlandish manners were beginning to attract undue attention. He could write Eliahu Golomb in Tel Aviv, but it would take a long while to get through to him, as he could not entrust a letter of this kind to the mail and would have to wait for a suitable courier. There was somebody in Yugoslavia who, he supposed, might be a junior member of the central staff. Agami happened to have his number, so he decided to try Aryeh Shindelmann.

The telephone operator registered Agami's call. The organization of illegal immigration was to be characterized by a series of enervating waiting periods sitting glued to the telephone. As our work expanded, the little black box became a living magnet that never let us out of its reach. We looked to it for the redeeming word, and when it kept silent we imagined the end of the world. This was the first of many such times: Agami was alternately drumming on the table, humming out of tune and violently scribbling on some piece of paper. Tension in the room increased steadily, until the shrill ring of the telephone at last cut the dense atmosphere. Shindelmann did not sound surprised when Agami identified himself. He agreed to come through Vienna on his way to Paris and would cable his arrival in a day or two.

'We are not alone any more,' Agami announced with a wry smile as he put down the phone. 'We have joined the unbeatable, dynamic and unrestricted rescue effort of the Jewish nation!'

Two evenings after the fateful call to Shindelmann, Agami took me with him to the Ostbahnhof Station to meet the man in the flesh. From there we hailed a cab and went to Pataki's Weinstube, a restaurant I had discovered the day before with no sign announcing 'Jews undesired.' Shindelmann had only two hours between trains, and as he was in Vienna on a Palestinian passport with a German transit visa, he had no intention of overstaying Germany's welcome. Agami talked to him intensely, and Shindelmann listened as seriously as Agami spoke. He made no notes – it was customary for Haganah operatives to put nothing on paper.

Meanwhile we were also served an exquisite meal. The *spécialité de la maison* was a sort of mixed grill called *Holztellerfleisch* served rustic fashion on a plate of carved wood. Out of it stuck a penknife which patrons were invited to carry home as a souvenir. In the course of the following months, I collected quite a number of those, as Pataki's was the only restaurant where we were always welcome guests. The owner was a Hungarian who could afford to disregard anti-Semitic excesses. And he had a fine gipsy band that clearly sympathized with us, as the gipsies' fate under the Nazis was so similar to ours. They loved to play 'Bel Ami', a hit-tune of the day, but for our sake they invariably played a number of sentimental Yiddish tunes on their sensitive violins.

Shindelmann promised to carry Agami's message to the Haganah chiefs. They would let him know their decision.

Two or three days after this meeting, Agami received a phone call from Paris. He understood immediately that the decision was favourable. Braginski, the senior member of the Haganah staff, announced that he would soon arrive in Vienna with Zvi Yehieli (who called himself Schechter on such excursions) to go into further detail with Agami.

In the summer of 1938, the Haganah High Command in Palestine had officially established the Mossad (Institution for *Parallel* Immigration, 'parallel' referring to the minute number of official entry permits granted to the Jewish Agency by the British Government every six months). Shaul Avigur, whom I met in London in 1936, was appointed head of the new organization. We were on our way into business.

(4)

'An Underground with Proper Characters'

NOW THAT THE PROJECT of illegal rescue work had become legal in the eyes of the Haganah authorities, our Vienna office faced a multitude of problems whose solutions lacked precedent: transit visas, the release of Jews already imprisoned – a whole series of unforeseeable hitches, all of which required the assent of the Nazi authorities.

An improbable chain of human beings led in short order to a high-ranking Austrian Nazi who became, of all things, a loyal friend to Agami and the rest of us. The chain began with Rudolf Loehner, a suave sophisticate who ran an ultra-fashionable men's clothing store. Through him it led to Gerta Haas, the beautiful Jewish wife of a Hungarian nobleman, who brought us to Giuseppe Matossiani, an Italian playboy, who was the connection with Wolfgang Karthaus, the high-ranking, esteemed Nazi who decided to save Jews.

The chain began to develop when Rudi Loehner suddenly appeared at our offices on Marc Aurel Strasse early in the summer of 1938. We all were familiar with his exclusive establishment and its clientele of artists, elegant industrialists and foreign diplomats, but Loehner had never had anything to do with the Palestine Office. Palestine was not the place for him; it was a place for Zionist fanatics devoted to idealism and sacrifice and a fondness for the hard life. None of this had ever had the slightest attraction for Rudi Loehner during the pleasant, easy-going years. His *milieu* had always been the peculiarly whimsical Austrian literature of Nestroy, Karl Kraus and Roda-Roda, and his customers liked him as much for the exquisite taste of his collections as for his specifically Viennese charm and easy humour.

But then everything changed for Rudolf Loehner. He explained to us that the *Anschluss* had been a triple shock for him, and the day Hitler's army rushed into Austria he suddenly felt like an outcast from the community of which he had always regarded himself a natural product. For a while, he was alone in the savage sea. Nothing 'personal' had yet happened to him, and as a veteran of the First World War, in which he served as an officer, he was assured by friends that nothing would ever happen to him. After all, he didn't look Jewish; he had a record of honest citizenship in the Republic, and, what's more, had excellent connections. A man of his position should not have to worry about his fate and that of his wife and only child, a boy of sixteen.

But in a way he was never able to comprehend or to explain, Rudolf Loehner felt suddenly drawn to his fellow-Jews, whom he had never before regarded with special affinity. He closed his store while the exultant celebrations of the 'liberation' of Austria were still in full swing. Suddenly he was without a country, without his business, in search of a refuge. He joined the crowd of frightened people who looked up the addresses of South American consulates in the telephone directory and went early in the morning to see them, one after another, starting with the most remote and ludicrous, in the hope that their migration policies would be less stern and pedantic than those of the more obvious countries. He soon realized the futility of it all. The evasive answers, the increasingly abrupt refusals, the hostile procrastination he encountered everywhere convinced him that he must find another way to security for his family.

Like a flash, an idea came to him. One of his former customers, Nicolas Haas, owned a farm in southern Austria. Rudolf Loehner took his sixteen-year-old son, Ernest, to Moosbrunn. Nicolas, a Hungarian nobleman, and his Jewish wife, Gerta, were glad to see their old friend. The idea of employing Ernest as an agricultural labourer on their farm amused them. But they understood Rudolf's reasoning: his boy would be safer in this remote place than in the streets of the capital, where Nazi storm-troopers had begun to hunt for Jews at random; and while his father was continuing his efforts to obtain papers for emigration, Ernest would be able to adapt himself for a new life in exile.

Gerta Haas, a striking beauty, was also an utterly practical woman. She suggested that in addition to Ernest, they could just as well take a whole group of Jewish youngsters who were in just as precarious a situation. And while they showed their new work-hand to his new quarters, Gerta Haas, now totally enthused by her ingenious scheme, announced that she was going to bring in Giuseppe Matossiani. 'Now that we are joining the underground we must establish contact with the proper characters.'

Matossiani, Gerta explained, was Italian, a refugee from Fascism who had been helpful in the past with her husband's wine business when it was necessary to open new markets or to win over reluctant buyers. He had incredible connections everywhere, including the new fascist establishment. A charmer of the highest order, he was also extremely adaptable, and underneath his mask of easy-going innocence there was a sharp, calculating brain.

Rudi Loehner returned to Vienna greatly satisfied. He had

found a haven for his son and was now able to do something
practical for the boys of other, less-fortunate people. Driving
in his white Daimler from Moosbrunn to Vienna, he decided
to contact the Palestine Office. He had never been there
before, but now he could think of no better channel for his
mission.

Agami was instantly excited with the prospect of working
with Matossiani. When Mirco Rudich reported to him about
the new connection, Agami immediately put in a call to
Moosbrunn, introduced himself in his strange Baltic German
to Gerta Haas and asked her to meet him that same morning
in front of the Opera. They entered the Opernkaffee as if
they had known one another for years. From there Gerta
telephoned Matossiani, who arrived in his red Alfa Romeo
within minutes, as if he had waited for her summons around
the corner. Agami's first impression of Matossiani seems to
have been a mixture of admiration for his audacity and
disappointment at his greed. But Matossiani lingered over the
description of the Gestapo hierarchy, particularly that of its
Jewish Department. Obviously he had a direct link to Herr
Kuchmann, the dreaded and notorious head of the growing
unit in charge of Jewish affairs.

'Affairs,' said Matossiani, 'has a double meaning in this
case. There is little that cannot be achieved with them if you
are ready to pay.' He agreed to prove his value by deeds: he
was going to submit a list of completely innocent Jews who
had been brought by the Gestapo to the Dachau concentration camp and have them transferred to one of Rudich's
farms, according to Agami's directions. He would receive
from Agami 1,000 marks for each person. Agami's head
swam in the face of this free-wheeling plotting. If all this
were possible, maybe he stood at the beginning of the road
that led to salvation. He had to press for more. His task was
not only to postpone the confrontation, but also to get the
young people over the frontier to safety.

Matossiani examined the variety of individuals who constituted the jumble of his countless connections. He was nost anxious to please Agami. He liked the man, 'was moved by the terrible trials Agami's fellow-Jews had to suffer', and knew that he was doing something for the salvation of his own sinful soul if he exerted himself in the service of an honourable cause. The inspiration came to him, while he was once again parading his candidates before his inner eye.

His choice was engineer Wolfgang Karthaus, an outstanding road-builder who was widely respected for his correctness and reliability. From our point of view there was one drawback: he was one of the founding members of Austrian Nazism. He had adhered to the Party when Austria, still a sovereign country, had outlawed the Nazis. Karthaus worked for them underground from that time until 'the liberation'. During that period, Matossiani told Agami, Engineer Karthaus had developed two foibles that were to be of great practical value to us: he had come to detest the vulgar, indiscriminate anti-Semitism of the Nazis; and now, since they took power, he had on several occasions – and at great risk even for an old fighter like himself – intervened on behalf of many victims of their outrageous policy. Most important of all, during the 'difficult years of the underground', he had become a very close friend of the man who today was *Gauleiter* of Vienna, the highest-ranking official in the Nazi hierarchy.

Agami was not sufficiently convinced by these credentials. 'In what particular way,' he asked Matossiani, 'do you think he can be of real help to our work?' Karthaus was, at the moment, building roads connecting some of Austria's highways with the desolate country roads in northern Yugoslavia.

'It is possible that the people who put up the budget for these developments have not only the flow of tourist motor cars in mind. His position with the Yugoslav authorities is very strong. Perhaps he could obtain visas for labourers on his road projects if he wanted to help.'

Agami's eyes lit up when he realized the potentialities of

transports of supposed labourers leaving (with their families?) for officially sanctioned work across the border . . . and then vanishing on a ship to faraway shores. 'You have my authorization to speak to the engineer,' Agami ventured. 'Don't go into any details at all. I shall do this myself – provided he agrees to see me and to work with me.'

Matossiani accompanied Agami to his first meeting with Karthaus at a coffee house that bore the notorious sign 'Jews not wanted here.' Agami immediately told the engineer that he would prefer to talk to him elsewhere. He could not bear to sit in a place that would evict him unceremoniously were it not for the protection of two members of the Nazi Party. Karthaus gave Agami a long and searching look; then they walked across the street into Karthaus' apartment.

More than anything that was said later on, Matossiani used to tell us time and again, this opening cemented the relationship between the two men. Karthaus respected Agami; he was not doing him a favour, condescendingly. Agami's proposition made sense to him. Austria wanted to 'purge' herself of her Jews, and Agami wanted to get Jews out of Austria, where they were 'undesirable', and transport them to Palestine. When the Mossad leader explained the need for Yugoslav transit visas so that the emigrants could reach the coast, where boats would be ready to transfer them to Palestine, Karthaus discarded Matossiani's idea of obtaining false work permits. These were unnecessary for people who wanted to cross through Yugoslav territory only in order to reach the coast. Instead he promised to obtain for Agami regular transit visas through Yugoslavia – provided, of course, there was a boat waiting when they arrived in port. To be completely safe, Karthaus offered to clear the matter with his friend, the *Gauleiter,* to have the Jewish Department of the Gestapo informed that the scheme had been approved by the highest authority in the land. When Agami asked

Karthaus how much time he thought he needed for the arrangements, the latter replied: 'Oh, just a few days.'

We could hardly grasp the ease with which Karthaus disposed of difficulties that appeared insurmountable to us. Karthaus, for his part, could not comprehend why we should be surprised: he was simply part of the ruling régime. He happened to be an honest man with no bias against Jews. He was able to help and glad to be given a chance. Suddenly, there was a man, all integrity and seriousness, who brought about the miracle of 20,000 Yugoslav transit visas within a few days. It was absolutely unheard of and quite incomprehensible, even when you saw the actual official document with the seal of the Yugoslav Consulate General in Vienna.

In thinly veiled language Agami reported to Braginski, eagerly awaiting news in Paris. Braginski was obviously fascinated. He told Agami that he was coming to Vienna to familiarize himself with the details and to check on the arrangements. 'The bride,' Braginski said, 'is too pretty. I must see if there is not a hidden hitch somewhere along the road.'

Agami knew that the Mossad was taking action towards acquiring a ship for his transport and that he need not worry about this problem. He was glad that Braginski and Zvi were coming to double check for hitches. They were the people with experience and authority. He could be certain that they would discover any weaknesses in the scheme. One was already perfectly clear: all arrangements had been made with two people, Matossiani and Karthaus, the one an unreliable, emotional, greedy fixer; the other, apparently highly dignified, undoubtedly reliable, and a man of his word, but an old-time Nazi nonetheless. It really was too good to be true. Agami did not think there was any reason to trust Dr Lange or Herr Kuchmann, the heads of the Jewish Department of the Gestapo. Maybe Karthaus trusted them, but Agami could not visualize Dr Lange's support if some other department crossed Agami's road. And Eichmann's Zentralstelle, the notorious institution devoted to the destruction of German Jewry, was looming large.

One more item needed Agami's attention: the alleged destination of the immigrants sailing from the Yugoslav port – provided, of course, that they ever got as far as that port. Here, clearly, was another job for Giuseppe Matossiani. When the question was raised Matossiani told Agami he had already thought of it. He had a close friend, the Consul of Mexico, a man full of understanding for people in distress. Naturally, Matossiani observed, the warm-hearted Consul would expect us to reciprocate his generosity. Agami was resigned to that by now.

'Just tell me how generous I shall have to be before you commit yourself,' he told Matossiani.

'I want you to understand that there can be two ways of compensating the Consul,' Matossiani replied. 'You can pay the official fee for each visa – a nominal amount. Since we are going to use a collective passport for the entire transport, there won't even be space for the Consul to stamp a visa opposite the name of every person on the list that makes up the collective passport. So he could collect for himself, say, 20,000 times the nominal fee per visa, and that, for him, would constitute a worth-while thing. Or you could propose another way,' Matossiani continued his lecture. 'The collective passport could be accompanied by a covering letter from the Consul stating that everyone on the list has the right to enter Mexico, and you could offer him a reasonable amount for that piece of stationery.'

Agami's decision, predictably, was in favour of the covering letter. This way it was not necessary to give to another unreliable person the real names of emigrants; he would offer a much smaller sum than if he had to reward the Consul for each visa; and 'I hope we shall have a departure now once every week,' he told Matossiani, 'so your man will make a lot of money with the large turnover, even if we pay him less per unit.' Agami could not have known then, but he had laid one of the foundations of our clandestine work, a routine that was helpful and more thrifty than the other method.

It took Matossiani only one day. Then there it was in our files, a letter signed and sealed as international courtesy and consular routine required: 'The holders of the attached collective visa are entitled to immigrate to Mexico. Any courtesy extended by the appropriate authorities to the holders of this visa, prospective citizens of Mexico, will be greatly appreciated by the Government.' Matossiani was given the equivalent of $1,000 in German marks. When he brought the priceless letter, he told Agami that 'the Honourable Consul General wants you to know that if the prospective holders of the visa should by any chance find themselves one day in Mexico, he will murder you and expect your heirs to pay him a monthly stipend until his last living day.' Agami, who never made light of these matters, merely locked the letter in the proper file.

(5)

The Adventures of
the *Attrato*

THE SHIP FINALLY acquired for this first large-scale illegal transport was the *Attrato,* and to us she seemed impressive, although her age was considerably more than that of any of the men of the Mossad. Built in Russia well before the First World War as a rescue vessel, she had a number of fairly large cabins (accommodating about twenty passengers, when we were thinking in terms of 400), first-class signalling implements and a record-breaking speed – for her day and for her original home port, Odessa. By the time our men discovered the *Attrato* her port was Piraeus and she was owned by a family of Greek shipowners, the Verenikos brothers.

The Verenikos family impressed the Mossad immediately: they had an honourable political past and had shown great personal courage. Just three years before Dani Shind and Yulik Braginski made contact with them, they had been involved in a daring exploit. The veteran democratic leader of Greece, Eleutherios Venizelos, had led an uprising against the fascist Greek régime of the day. The rebellion was poorly prepared and collapsed under the overwhelming might of the government it had set out to topple. The Verenikos brothers, in admiration of the leader who was often called 'the Saviour of Greece,' saved his life by risking their own, for it was one of their small boats that brought Venizelos to the relative safety of the island of Rhodes. In the general appeasement that followed the abortive revolt, the Verenikos brothers demonstrated another of their abilities: using just the right connections – and vast sums of money – they bought their way back to respectability under a régime that appreciated astuteness as much as it abhorred nonconformist disobedience. Thereafter the Verenikos family turned to revolutions farther from home and lent its extensive services to the Spanish Loyalists fighting against the Franco rebellion. The men of the Mossad had found what they were looking for: audacious seafarers who understood the value of money but preferred to obtain it for honourable causes.

Greece had for some time been the centre of activities for illegal departures. Both the Mossad and the Revisionists had organized transports from the small inlets along the picturesque coast, helped by the warm-hearted population who were themselves used to hardships and therefore full of understanding for the plight of the Jews. We even had 'our man' in Piraeus, Aristo Chorilos, who had simply attached himself to the men of the Mossad working at the port. He had noticed the strange foreigners hanging about the coffeehouses of the port area. They seemed different from other outsiders who came to the port looking for opportunities of various kinds. They were more generous and kind, and they were more naïve and inexperienced. Chorilos appointed himself their mentor in the ways of Greek ports, and gradually the Mossad could not imagine working in Athens without this man. The Mossad decided to give him a monthly salary, and he responded by pressing his trousers, putting on a tie and making himself the respectable interpreter of a cause which he knew next to nothing about. When the first groups of Polish pioneers arrived in Athens – posing as tourists on a pleasure trip so they could disappear soon after by train or from an obscure inlet on the shore in one of the little boats – it was Chorilos who instructed the bewildered boys and girls from small towns in Poland in the appropriate behaviour of tourists on a cruise. And it was Chorilos who established the first contact between the Mossad and the Verenikos brothers.

The men of the Mossad were particularly pleased with this contact because for the first time they had found a real shipping company, rather than the lone pirates who sold their services only to vanish without leaving so much as an address. At the same time, however, the importance of Greece as a departure point was, unfortunately, coming to an end, as Greece became the main target of British actions against illegal transports to Palestine. In the summer of 1938, Britain ordered her Missions in Europe to obtain promises from every government in question that it would do all in its power to thwart our efforts to move Jews to places from which they could depart for Palestine. The men of the Mossad were sternly warned by their Greek contacts to discontinue their embarrassing activities and leave Greece altogether.

Braginski and Shind therefore decided to transfer the *Attrato* from Greece to Italy. Polish tourists needed no entry visas to Italy, and the Italian authorities were eager to attract foreign travellers. The Verenikos brothers accepted an advance payment of £1,000 – a tremendous amount for the Mossad – and, under the experienced command of Captain Dimitriu, the *Attrato,* empty and with the blessing of the Greek port authorities, set sail for Venice.

The *Attrato* had already completed her refitting for the voyage in the port of Venice when Captain Dimitriu returned from a trip to France, where he had completed the rather bizarre procedure of registering the vessel to the Panama Life-Lines, a shipping company in neutral Liechtenstein. The *Attrato's* Panamanian character properly vouchsafed, the flag of Panama was handed to Captain Dimitriu by the Consul of that country in Paris, and he brought it to Venice like a trophy. After hoisting the *Attrato's* new national banner, Captain Dimitriu, in full accord with the Mossad's men, decided to move the ship from the beauty of Venice into the more mercantile surroundings of the port of Bari. Since his return from Paris Captain Dimitriu was inclined to see in every tourist along the winding canals of Venice a super-spy planted there to follow the nefarious transactions of the Panama Life-Line. It would be healthier to follow in Scipio's footsteps and depart from Puglia towards the east. The 'tourists' were redirected on their train journey to Bari. There, in the safety of Italy's remotest port, and under the benevolent eyes of Captain Dimitriu's newly acquired friends among the Italian police, the transport departed into the unknown.

When Braginski and Zvi Yehieli arrived at Vienna's western railway station, Agami and I went to meet them. So did Giuseppe Matossiani. He wanted to observe their safe arrival for a special reason: he had obtained German entry visas for them within a day of their call from Paris. We all gasped unbelievingly when Matossiani showed us a copy of the telegram sent by Dr Lange's office to the visa section of the German embassy in Paris.

'When we see them arriving at the station,' Agami had remarked to Matossiani, sceptical as usual, 'we shall have proof, for the first time since we've begun working together, that you can deliver the goods.'

They both were of medium height and a little plump. Braginski's keen, blue eyes behind dark-rimmed glasses and slightly greying hair gave him the air of a visiting professor far from his homeground. He had never been in 'Nazi-land' before.

Zvi Yehieli was more at ease. He had travelled through Germany and had been in Vienna often before the *Anschluss*. His eyes belied the air of cool indifference he assumed for security reasons, for he was bursting to hear details of the arrangements Agami had been able to conjure up in a matter of weeks.

Although we were in Matossiani's car – and our guests knew that few secrets about our work were withheld from Matossiani – no word was said about what mattered most until we reached the hotel room and Matossiani had departed. Braginski fussed with a telegram Agami had received for him just as we were leaving for the railway station. Finally he was ready to read it. 'GOOD LUCK STOP YOUR TENT WITH 386 BOOKS ARRIVED SAFELY AND EN ROUTE TO YOU NOW.' We knew that in Mossad code this meant that the *Attrato* had safely delivered its passengers, turned round, and was now on her way to Yugoslavia for another group. There could have been no more auspicious beginning for Agami's interrogation, which went on through most of that night. Nothing resembling Agami's scheme had ever succeeded. Braginski and Yehieli were used to working under conditions of great hardship, in miserable solitude, without any high-powered contacts with the governments of the countries from which illegal transports had so far departed, Poland in particular.

It was obvious that the last country where one would have expected to find trustworthy intermediaries with good connections was Nazi Austria. It was a paradox hard to grasp: the bestiality of the Nazis had brought out human instincts in a few individuals and the necessary courage to apply them, in spite of terrible personal consequences should they go wrong. Driven by the scepticism of many disappointed hopes and the gruelling experience of clandestine work under the most adverse circumstances, Braginski and Yehieli exposed Agami to a veritable inquisition. Although he answered all questions to their satisfaction, it was clear that we would know the real value of our agreements only when they actually had been tested. We were still elated by the good news that had arrived at the beginning of our talk. No one was worrying about the *Attrato*. She was slowly but surely approaching the port of Susak in Yugoslavia.

Early the following morning Agami sent messengers to the farms where youngsters were waiting anxiously for the word to move. The number of these farms had grown: there were now fourteen in various parts of former Austria, with over 1,000 young people who knew that their security increased if they made themselves indispensable to their farmer hosts. They had made great efforts to convince their hostile hosts that Jews were capable of hard work and could be something besides tradesmen, misers and intellectuals.

Each farm was allotted a certain number of places on the transport that was to leave for Susak. The names were determined by the farm committee, whose decision was based on length of stay on the farm, physical ability to withstand the strenuous trip and willingness to risk illegal immigration. The candidates for departure parted from their friends and rushed to their parents' homes to say good-bye. Each knew that it was very doubtful whether he would ever see his family again. Yet only a very few found it impossible to part. The certainty that the gates would sooner or later be locked gave parents the strength to encourage their children to leave.

It was Agami's idea that the first person to go to Susak should be Karthaus himself. He was, after all, the father of the whole arrangement and the man with the most influence in Yugoslavia. Karthaus hesitated. The ordeal of a night trip to the remote port did not appeal to him, and his influence was not really with the lower-ranking port officials and frontier authorities in Susak; he knew the Prime Minister and several other important people, mostly in the capital. But finally he accepted Agami's plan. As a German citizen, with the private telephone numbers of members of the Yugoslav Government in his pocket, he was sure to impress even the lowly officials – in whose hands our fate actually lay – if something went wrong. He even added another touch to Agami's scheme: he would make a stop at the frontier station to prepare the inspectors there for the arrival of the emigrant Jews.

On the evening that Karthaus left, Braginski returned from his Paris headquarters, where he had been called to attend to some urgent business. He brought important news: Yehieli had acquired another boat from the Verenikos family. The Yugoslav port authorities were known in the shipping world as sticklers for meticulous inspection of the ships that passed through their ports. The *Attrato,* he feared, might not pass the test, for we had crowded over 400 passengers into specially installed narrow berths. The Verenikos brothers now offered the Mossad a real passenger ship. It was not capable of making the trip to Palestine – nor would it look to the port authorities like a ship that could take 400 passengers to Mexico as their documents indicated – but she was a beautiful passenger ship, the kind used for short excursions along the coast. It would satisfy the pedantic Yugoslavs more than the *Attrato,* and the passengers would be transferred to the *Attrato* once the new ship – the *Colorado* – was safely out of the sight of the inquisitive Susak port authorities.

Agami took in this news with mixed feelings. He disliked last-minute changes. He had got used to the idea of his transport departing on the *Attrato,* the lucky one that had just delivered a group of illegal passengers without detection by the British Navy and was on her way back for new people. Of course, Braginski's reasoning made sense, and he found that Braginski had prudently added an extra thirty-six hours for the *Colorado*'s expected arrival time at Susak after the relatively short trip from her home port of Piraeus.

The operation had to go on. Two hundred and eighty passengers from Germany were already on their way to Vienna. Agami had included them in this transport because they had waited longer than Vienna's Jews for a chance to go to Palestine, and the Jewish community of Berlin was financing their trip to the extent that Agami was able to subsidize the more destitute passengers leaving from Vienna.

The people from our farms gathered in our office. We had removed the furniture to make room for them to spend their last night in Vienna there. The transport was divided into groups of twenty persons, each group with a leader, and the group leaders assembled for last-minute briefings. From outside the building one could not hear a whisper or see a shadow moving – so careful were they not to attract the attention of the onlookers from across the street: the Gestapo, stationed in the Hotel Metropol.

At dawn the groups were awakened and formed a column that marched down the street to catch the early tram to the southern station. The train from Berlin carrying the 280 passengers had arrived exactly on time. So far everything was going without a hitch. Matossiani took Agami to the station in his car. I came along with them and sensed the extreme tension as we approached the station and saw the 400 passengers that were to leave in a few minutes – and to be saved.

Not a word had been exchanged, but as we approached the train both Agami and Matossiani said good-bye to me. They had – quite independently – decided to join the train as far as the border to see that all went well and to be present at the first critical stage of the long trip into an unknown future: the crossing from Austria into Yugoslavia.

When I returned to the office I found Braginski planted firmly near the telephone on Agami's desk. Willi Ritter, the head of Hehalutz, was with him, and he had a huge box of French cigarettes at his side. He tried to appear calm, but could hardly suppress his anxiety about the outcome of this adventure, although for the next seven hours, until the train reached the border, there was no news to expect. Still, Braginski waited for the call from Susak, confirming the *Colorado*'s arrival in port.

Finally, the tension was broken by the telephone. As Renée Wiesner, our secretary, transferred the call from the outer office to Braginski, he knew that something had gone wrong. We could hear Agami's voice shouting from the border station. The train had been stopped by the Yugoslav frontier guards. They had expected the train, but they were supposed to receive clearance from Susak before letting the passengers cross the border – on the ground that a ship was waiting for them in port. But there was no ship in Susak.

Agami was desperate. The passengers had been cleared by the German frontier police; they had left the Third Reich, but they were now stuck in no-man's-land. Even the presence of Matossiani had not produced a way of swaying the severe Yugoslavs.

Braginski fumbled with the telephone. It was futile even to try to call Yehieli in Athens. The *Colorado* had left there four days before. By all counts she should have been safely at Susak; but she was nowhere near the port.

Meanwhile, Matossiani was furiously phoning Karthaus in Susak. He spoke as if the *Colorado*'s failure to appear was Karthaus' personal fault. He would hold Karthaus responsible if the Yugoslavs did not let the transport go through their frontier. After all, the passengers were in possession of proper visas both for transit and for destination. He had never heard of such impudence: the train on which the passengers travelled had left, the carriages had been detached on a sideline in no-man's-land, but they were urgently required in Vienna for further duty. And here some little Yugoslav frontier guard permitted himself to keep German railway carriages idle because of the pedantic stubbornness of another little Yugoslav guard in the lousy port of Susak, where grass was growing in the streets!

Karthaus was no less desperate as he saw his scheme collapse. Why had he not insisted on waiting for confirmation from Susak that the boat was safely in port before the visas he had obtained were put to use? Unable to get in a word during Matossiani's tirades, he used the time between Matossiani's calls to cultivate the 'little Yugoslav guard'. Together they stood at the quayside and stared into the infinite expanse of the Adriatic, interrupting their watch only when Karthaus was summoned to the nearby office to receive another impatient call from the other end of Yugoslavia.

In Vienna, Braginski was by now quite unable to control his rage. His greatest frustration was that there was no one in particular to blame. The *Colorado* had left Piraeus four days before. He had insisted that the transport leave thirty-six hours later than the time the ship normally should have arrived in Susak. All reasonable precautions had been taken. It was incredible that something completely unforeseen should have detained the ship. It was a tragedy that so beautiful an operation should be marred by the most unlikely defect in the fragile links of this delicate chain. And it was quite a defeat for the Mossad that it should be its part in the bargain that imperiled the well-conceived plan.

Unperturbed and cool as ever, Moshe Green, the Secretary of the Palestine Office, stuck his bespectacled head through the door and, quite unnecessarily, asked whether he was interrupting anything. Dr Green, the ranking official of the Palestine Office, was an old hand at emergencies and a soft-spoken man with nerves of steel. When others lost their heads, it was always Dr Green who kept his composure and was able to suggest a constructive solution. But this time he had just a message to deliver. 'There was a call for you,' he told Braginski, 'from Dr Lange's office. The Gestapo wants you to report at once. A routine check on foreigners, they said.'

This, we all thought, is the end.

I took over the telephone from Braginski as he left with Dr Green to cross over to the 'other office'. I was just asking to be connected with Agami at his border station to break the news of this latest development, but Agami got through first with his own bad news: orders had been received from the Central Railways to start the five carriages on their return trip to Vienna at four in the afternoon. We had another two hours before a locomotive would come for them, and if the passengers were unable to move towards Yugoslavia by then, they would be attached to a train returning to the city shortly after four. When I told him my news, Agami regarded Braginski's summons in light of this definite threat. He sounded quite grim when he said, 'Pretty as the bride might be, it seems to be the groom's fault if the wedding is not coming off.'

Somehow, three hours passed after that conversation, and Agami had still not reported the return of the passengers. Just as Braginski returned from his enforced absence, he phoned.

It *was* a routine check on foreigners, Braginski said beaming, but he was showing the strain. 'The fellow wanted to know what I was doing here. And when I explained that I had come to inspect the farms prior to the emigration of some of their inmates, as we had agreed, the SA man laughed at me sardonically: "Farms? Have you ever seen a Jewish farmer?" We had quite a talk,' he added.

Agami was relieved to hear the real reason for his chief's absence. And at his end, too, things were looking a bit brighter. Matossiani – invoking every prestigious name he knew in the Nazi hierarchy, and continuously bombarding the railway people with threats to their careers if they committed the unforgiveable blunder of returning a group travelling under the highest auspices ever – had secured an extension for the railway carriages. They were now to be allowed to stay until 7.30 and await news from Susak.

Karthaus himself gave us the final word: the *Colorado* had arrived in port. She was a little slower than Captain Dimitriu had cared to admit, but now she was here and had already been inspected by the Yugoslavs. The friendly relations established during the hectic day had paid off in something less than a cursory examination of her seaworthiness. Yes, he said, he had already advised Agami at his frontier post. The train should be on its way by now. The ring of the phone bringing this news was a classic example of 'saved by the bell': it was twenty minutes past seven when Karthaus called.

We remained in the office through the night. Although we knew that Agami could not possibly arrive before the next morning, we simply could not leave. We just waited for any news at all, consuming countless cups of coffee, and dozing off periodically. Finally, Agami and Matossiani returned.

'We must make arrangements for the next transport to leave in ten days time,' Agami pronounced as he sat down at his desk.

'Make it thirteen,' Braginski said, 'just to be on the safe side.'

The first sailing of the *Attrato* came after the most severe outrage against Germany's Jews since Hitler had taken power in 1933. On 7 November 1938 a Jewish youngster, Herschel Grynszpan, entered the German Embassy in Paris and asked to be received by the Ambassador. A young Second Secretary, Ernst Vom Rath, received the visitor on behalf of the head of the German Mission. Grynszpan shot and killed Vom Rath.

Terrible revenge was taken by the Nazis on Jews living in the Greater Reich. On the night of 9/10 October, 20,000 male hostages were arrested at random and shipped off to concentration camps; 138 synagogues were stormed and burnt; the windows of Jewish shops were shattered and their goods looted. When it was over, the German Government imposed a 'fine' of one billion Reichsmarks ($400,000,000) on the Jews of Germany. This, and other astronomical amounts far in excess of the total of Jewish property, spelt the ruin of the once prosperous and tranquil community. The outrage became known as *Kristallnacht* ('The Night of Broken Glass'). Yet the outrages were more ferocious in Austria than in any other area of Hitler's rule. Any remaining illusions about our fate were finally obliterated. As desperation grew, the demand for emigration facilities became overwhelming.

The *Colorado* was less than a drop in the ocean, but it was a concrete reply to what had become a hopeless situation. She was ferrying passengers dutifully when the British Government announced its new plan for the settlement of the Palestine problem.

In November 1938 a report was published by the Palestine Partition Commission, headed by the distinguished Indian civil servant Sir John Woodhead. Since February 1938, the eve of the *Anschluss,* it had laboured over the complicated problem of how to recommend practical implementation of Lord Peel's partition plan and yet propose nothing that would confront the British Government with the clear necessity to solve the Palestine problem by the establishment of an independent Jewish State, however small. It was a hopeless assignment, as independent statehood was the only reason why the Peel partition plan had been accepted by a slight majority of Jewish opinion in the first place. But it was a procedure that befitted the 'Government of Appeasers' who sought patched-up compromise in every field. The new commission defined a small, useless area as the Jewish State: a ghetto, really, that comprised Tel Aviv and a small portion of the surrounding land. After the cynical apathy of the Evian Conference, the new development came as another blow.

Yet the intoxication of success with our own illegal transport persisted even as we returned to the misery of reality. The fact that we had been able to combine the various elements necessary to save people's lives left us elated. We scrutinized every detail of the past operation with the trust one has in a reliable engine – no longer just with the faith one places in chance and good fortune. Agami decided that we must do everything possible to avoid the repetition of our mistakes. 'There will be new mistakes each time,' he used to say, 'but for God's sake, let's not make the same ones twice.'

Just five days after *Colorado*'s departure from Susak – and after she had transferred her passengers to the much faster *Attrato* – we received the cabled message for which we had been waiting. But this time the 'books that had arrived in the tent' were our own comrades, people we had seen leaving just a few days earlier. The small group of people that had been involved in the preparation of their rescue was drawn closely together. I felt – and I know Agami, Braginski, Yehieli and Willi Ritter felt – like a member of a particularly privileged order, and we loved one another very much.

(6)

A Short Trip 'Home'

ONE DAY in the winter of 1938, Willi Ritter asked me whether I would like to accompany one of the youth groups on their way to Palestine. We had a number of special immigration certificates for youngsters from the separately functioning body of Youth Aliyah, under the leadership of Henrietta Szold. The boys and girls were brought to kibutzim, where they studied in the framework of their own group, but were in close contact with kibbutz children of their age. At the height of the catastrophe, after the *Anschluss*, we in Vienna received 300 such places and were sending groups of about forty children each. Willi Ritter had learned that it was possible for one adult to accompany these groups, free of charge. Even more important, a chaperone on such a trip could return to Germany without forgoing his German exit permit, which was given to any emigrating Jew just once.

I accepted the idea with enthusiasm and prepared to leave almost immediately. The very chance of being away from the oppressing fear and tension in Nazi Austria would have been enough to justify such a trip. But there was more. I would see my parents in Jerusalem, encounter the reality of the country of my dreams and set foot in a kibbutz for the first time. And I was going to see Hanna again. She had left almost immediately after the *Anschluss* and was living in an agricultural school in Palestine.

I had met Hanna when I was seventeen and she was fourteen (five years later we were married). I am quite sure that I fell in love with her the moment I saw her appear as an Eskimo in a play she had written. We had been in Tchelet-Lavan together, as she and her parents had left Munich for Vienna in 1933, the year in which Hitler came to power. Her father was not only a Jew but a well-known psychoanalyst, and the family realized that they would be open to persecution on both counts. Hanna had left for Palestine almost immediately after the *Anschluss* and was studying in an agricultural school.

I have forgotten all the details of the trip itself, perhaps because I was so eager to arrive at the destination. The first image I remember is the top of Mount Carmel with a cluster of little houses and green trees coming closer as the *Gerusalemme,* the Italian steamer from Trieste, moved into Haifa port. Suddenly I spotted in the waiting crowd a lovely girl with auburn hair, in a traditional brown leather coat, searching intensely with eyes that seemed on the verge of erupting into hearty laughter. A warm wave of love for all mankind, for my country, and for the fellow who stood next to me at the railing swept over me.

Having come with my charges, I first had to deliver them into the hands of the Youth Aliyah representative, who was to take them to Tel Yosef, a veteran kibbutz in the Jezreel Valley. I promised to look them up there before I returned to Vienna – a moment that seemed as absurd as it was far removed at that time – and only then was I free to take Hanna's hand and to break away from the goings-on.

At my parents' home in Jerusalem, a message was waiting for me. Shaul Avigur, head of the Mossad, wanted to see me.

Messengers who seemed to know my every step arranged for me to be taken to Tel Aviv. There I had a long conversation – or rather interrogation – with the Chief during which I was asked about even the smallest and least significant aspect of our situation in Vienna.

Shaul Avigur appeared more sceptical than he possibly could have been. But the heads of the Haganah had had so many rosy hopes smashed by conditions more severe than they had been able to foresee that they took nothing for granted. I felt like the young recruit admitted to the real centre of responsibility, and had the marvellous revelation that our every movement and train of thought over there, thousands of miles away and under circumstances that even I – at that distance in time and space – found hard to grasp, was meticulously followed and observed by a sharp and deeply concerned mind. Avigur was satisfied with my report about the opportunities to channel people through Yugoslavia via the arrangement with Karthaus and Matossiani and promised that the Mossad would do all it could to get ships for our operation.

Avigur wanted me to see as much of the country as I could and to enjoy my stay to the full, but he was also gently and discreetly prodding me to return to my duties soon. Travelling in armoured buses (at that time Palestine was in the throes of the 'Arab Rebellion', which expressed itself in various terrorist activities), I visited every place where youngsters from Vienna had been placed. From most I took messages of encouragement to the families they had left behind in the clutches of the Nazis.

With Hanna I visited Agami's family in Kfar Giladi, the kibbutz on the Syrian frontier high in the rugged hills of Upper Galilee. It was the place I then regarded as my own eventual home, and Hanna and I made plans about our future – provided I was able to leave Vienna for good and join her. But two short weeks after my arrival, I found myself bidding good-bye to Hanna, my parents and friends and in Haifa once more for the absurd trip back to hell. I was young, optimistic and could not have known the real horror of the years ahead, but at the same time I was returning to a place from which I had no real hope of ever leaving again.

We were just a handful of passengers on the trip from Haifa to Bari, where I disembarked from the serenity of the sea voyage and arranged for the continuation of my trip by train. Going from Bari northwards towards the German border, I found myself next to an Italian officer of apparently fairly high rank. I introduced myself mainly to get his name and rank, but he would reveal neither. When we got to talking, he interrogated me almost as meticulously about my trip to Palestine as Avigur had about the situation in Vienna. He spoke almost flawless German, yet from the beginning of our talk I had the vague feeling that this Italian officer was on my side, rather than on that of his Nazi allies. Proof came when he prepared to leave the train as we were moving into Venice. He drew a many-folded page of newspaper from his breast pocket. 'Read this when you are alone,' he whispered, pressing it into my hand. He wished me good luck and left.

A little later I was reading the lead article from the 23 November 1938 issue of the SS paper *Das Schwarze Korps:* 'As early as 1933, the year in which we took power, we claimed that the Jewish Question should be solved with the most brutal methods and completely. We were right then but were not able to implement our view because we lacked the military strength we possess today. It is essential, it is inevitable. We no longer hear the whining of the world. No power on earth can now keep us from bringing the Jewish Question to its total solution.'

The train pulled northwards toward the border of the Greater German Reich.

(7)

The End of the *Attrato*

BACK IN VIENNA, as usual I was sitting in Agami's office with the rest of the staff, clustered around his desk, making plans for our future exploits and confident that all was going well. Waiting for the message that 'the books had been transferred to the slower tent' had become routine for us, but this time the telephone call from Susak was a little late. Agami was going to lunch with Karthaus that day and was beginning to wonder whether he would be late for the appointment.

The end came suddenly. Renée Wiesner rushed into the office waving a newspaper, unable to utter a word. She placed that day's issue of *Der Angriff* before Agami. Goebbels' afternoon paper, 'the most widely read paper in the Third Reich', carried a banner headline announcing 'Ghost-ship disappears in Adriatic . . . Discovery of ingenious Jewish plot to trick authorities . . . ' Following it was the story, detailed enough, of the trans-shipment of the refugees we had sent the day before from the *Colorado* to the *Attrato* at Susak.

'We've finally made the front page!' Zvi Rechter said, but under Agami's grim glance he immediately regretted the frivolous remark.

Captain Dimitriu had become too sure of himself. He had neglected the standing order that trans-shipment must take place well outside the port of Susak, in a hidden bay and during the night following the clearly visible departure of the *Colorado* on its pleasure cruise. The *Colorado* was not to return to port for three days, to make it plausible that she had carried her tourists to the southern port of Dubrovnik and returned empty for a new load of sightseers in search of distraction. But his girl-friend was waiting for him in Susak. All had gone so well with the trans-shipments from the *Colorado* to the *Attrato* that he thought he could afford a little less conspiratorial prudence for once, get rid of his charges and hurry back to the arms of his woman.

His rashness had been observed by the keen eyes of the *Angriff*'s reporter, who smelled a fine story involving the smuggling of Jews out of Yugoslavia, and perhaps a bonus for bringing to light a new conspiracy of the world's 'Enemy Number One'.

'This is the end of the Yugoslav traffic,' Agami observed dryly. Without another word he left for his meeting with Karthaus, the man who had risked so much to make this traffic possible.

A few days later, we were informed by Szime Spitzer, Deputy President of the Yugoslav Jewish community, that on that same day another meeting had taken place in Belgrade which had decisive bearing on our efforts and was another nail in the coffin of the comfortable transit route to the Adriatic port. The British Ambassador, M. Campbell, had sent his First Secretary, T. A. Shone, to call on Imre Kovacs of the Yugoslav Foreign Office. Campbell, along with his colleagues 'in countries adjacent to the Greater German Reich', had received urgent instructions from London to enlist the understanding and help of the local governments in the struggle against illegal immigration to Palestine.

Campbell was a fine human being and an experienced

diplomat. From his contacts with Yugoslav Jews, he was well informed about their situation, as well as that of the Jews in Greater Germany. Many of the latter had been trying to cross over into Yugoslavia, where a more liberal attitude towards Jews still prevailed, in spite of an anti-Semitic government and fascist policies. But since they could not be refugees in Yugoslavia forever, what they probably planned was to join together and form illegal transports to Palestine. Mr Campbell shuddered when he thought of the problem that faced his government. Here were the destitute, sorely in need of help, ranged against the obligations of His Majesty's Government towards the Arab population of Palestine. Yet he knew that Nazi Germany, together with fascist Italy and independently, was taking an active interest in the Arab Nationalist movement. He also knew that the Nazis were mercilessly expelling Jews from their state and that most countries in Europe and overseas had turned down requests to accept these victims of Nazi brutality. It was all terribly confusing. But this was part of the price Great Britain had to pay for being a major power. So the representative of the major power had to dispatch his First Secretary to meet his contact in the Yugoslav Foreign Office.

In subtle diplomatic language Mr Shone explained that His Majesty's Government expected Yugoslavia not to abet illegal transports. They were criminal, like everything that was against the law and contrary to existing rules. These activities were particularly damnable because of the unseaworthy ships on which greedy and adventurous pirates were transporting the poor refugees, taking undue advantage of their plight. Yugoslavia was in fact only rendering the victims of these insatiable extortionists a service if they prevented them from falling into such well-prepared traps.

The next visitor Imre Kovacs was to receive would be Szime Spitzer. Kovacs and Spitzer had been to school together and were life-long friends. So Kovacs decided that before he reported to his superior about the British support for the German policy against the Jews, it was his duty to warn the Jewish community. There were, Kovacs discreetly told Spitzer, new pressures. He described his meeting with Shone and noted that the Yugoslav Government was likely to fall in line with the British request. As Spitzer knew, the government had few qualms where anti-Jewish tendencies were concerned, and there was no reason to add another item to the long list of irritating subjects that marred their relations with Britain. The Jewish community was obliged, Kovacs warned, to be more careful in the camouflage of border crossings from Greater Germany into Yugoslavia. He concluded the conversation by asserting that if there was anything at all he personally could do to help, the Jewish community had just to let him know what was expected from him. Kovacs then excused himself to report to his superiors about the British intervention.

But the day was not over yet. While Agami was out to lunch with Karthaus, a uniformed policeman arrived at our office and delivered a summons for him to report to Gestapo headquarters at once. Agami had been to the awesome building across the street on previous occasions, but had always gone by appointment with the official he needed to talk to and never by summons. On his many visits to the 'Lion's Jaw', he had dealt with urgent matters of people in jail or in concentration camps, pleading for their release so they could be attached to a convoy on its way to Palestine or to a group for which we had obtained temporary visas for agricultural training in various European countries. Each time we nervously awaited Agami's return, uncertain whether we would ever see him again after his disappearance behind the forbidding doors. But this time the tension was graver than ever. The formal summons was a bad omen. Having made the front page of Goebbels' paper recently was the worst publicity possible.

After signing various registers and receiving a temporary pass, Agami was escorted by a silent, uniformed blackshirt. The guard opened the door of a completely empty, high-ceilinged room for him with a 'Wait here. You will be called.' Agami was careful not to light one cigarette with another, for he only had half a pack with him. But his store was exhausted when, six hours after his arrival in the huge room, he heard a voice. The door had opened – not sufficiently for him to see who was speaking – and a voice said 'Be quiet!' He tortured his brain to identify the voice. Matossiani? Karthaus? It had not been a threatening tone in which the unknown voice had addressed him.

At exactly eight o'clock the door finally opened and an officer called for Agami. His senses were dulled by the long wait, standing in the empty room or walking up and down. He was hungry, thirsty and his nerves were on edge. Walking through the long and quiet corridors of the frightful building, Agami finally reached the elegant room of Dr Lange. Meticulously dressed in a dark business suit and with rimless glasses on his eager eyes, Dr Lange might have been an executive of a commercial firm. The notorious head of the Gestapo's Jewish Department was seated behind an ebony desk covered with files and papers. Each must have contained the fate of a Jewish family. He waved Agami into an easy chair. At least the forms of courtesy are being observed, Agami thought.

When Dr Lange began to speak, however, it was clear that this was an interrogation, not an interview. He asked every routine question about Agami's activities and his personal circumstances as if just this evening the Gestapo had become aware of the existence of an active rescue mission whose front door could be clearly seen from Dr Lange's windows. Finally, after repetitious inquiries about the nature of Agami's work, Lange said, 'Incidentally, your last transport to Palestine was not such a brilliant success.' Agami had expected some reference to the incident and was not surprised, but at the same time he mused on Lange's statement.

If it is Palestine, Eichmann gets the credit for having cleansed Vienna of another bunch of Jews, but you need a destination other than Palestine for your own advancement. Out loud he said: 'Excuse me, the destination of the convoy that received undue publicity was Mexico, not Palestine. You know the person who obtains the visas for me. Ask him. Matossiani will corroborate my assertion.'

It seemed that the respect Matossiani had often expressed for the head of the Jewish Department was not fully reciprocated. Lange waved Matossiani's name aside and continued to dissect every sentence of Agami's replies. It was past midnight when the interrogation ended.

'All right, so it was Mexico,' he said. 'But you must know that there is strong British pressure on Yugoslavia to discontinue transit of Jews over its territory. The British, in any case, seem to think that these convoys end up in Palestine.' Then he handed Agami a typewritten statement that had been lying before him throughout the interrogation. 'Sign this,' he said curtly.

'I, the undersigned, a citizen of Palestine engaged in organizing the emigration of Jews from the Greater German Reich to the Western Hemisphere, affirm that the destination of the convoys at the present time is Mexico.' Agami complied.

We had waited for Agami in his office, discussing his chances. We were all sure that we had seen him for the last time. At last he dragged himself into the room. Slowly and patiently, over tea and cigarettes, he went over every moment of his long ordeal, not so much to retell the story for our benefit as to judge, and let us judge, whether he had stood up to his interrogator correctly and whether there were any hidden catches in what had passed between him and Lange that he had not observed in the tension of his confrontation.

'If you ask me,' said Jukel, one of the leading members of our group, 'the game is up.'

'We are in a new phase,' countered Willi Ritter. 'The

transit through Yugoslavia is finished, of course. But what worries me more is that it seems there is keen competition for patronage of our work among the Nazis. They are dangerous enough when they come singly.'

Agami was deep in thought. Before we dispersed he announced, 'Tomorrow we shall begin to organize a convoy down the Danube through the Black Sea.'

But the next day we were to attend to a quite different matter. Dr Green came in to say that he had just returned from a 'command performance' with *Hauptsturmführer* Eichmann, head of the Centre for Jewish Emigration, where he had been informed that new measures were now in force to expedite the emigration of superfluous Jews. A central office for illegal convoys to Palestine was to be established under the leadership of *Kommerzialrat* Storfer, Eichmann's assistant. Both we and the Revisionists were to cease our private operations. Order would now prevail. He, and he alone, would determine who was to leave and who was to stay. The random selection of youngsters without means was over. Whoever could contribute the price of the trip was to go. Emigration was not a charitable feast; it was to be accelerated and made totally effective. And Agami, this wild man from the Syrian border, had to leave the Reich at once. There was to be no interference with the job by outsiders with special interests.

We listened to Dr Green's account with sinking hearts. We had been caught in the nets of inter-Nazi competition, and Eichmann had emerged as the stronger side. Not that we cared which of the Nazi departments was the channel for processing our travel documents and facilities for accelerated emigration, but we resented Storfer, Eichmann's unscrupulous proconsul, who had no regard for our selective process (which did not diminish the number of emigrants but selected those most apt for the hardships of the trip and for the difficult landing off the shores of Palestine). And we were worried that, just to get rid of as many Jews as possible, Storfer would use unseaworthy ships that would endanger the very lives we were trying to save.

Agami remained calm and philosophical. 'Listen, my children.' He turned to all of us. 'There is one piece of wisdom to which I have become accustomed throughout my life in Kfar Giladi: nothing is as good as it looks at first – but neither is it as bad as it looks at first.'

In spite of the Yugoslav disaster and the embarrassment we had caused him in Yugoslavia, Karthaus promised to protect Agami. He advised Agami not to leave the borders of the German Reich but to go to Berlin for a few days, during which time he would sort things out. 'Who is this upstart Eichmann, anyway?' he exclaimed in annoyance. Agami followed his advice. He was going to use a few days in Berlin to compare notes with our friends there, to co-ordinate work for future contingencies and to try and get information as to what was going on behind the scenes. Agami left that same morning. Barely a week later Karthaus telephoned to say that he had arranged everything and Agami could return to his work in Vienna. The old preferences were still in order, and we had nothing to fear from power-hungry, inexperienced upstarts.

When Agami returned he found an urgent summons to come to the Rothschild Palace: the master of the Zentralstelle demanded his immediate presence there. He was led by an SS guard into a large room wallpapered with dark red silk that not so long ago had been the cabinet of Vienna's ruling Baron Rothschild, Luis. There he encountered Eichmann in his black SS uniform and boots, whip in hand, first impetuously commanding Agami to come nearer, then suddenly detaining him 'three steps from my body'.

'Either you disappear or I shall make you disappear!' Eichmann shouted at Agami, indicating that it was not only the interview that was over.

The same afternoon Agami left by plane for Geneva, where he joined Zvi Yehieli. In the evening he telephoned me in Vienna, urging me on to renewed efforts and indicating that he would support from there the work he had begun in Vienna.

Shortly after Agami's departure I was asked to attend a meeting at *Kommerzialrat* Storfer's office. Zvi Rechter 'the indispensable', my closest friend in the group, agreed to come with me.

When we walked into the enormous conference room, arrayed around a large table covered with green felt were all the representatives of organizations that had anything at all to do with transport to Palestine. Our prestige was at its lowest possible level at the moment: the Yugoslav transport blown, transit facilities in all probability gone forever and Agami banished. Yet Zvi and I felt that we enjoyed a special position in this macabre group. We were the representatives of the Haganah, of the Jewish Agency, of the organized body representing the Jewish people. And we were linked to what counted most: the best disembarkation organization on the shores of Palestine. Everyone around this table, whatever his motives for organizing illegal immigration – political or human concern, the fight against Britain's restrictive immigration policies, or greedy determination to exploit the tragic situation – knew that the essential problem was to land without being detected by the British ships that blockaded the Palestine coast. Of all the elements needed to make rescue by illegal immigration possible, the hardest to come by and the most scarce was ships. Therefore the value of the Haganah's disembarkation unit was highly respected in this room.

Zvi and I decided to take advantage of our privileged position by insisting on the continuation of our own work, even if it would have to be in co-ordination with Storfer. We demanded our share in any transport organized by him and insisted on the use of seaworthy ships as a minimal requirement. In return, we promised to obtain the services of the landing unit for any transport from Austria, no matter the originator of the departure.

Storfer belonged to the class of international businessmen who were convinced that it was they who actually run the world – regardless of the régime of the day. During the post-war period, while Austria was independent but weak, he had established himself as one of her leading tycoons, with tremendous self-assurance and boundless connections in every corner of the world. Since the *Anschluss* he had been – as we well knew – in league with the devil. He understood power – he was convinced that power was a constant condition, whoever wielded it. He had only scorn for the Nazis' narcissistic delight in uniforms and emblems. His shrewdness told him that they concealed insecurity about the things that really matter – the things he understood best – and that a man of his talents was inexpendable to an ambitious régime.

As mass emigration was the order of the day, he, and he alone, was capable of managing this new order on a scale satisfactory to the new masters, and he offered Eichmann his services in the 'purification' of Austria. Storfer was ruthless, ready to shove everybody else aside. He had no time for amateurs and for idealists. He competed, quite clumsily, with the hard-won contacts of the Mossad in the shipping business and caused the price of boats – in such short supply already – to skyrocket. (For all his loyal service to the Third Reich, he was liquidated by Eichmann just before the end of the war.)

In our private code we reported the results of the meeting to Agami by phone. He was quite satisfied with our activities in his absence, though he warned us not to be too optimistic, to work on practical facts, not smooth formulae.

'Try to persuade Storfer to come and see me in Zurich,' Agami said, 'I want to impress on him as strongly as I can who is really in charge among the Jews.'

It was surprisingly easy to induce Storfer to go to Zurich.

He returned impressed by Agami's firmness, and we knew that for a few weeks, at least, he was going to retain his respect for our organization.

The Mossad had transferred the *Colorado* and *Attrato* to the Black Sea, as the Yugoslav disaster had made the continuation of departure from Susak impossible. In spite of the publicity that surrounded the last departure from the Adriatic coast, Captain Dimitriu once again was able to slip through the British warships lying in ambush for him along the Palestine coast. He turned around and raced to Constantsa, determined to make up for his irresponsibility in Susak by extra zeal in his performance from now on. Without delay the two ships were filled in Constantsa with refugees from Germany and from Poland who had found their way to Rumania. A few Rumanian Jews were added to the transport, which was to be the *Attrato*'s seventh, and last, trip to Palestine.

Levi Schwartz, the veteran escort of illegal Haganah ships, was on board the *Attrato* on this occasion. This last trip had had an ominous beginning. Over 100 additional passengers, newly arrived refugees from Austria, had been pressed on the already overcrowded boat just before she left the port of Constantsa. The filth and congestion exceeded the worst precedents. To cap the difficulties, the captain took ill soon after the *Attrato* crossed the Bosporus. He had his sick-bed moved to the bridge and supervised the running of his ship from there. Twice the *Attrato* struck reefs. The inexperienced sailors who did their best to replace their sick captain kept the ship on course near the shore, but their prudence was rewarded by the sharp rocks that run along the Turkish coast. However, the ship's strong engines and the brave captain's instructions twice succeeded in freeing the ship from its trap.

Near Cyprus they ran into a storm so strong that the ship had to take shelter, lying at anchor in a bay closely guarded by units of the British Army and Navy. On the third day a coded cable was received by the ship's wireless: EQUIP 100 MEN WITH LIFEBELTS, APPROACH TEL AVIV, STOP AT A DISTANCE OF 2 MILES AND LOWER THEM IN BOATS. WARN THEM TO BE READY FOR ANYTHING.' The message was an expression of the determination to stand firm against the British.

Levi Schwartz called all the men on board to the upper deck and read the cable, and asked for 100 volunteers. Many more than the required number rose from the cramped position in which they were penned up on the narrow deck. Levi warned them of the danger they were going to meet. But only one, a married man and father of two little children, withdrew voluntarily.

The *Attrato* was to move to a point directly opposite the beach of Tel Aviv. There she was to unload her passengers under the cover of darkness and, it was hoped, slip away for a new trip to Constantsa. Captain Dimitriu did all he could, in his miserable condition, to steer the ship to the point indicated to him by wireless from the shore. It was a pitch-black night, but the sky was bright with shining stars. Levi suddenly observed two stars that moved; they were man-made: the searchlights of a British cruiser blocking the *Attrato*'s approach to the beach – now just a stone's throw away. The cruiser, almost ramming the little ship, pushed her in the direction of Haifa port. Stern warnings were broadcast over the cruiser's loudspeaker: 'Proceed to Haifa and your passengers will be disembarked unharmed. Then they shall be detained.' Once inside Palestinian territorial waters, the *Attrato* was unceremoniously sequestered by the British Navy as soon as she entered port.

Two months later, the *Colorado* shared her sister's fate. On 28 July 1939, the ship's fifth trip to Palestine, with 377 passengers on board, she was stopped by the British warship *Hotspur*, asked to identify herself, and brought in forcibly under escort of three British Men o' War – the *Hotspur,* the

Hereward and the *Havoc* – which in April had been assigned the mission of intercepting illegal arrivals.

With Agami banished from Vienna, Zvi and I took over the operation of the office, and when the Twenty-first Zionist Congress opened on 16 August 1939, we found ourselves in Geneva attending a meeting of Mossad operatives convened under the auspices of the Congress. The Congress and our parallel gathering were held under the terrifying shadow of impending war. Plans for Jewish participation in the Allied cause were gravely drawn up side by side with programmes to accelerate our rescue efforts in Europe and step up the struggle against the British White Paper. The tension mounted steadily throughout the days of deliberation, and on the day the Congress closed, Switzerland mobilized its citizens' army. A special committee on behalf of the Haganah decided which emissaries and local activists were to continue their operations in Europe and which were to return to Palestine. Zvi and I were instructed to continue in Vienna, and as our plane from Geneva landed in Salzburg we heard Hitler's final threat against Poland. A few hours later, when we had reached Vienna, the German Army was sweeping into Poland. The world was at war.

In Geneva I learned that on 8 May 1939 members of the Jewish Agency Executive met in closed session in Jerusalem. Ben Gurion presided over their meeting, and everyone present sensed that he was living through a crucial moment. Ben Gurion reviewed the sequence of harrowing events that had led up to the present deliberations: another Royal Commission had returned from Palestine, this time reporting that partition was impractical and that there was no solution in sight. Thereupon the British Prime Minister called a conference of Jews, Arabs and British at which each side was supposed to put all its cards on the round table, and somehow a compromise would miraculously emerge. Neville Chamberlain, who had just sacrificed Britain's ally Czechoslovakia to Hitler at Munich, was not in a position to command the respect of the Arab delegations. Their threats to join Hitler's Axis turned the conference into a shambles. Ben Gurion and his colleagues became convinced that Britain was preparing the abrogation of the Mandate and, in fact, the repeal of the Balfour Declaration.

As the British despaired of achieving any agreement between the Jews and the Arabs, they were now proposing a plan of their own: during the next five years, 75,000 more Jews would be allowed to enter Palestine, but thereafter immigration would be dependent upon Arab consent; on the other hand, Palestine could not become an independent Arab state without Jewish consent. As Ben Gurion said, a more wicked, more shortsighted policy is difficult to imagine: the British deny the Jews what they want most – immigration – and they deny the Arabs what they want most – Palestine as an independent Arab state. For the first time since the destruction of the Temple, Ben Gurion told his colleagues, the Jews were engaged in a serious struggle with a Great Power and did not ask for pity, they demanded justice. The British ministers could not believe their ears when Ben Gurion declared at the London Conference that 'the Jewish minority in Palestine needed no guarantees and that this minority is capable of looking after itself.' In the horrified silence of the council chamber, where the Jewish delegation from Palestine confronted the British Government, Ben Gurion had said: 'Jewish immigration can be stopped only by British bayonets. Nor can Palestine be turned into an Arab state, against the resistance of the Jews, without the permanent presence of those bayonets.'

Ben Gurion informed his colleagues that in a few days the government would publish a White Paper embodying the ideas on which the Jewish Agency had declared war. The

British proposals were now to become official policy. The session became a council of war. The Executive of the Jewish Agency began to act as if it were the government of a sovereign state. It decided not to wait any longer for British concessions on immigration: The Jewish Agency was to instruct the Haganah to step up unfettered, free immigration, without regard for British restrictions. Every settlement along the coast was to be given its store of arms, rations for an emergency and standing orders for the moment when the night might be disturbed by the unannounced arrival of clandestine immigrants. The White Paper was promulgated on 17 May 1939 and remained in force, officially, until the dying day of Britain's Mandate over Palestine.

(8)

You Haven't Much
to Lose

RENÉE WIESNER, our secretary, came into my room in a
flurry of excitement and leaned over to whisper into my ear
because, as usual, my office was crowded with people coming
and going, everyone looking for everyone else with an urgent
message or a desperate inquiry.

'There is a man outside,' she said, 'a well-dressed Gentile.
He murmured something about representing a travel agency,
but he also mentioned the Gestapo. Anyway, he wants to see
you.'

I was quite calm as I received him while Renée cleared the
room. He was a strange mixture of a man, burly and somehow slim at the same time. He wore a well-tailored dark grey
herringbone tweed suit and with it – somewhat incongru-
ously – a 'Styrer Hut'. I remember feeling that the hat was
supposed to symbolize his Nazi loyalty, in the absence of any
other identifying emblem. I remained seated and waved the
stranger into the chair opposite me.

'My name is Ceipek,' he began, 'and I have some important connections. Never mind the details. I was a Nazi in the Austrian underground for more than ten years. I always supported the union between Austria and Germany: Austrians are Germans, and Austria has been decadent and in permanent decay since the last war. But now that the Nazis are here, I see what they are doing: indiscriminate arrests, Jews having to sweep Schuschnig's plebiscite slogans off the streets, jealous neighbours allowed to rob Jewish property, people tortured and mishandled only because they are Jews. I have fallen out of love with my Party. They are exactly as evil as they have been made out to be by what, until now, I always considered enemy propaganda.'

'A likely story,' I said to Ceipek after listening to this confession.

'Don't look at me so sceptically. If I were less than sincere, would I have come here to your office in mufti? Wouldn't I have come in my SS uniform and taken you and the rest of them? Think a bit! I want to make up, in a small way, for having helped to bring this about.'

He had considered the problem for some time, he continued. To stand up against the Nazis openly would be suicide. So he had decided that, rather than killing himself, he was going to do something for their principal victims.

'This way I am also going to take revenge on them for having deceived me. I wanted the Greater German Reich, but not this bestial nightmare of sadistic atrocities,' he said in a matter-of-fact voice with a playful Austrian accent and a slight Hungarian inflection, smoking all the while through an unusually long gilded cigarette holder.

We had the great advantage, at that time, of being impervious to fear. We knew that we were lost anyway, so there was no need to take fright in any single case. If we had had such a thing as hope for our own survival, we would have been much more cautious about taking huge risks.

'All right. We'll try you out,' I said.

Thereupon, without further ado, he moved closer and said, 'Now then, what are your immediate needs?'

'First of all, I want you to meet my closest colleague. Don't say you are too conspiratorial to work with two of us, because either of us can be caught at any moment by your friends, and if you knew only one of us, the contact you want to establish so badly in order to salve your conscience would be finished.'

He agreed and I called for Zvi. Eminently perceptive and quick-witted, Zvi understood the situation as soon as he sat down with us. 'There is, of course, the problem of "The Twelve",' he said. The Gestapo was indiscriminately arresting Jews in the streets. Stateless persons were even more severely persecuted than Austrian Jews. Those who could not prove on the spot that they had concrete plans for early departure from the Greater German Reich were carried off to a concentration camp. In their desperation one after another had come to see us. They all had talked themselves out of arrest several times, but they could escape arrest no longer; they had to show the Gestapo some sort of visa.

Zvi had sat down at the typewriter and produced a document breathing authority which said that so and so, a stateless person, 'had been accepted for emigration overseas' and would be able to leave the German Reich within a fortnight. With this 'document' victims were able to gain a little extra time. But the fourteen days were running out, and Zvi was terribly worried.

Ceipek listened attentively. 'Have these people here at your office tomorrow at nightfall,' he said. 'I shall send three cabs. Pay the drivers whatever they charge for the trip. Your people will be taken to Hungary.'

Zvi and I heard his proposal with wonder – and some suspicion. Reading our thoughts, Ceipek waved them away with an impatient gesture of his hand: 'You haven't much to lose. Try me out.'

'This is nerve-racking,' Zvi complained when Ceipek had left. 'Let's take the day off!'

Sitting in the tense atmosphere of the darkened room, we had not noticed that outside it was a luscious day. This was definitely an occasion for the 'grand promenade'. We took the tram to Grinzing, feeling like two youngsters running away from school. This frivolous mood persisted until we began our ascent of the Kahlenberg. In the stillness of the Wienerwald, we gathered our wits and recapitulated the talk with our newest collaborator.

It was not only what he had said that impressed us with the obvious scope of his capabilities. 'He has a deadly poignancy about himself,' Zvi said. 'He must be very high up in their hierarchy. Otherwise he could not afford to play this fatal double game.' Of course, it was too early to judge. So far we had only talked. But if he was capable of getting stateless individuals without documents to Hungary and to safety, here was an outlet of which we had never dreamt. And if he could achieve this, there would be other schemes that he could devise. It was our duty to discover – and to exploit – them fully, not to lose time. There was no way of knowing how long we could enjoy this newest acquisition.

When we reached a bench and sat down, and the stillness of the forest was disturbed only by the chirping of the crickets, we resolved that the time had come to begin preparations for the evacuation of the last of our old leadership. The certainty of war was growing every day. In the middle of March 1939, six months after the Munich Pact, Czechoslovakia was occupied by Germany. Then Germany took over Hungary and large parts of Poland, while a puppet state was set up in the remaining area – the 'Independent Republic of Slovakia' – under the rule of a Nazi-type organization, the Hlinka Guard. A Catholic priest, Father Joseph Tiso, became dictator in Bratislava, the capital of the new 'republic', a charming town that had always been a kind of suburb of

Vienna. From that day on, we waited for war to begin.

Soon we would be cut off from Palestine and from the roads leading there. We had to provide a ship for those of our comrades who had agreed to postpone their own departure in order to be of service on the farms and in the office. We had to ask Jukel, our senior colleague, to come to Vienna. If he agreed – and there was no doubt about the position he would take – we would proceed.

After a few hours in the outer world, we returned to the office and I phoned Moosbrunn. Jukel was still at work in the fields, but the message would be delivered when he returned to his quarters. He arrived in Vienna at lunchtime the next day, his keen eyes looking forward to receive news about the general situation. With a warm smile on his kind face he said: 'Greetings, you city-dwellers. If you are really the big shots you are supposed to be, can you provide a meal for a hungry farmhand who has the chance to spend one day in the great metropolis?'

'We've thought of that,' I said, 'and were lucky enough to find a place that is good enough to feed sub-humans like you and me.' Jukel's spirits rose when we arrived at Pataki's; all he had expected was some third-rate café. The headwaiter received us as honoured guests, the orchestra played 'Bel Ami' and as we ordered the day's specialty we settled down comfortably to outline our plans.

When all was set, we waited for confirmation of the arrival of the boat coming to Constantsa to take Jukel's group. I tried to put a call through to Ruth Aliav, the legendary Mossad representative in Bucharest. If all went well and there had been news, Ruth would have sent a telegram in the absence of telephone lines. The fact that there was no news at all was a sinister omen. Our preparations for the departure of well over 1,000 people were almost complete, but they could not move before we were certain that the ship was waiting for them.

A tall, lanky, red-haired youth had entered my room as I was frantically fumbling with the telephone. His eyes were inflamed and a strange smile was stamped on his face.

'A new state has come into existence. Go and see the Slovak Consul. He is new on the job, and he needs money. He will let you use his diplomatic telephone if you pay him for it.'

It took me a moment to recognize that this red-headed youth was Joszi Friedmann. A few years earlier we had ostracized him from our youth organization for he had turned communist and was undermining the discipline of our group, which was based on Zionist Socialism. But he was a sensitive boy, a gifted artist with a magnetic personality, a charmer who had won my mother's heart. She let him come to our house to do his homework and to paint even after we had had our political row.

'You must help me and my family get out of here,' he now said. 'Forget our past political differences. I must save my skin.'

To my delight, we had a few places in Holland at our disposal, and I was able to tell Joszi that he could go to Holland and apply for entry permits for his family as soon as he had started to work on a Dutch farm. The fine tip about Slovakia was just the first in a long row of Joszi's brilliant ideas.

Now I needed Ceipek. He arrived immediately after I phoned, almost as though he had been waiting behind the door. Putting his black Eden hat on the table, he took his extra-long cigarette holder from his coat pocket and analysed our summons in his unperturbed manner: 'You want to take advantage of the change. Give me your orders.'

Joszi's suggestion appealed to him. He had seen us suffering the agonies of interrupted telephone calls, the interference of hostile censors. Ceipek dialed a number and spoke softly to someone who gave him detailed information about the new Slovak staff. Then he phoned the new consulate and announced our visit.

We hailed a cab and drove to the Slovak consulate. It seemed to me that Ceipek had never met the new Consul General, and I do not know exactly what he told the diplomat or how he explained my presence, but after they had spoken for a few minutes the Consul offered me his seat, moved the telephone across the desk and, together with Ceipek, left the room. I had taken over the switchboard of the young sovereign State of Slovakia's Consulate General in Vienna.

Diplomatic calls received priority, and in a little while I heard Ruth's voice. It sounded like celestial music – but the news was very bad. For the first time we were able to speak at length without using code words, which sometimes were confusing. Ruth was obviously not quite able to grasp how I was taking such liberties, but she accepted the situation. Finally she told me that there was absolutely no ship in sight. Most flags had already been called up by the various countries for service of some sort. Crews were reluctant to take risks with human cargo under clandestine conditions, when it was so easy to sell one's services for more conventional jobs at equally exorbitant prices. Jewish refugees were an especially unwelcome commodity: the Germans wanted to get rid to them at all cost, and the British refused them admission to territory under their control. There was no ship in Constantsa, and none likely to turn up.

The call over, Ceipek and my host returned to the room. Not a word was said about the content of my telephone communication. The Consul General treated us to some very strong barazk to celebrate his country's newly won independence and to cement our recent friendship. Ceipek informed the Slovak that I would use his phone from time to time. Money was not mentioned. But in the cab on the way back to the office, Ceipek gave me a slip of paper with the number of a bank account in Zurich, to which I was to transfer £ 10 after each call.

Zvi was waiting for me back in the crowded office. He had entertained no illusions, so he was not disappointed by what I had to tell him.

'This is a hard time for getting ships,' he agreed. 'But let's wait. They will swing it. They always do.'

We decided to go to Moosbrunn personally to talk the situation over with Jukel. His reaction to our latest snag was directly contrary to Zvi's faith in patience.

'We must move,' Jukel summed up. 'The sooner we take the people out of the boundaries of Germany and even into Slovakia, the better.'

I tended to agree with him.

'It's true that we're giving up the relative advantage of our knowledge of the "local scene"; here, at least, we know whom to alert in an emergency, though it might be quite futile to do so. But Slovakia sounds like a place where we could bluff our way through, at least for a while.'

Zvi still had his reservations, though.

'Sending 1,000 people to Slovakia is a plunge into uncertainty. To get them from there down to the Black Sea we need Danube ships. And if that's what we decide to do, the sooner we hire them – before the war reaches Rumania and the river freezes over – the better for all of us.'

We decided to move the 1,000 on Danube boats to Bratislava, in order to have them out of the Greater German Reich; to pressure the Mossad for a ship; and to cultivate our contacts with the Danube Steamboat Company – and with the new Slovak régime – so that they would hold our people on their steamers for a maximal period and give us all the time needed to obtain a seaworthy ship for the emigrants.

On the slow drive back to Vienna, Zvi and I hardly exchanged a word. As I entered my office, I spotted an envelope crossed with red and bearing the ominous sign of the swastika. I opened it with trembling hands. It was an order to present myself immediately at the office of one of the new masters of the city of Vienna, an official – still somewhat obscure – whose name was to become synonymous with the most outrageous barbarism in recorded history. Now it was my turn to meet Adolf Eichmann.

The SS guard took me from the gate through a winding hallway up a wide staircase. The Rothschild Palace was dimly lit. Most of the rare treasures had been carried off by the conquerors. Here and there a relief laid into the wall or a piece of tapestry overlooked during removal gave the place the ambiguous air of a deserted showpiece turned office building. Signs and notices stuck into the expensive panelling indicated where Adolf Eichmann's men worked. It was a long, still walk until my guard and I reached the large and rather narrow room in which Eichmann waited. He stood at the far end in black boots and uniform, whip in hand, one foot on a chair.

'Closer!' he shouted as I moved towards him. 'Closer!' Then suddenly like thunder, 'Three steps away!' and the whip cut the air with a vicious whistling sound as if to demarcate the line between us. He sat down. I remained standing in front of his desk.

'Progress is too slow!' he barked at me. We did not work quickly enough. Why did we get so few people down the Danube to the Black Sea and through Yugoslavia to the Adriatic and from there to Palestine? And why did we not push more people into England and America? Were we not aware that he had had enough of us? It was time to make the place *judenrein* – and soon!

'We do all we can,' I said. There were certain facilities for Western Europe, which we used up as soon as we received travel documents from his office. Sometimes, however, his office delayed these urgently needed papers. As for Palestine, there were additional obstacles: it was increasingly difficult to obtain ships, in view of the growing tension in the world; and we had to move our ships secretly, otherwise they were captured by the British.

'Mere excuses!' Eichmann shouted, as if he were addressing me across the ocean. I was protecting a political interest. We moved so slowly because we insisted on young people only. But they were poor, and we were impeded by a constant lack of money for our work. We also had to take some of the wealthy, even though they might be sick and old. He had no time to lose while we were indulging our caprices.

I insisted that the only reason for our selectivity was the hardship of the trip. The passengers had to be able to jump into the sea near the shore to escape the British. But unable to concede a point in this 'debate', he shrieked, 'You and Agami are the only Jews who ever answer back. Let the old and the sick jump into the water too! From now on you will have to take them!' He ordered me to contact his 'handy-man', Storfer, who would co-ordinate the work and speed up emigration. And with that I was dismissed.

We were determined to avoid cooperation with Storfer – which meant collaboration with Eichmann. When I told Zvi and Jukel about the orders I had been given by Eichmann, we agreed that this new development made the departure of Jukel's transport even more urgent and that we had taken the right decision just in time.

Early the following morning Zvi entered my office carrying two suitcases. He had come up from the cellar and was on his way to the Danube Steamboat Company. In the cellar we had stored several huge wooden crates jammed with ever-growing bundles of German money in bank-notes. Some of the wealthy Jews – and some who had very little – brought us their money before they fled. Rather than let it fall into the hands of the Nazis – to whom they were leaving all their possessions in their abandoned flats – they wanted us to use their savings to help other people who had less. Zvi had filled up two suitcases with the money needed for the hire of the Danube Steamers, and he was on his way.

'Funny,' he said, lifting his two valises to demonstrate their weight, 'I couldn't get a sandwich for all this in one of the racially pure joints on my way.'

'Don't tempt the innkeepers,' I said. 'The contents of your suitcases might make them forget the Nuremberg laws.'

'See you in hell,' Zvi said as he went out on what actually was a hair-raising mission. What if the police should stop him – for any reason whatsoever?

When we applied for 1,000 passports at Eichmann's Central Office, we were treated like preferred customers. Our man who brought the list was even invited by the SS corporal to take a seat! And to save work and time for everybody, Eichmann's office proposed issuing us a collective passport. There would be a list of 1,000 names with particulars and photographs attached; just one passport form would be valid for the entire group. We accepted this arrangement joyfully. Our emigrants only needed the passport to cross from Greater Germany into the satellite puppet state of Slovakia on board German Danube boats. From there they would travel down the Danube to a boat that would be waiting to take them to a landing place where no one would bother about passport formalities anyway.

After some serious deliberation, Jukel appointed his general staff. As usual, the transport was sub-divided into groups of twenty people, each with a group commander. Fifty such group commanders were selected and briefed for their duties on board. It turned out that the conscientious preparation of the infrastructure of this huge transport was of far greater importance than Jukel had thought when he took routine measures in their preparation. The date was fixed for the departure to Bratislava, for, first of all, we wanted our people beyond the confines of the Greater German Reich. We still had no word about a seagoing vessel from Rumania.

After receiving exaggerated payment for the trip down the river, the Danube Steamboat Company suddenly changed its mind. Their boat would not leave before they had word from their *own* representative in the Black Sea port of Sulina that the seagoing ship was there to receive the passengers. They returned the money and cancelled our reservations. Every morning we tried to phone both Geneva and Bucharest, hoping against hope that we would get the answer we so anxiously awaited.

In desperation we turned to Ceipek, and he again saved the day. He brought the collective passport we had received from Eichmann's office to his friend, the Slovak Consul, and received from him regular Slovak entry visas for the 1,000 persons on the list.

'A much better arrangement,' Ceipek said in the matter-of-fact voice he reserved for the announcement of great achievements, 'than having your people crammed into a ship that rocks and pitches in the middle of the Danube. This way they will be allowed to stay in Slovakia until your contacts in Bucharest can find a ship for them.' The visas cost us 3 marks each, a negligible amount. But the Slovak Consul was eager for more of these illegal transports.

From Geneva, Agami informed us that the Mossad fully supported our decision to get the transport going. He and his colleagues calculated that their days were numbered, and the sooner we brought about the emigration of Hehalutz from Austria, the safer for all involved.

When our transport finally left for Slovakia, Zvi, I and the few others who remained behind had the bitter feeling of being the last rats on a sinking ship. We now organized ourselves for the predictable problems we would encounter if the Slovaks became impatient with their guests. Sooner or later they would threaten to send them back to where they had come from unless we could move them on towards the Black Sea, the Mediterranean and Palestine.

Still, no ship in Constantsa. From day to day it became more difficult to telephone abroad. Sometimes it took three days before we could contact either Agami in Geneva or Ruth in Bucharest. Zvi and I tried hard to discipline ourselves and not to mention our problems needlessly. We applied our time to the different chores of mopping up after the departure of the remnants of the Austrian Hehalutz. Bills had to be paid, property of various kinds liquidated, and we had to be careful not to get ourselves arrested by mistake, now that we were beginning to believe that maybe we, too, would be able to get out.

As often as I dared, I went to the Slovak Consulate to telephone when other lines were cut or when the censors would not allow private communications, so I was also able to keep in touch with Bratislava. The Consul told me that his authorities were gradually becoming fed up with so many Jews in the town. Ours were not the only 'temporary residents'. There was a transport from Prague and one from Berlin and Danzig, all there on sufferance of the Slovak Government. They, too, were waiting for boats to carry them downstream.

'In fact,' the Consul said, 'the Danube is going to freeze over soon. And if they are still in Bratislava when that happens, you may rest assured that you will meet those people in Vienna again. They will not be allowed to hibernate in Slovakia.'

I decided to go to Bratislava personally. If our transport were sent back, we would never meet its members again; they would be sent directly to a concentration camp. Once again I turned to Ceipek for help and explained the problem to him. If I used my German passport for the trip, I could never again obtain an exit permit, even if I somehow managed to return from Bratislava to Vienna – which was doubtful. Then I would have lost my most treasured possession – the exit permit – for a trip of uncertain value. But I had to go; I felt that I must encourage our people in their transit camp and prevent their return to Austria.

Ceipek, as always, was quite unperturbed. 'So we shall go there tonight. Be ready at seven. My car will pick you up. Go buy yourself one of these grey leather greatcoats, the kind the *Luftwaffe* wears. And don't take any documents except your soldier's paybook.'

Precisely at seven, a black 'Graef und Stift' car stopped in front of the house. Attired in my grey leather coat, I leaped downstairs. An SS driver, saluting smartly, opened the car door for me. On the fender there was a Gestapo pennon neatly ensconced on a celluloid folder. And in the back seat of the car, with all the dignity of high office and the full regalia of elevated rank, sat an SS officer. With a whimsical smile under his mustache, he waved me to his side. My sinking heart began to beat again. It was Ferdinand Ceipek. The driver obviously took me for my cover – a high-ranking *Luftwaffe* officer on a secret mission to Bratislava. Deferentially, he rolled up the dividing pane between his seat and ours and we drove into the night.

Just about one hour later we stopped at the German frontier control. At once Ceipek got out, taking my soldier's paybook with him. I was the honoured VIP, too distinguished to look after frontier formalities myself. Ceipek identified himself by some document that, in addition to his splendid uniform, convinced the guard that everything was in order. Ceipek and the guard exchanged salutes. We were in Slovakia.

After the blackout in Vienna and the tension of the ride, Bratislava, all lit up and gay, looked like a fairy-tale city to me. We drove to the Palace Hotel, where Ceipek had reserved rooms for us. After a respectable few minutes in my room, I went out and took a cab to the transit camp.

Jukel received me like an apparition from another world, but we soon settled down to serious talk. The Jewish community of Bratislava had established a special welfare committee which had brought mattresses to this abandoned factory building, and the floor of the huge hall was covered with sleeping people. A child cried, and in a corner a sick man moaned in his sleep. Jukel occupied the porter's lodge, where he had his little office and a mattress.

To remain as unobtrusive as possible, no one left the hall during the day. The place was littered with their belongings and with the refuse of a temporary stay that had turned into a long drawn-out nightmare. The Slovak police, Jukel told me, were losing patience with the Jewish squatters from Vienna. The Danube was due to freeze over in a few weeks. Then the Jews would not be able to move down the river until spring. If they were held up in Bratislava because no boat was available in Constantsa now, at this early stage of the war, was it likely, the authorities asked, that their foreign patrons would be able to supply one in a few months, when the war would no doubt be at its height? The last thing they needed was a lot of Austrian Jews around at a time when they were beginning to see to the removal 'of their own Jews'. The police officer who inspected the camp every morning had, in fact, given Jukel an ultimatum: move down to Yugoslavia or up to Austria within ten days.

But Jukel thought he had a solution to the latest dilemma.

'These people are new on their jobs. Their salaries are small, and most of them think that their days are numbered because sooner or later the Germans are going to take over Slovakia. So we must try to bribe their chief, Colonel Houssek, the supposed strong man who will decide our fate.'

Anticipating an emergency, Jukel had hoarded the necessary money. The women of the Bratislava Jewish community who looked after the camp had smuggled in bundles of Slovak currency. Jukel showed me the pile of money he had stored away in a wooden box; it looked like an impressive amount. My unexpected arrival provided the missing link – the vehicle of remittance.

'Your Gestapo aide will get you into police headquarters,

and you are the best per_on to deliver the bribe,' he said. 'If Houssek shows any false pride and feels insulted by your attention, only you will have to answer for your indiscretion, and the camp will not be implicated in the manoeuvre.'

To implement his plan Jukel went into the hall where the people slept and, careful not to step on anyone, walked to the men's area and woke one of the sleepers. 'Dr Schechter,' he said to the young man whose dreams had been abruptly interrupted, 'I need your black briefcase, for a public purpose.' Dr Schechter reached behind his head and gave Jukel the case that he used as a pillow. In former years this elegant and efficient looking briefcase had served one of Vienna's most promising young surgeons.

Ceipek was waiting for me in the lobby of the Palace Hotel. 'With this distinguished briefcase in your hands and your grey leather coat, you really do look like one of those pompous, inflated Air Force staff officers who move around the Greater German Reich as if the survival of humanity depended on their brilliant schemes,' he commented.

'The future of a tiny part of it does indeed,' I replied.

We went into the hotel's grill room for a luxurious supper and plotted our brilliant scheme. The more I saw of Ceipek, the less I understood who he was.

The next morning I found him in his room on the phone to the local police. He had made an appointment for himself – strictly on business – so we would be expected at the gate. He had implied that he was in the company of an important emissary from Vienna who had come specially to see Colonel Houssek.

Ceipek's car was on hand and we drove to police headquarters. The Hlinka guard was not satisfied with Ceipek's credentials alone – he wanted mine, too. The grey coat and the black attaché case looked fine, but he must have become suspicious because I wore no uniform cap and no insignia of rank whatsoever. But Ceipek, all authority and Greater

German might, waved him aside with one arrogant growl. With the offended glare of the rejected guard burning in my back, we strode up the stairs to the awesome place.

Ceipek brought me to Colonel Houssek's room, introduced me vaguely as the man who had been sent over specially from across the border and left us. I put the briefcase on the floor under Houssek's table and got straight to the point. We did not expect Slovakia to become a haven for these Jews from Greater Germany, I explained. But those who were already here would have to stay until they could move on. Everybody in Vienna expected Slovakia to show that much goodwill and cooperation. We were also, however, ready to do something for the Slovak Police Pension Fund, and imperceptibly I pushed the briefcase so that it just touched Colonel Houssek's foot. For the briefest second a warm glimmer appeared in his eye. He would do what he could, he said. He would give them another three months so that they could arrange for the continuation of their trip. He had always hoped he would be able to oblige the authorities across the border on some important matter. After all, we were all in the same boat.

I thanked him warmly for his patriotic understanding and hoped that Ceipek would come in and take me away. The colonel was just as anxious for me to go as I was. After what seemed an eternity of small talk and pleasantries, Ceipek arrived. We took leave, and before closing the door we caught a glimpse of Colonel Houssek coming up from his reverent bow with my briefcase in hand, eagerly examining its contents.

I then went to the best leather shop in town, bought Dr Schechter a new briefcase, and took a cab to the transit camp to give Jukel the good news and bid him good-bye for the last time.

Ceipek waited for me patiently at the Palace Hotel. Our mission had been a complete success – so far. But one perilous hurdle was still before us: we had to get me back into Germany in my deficient uniform and on my dubious soldier's paybook. This time both of us were tense. We lunched on roast goose – the Slovak specialty and a dream for anyone living on German war rations, not yet in effect in the sovereign State of Slovakia. Then we began our return journey.

Our car reached the border after a short drive. We merely saluted the Slovak guards; they did not worry about travellers going into Germany, knowing the real authorities would take care of them in any case. And in a moment we faced the red-and-white barrier of Greater Germany, the Nazi flag, the guard. He immediately asked both of us to follow him into his small hut. After carefully scrutinizing Ceipek's documents, he handed them back and reached for mine. Trying to control my trembling hand, I gave him my paybook. He looked at it and then at me. Carefully he studied the first page of the paybook – all he was allowed by law to see of it, as the following pages might contain information about the bearer's posting, accessible only to his superior officer. And there he made his mistake. Obviously dissatisfied with the remark 'released from armed service' he began to turn the page.

Spurned by desperation I tore the book away from him and shouted, 'Don't you know your regulations, man?' Nothing impressed a German soldier more than arrogance. The guard saluted, bounded ahead and opened the car door for us both. For the rest of the trip, neither Ceipek nor I were able to utter a word. Ceipek's driver, cool and unperturbed, drove on towards the city of my birth.

When the danger that our convoy might be returned to Vienna was removed – thanks to the gift to the 'Pension Fund' of the Slovak Police – we began to look for a solution in a new direction: farther downstream, towards the Black Sea. The general attitude of the Slovak police seemed to improve immediately after our excursion. Not only did that one Viennese convoy profit from the more lenient attitude of Colonel Houssek's gratitude, but Bratislava became a central transit point. At first only rare convoys organized by the Revisionists had passed through the sleepy town. As their successful route down the Danube and to the Black Sea became known, other organizers of illegal convoys began to use it. Furthermore, when Yugoslavia shut her land frontiers to the transit of organized groups of refugees, the relative autonomy of Slovakia, the readiness of the Slovakian authorities to accommodate well-paying guests, the help of the Jewish community of Bratislava and the Danube all combined to make this new escape route popular.

Agami maintained constant contact with the Jewish community in Yugoslavia, and their efforts were what finally brought about what then seemed to be a happy development. Szime Spitzer, the deputy head of the Organization of Yugoslav Jewish Communities, succeeded in chartering from the Yugoslav Government Corporation three small vessels used for excursions along the Danube. These pleasure boats were sent from Yugoslavia to Bratislava, where the stranded travellers boarded them with excitement. But their joy was short-lived. On 30 December 1939, just as they were about to leave Yugoslav territory for the Rumanian stretch of the trip down the Danube, the river began to freeze over, and the little riverboats were forced to speed to the nearest shelter, the port of Cladovo, on the border between Yugoslavia and Rumania.

The land border was closed: Rumania wanted no refugees to travel through its territory. The British Government, in the early days of the war still a powerful opponent for a small country like Rumania, had made the purchase of Rumanian oil (which was more vital for Britain than its sale was for Rumania) conditional on Rumania's obligation not to allow any more refugees to pass through her territory for the purpose of illegal immigration to Palestine. The Danube was at that time still considered an international waterway. The Yugoslavs showed great patience and understanding in allowing their riverboats to lay over in the frozen port of Cladovo. It was clear that much time would go by before they were able to leave. Not only did the ice have to melt; a ship had to reach the Black Sea port and receive the convoy held up in Cladovo.

In the spring of 1940, the Yugoslav authorities, again under the influence of Spitzer's pleading, permitted the refugees to disembark from the tiny vessels on which they had spent the difficult winter. A camp was established at the outskirts of the town of Cladovo, and while they enjoyed its relative comfort, they also realized that they had been allowed to disembark only because hope for the continuation of their trip was very slender.

Agami, still in exile in Geneva, was determined to find a ship for the people in Cladovo. He obtained from the American Joint Distribution Committee the money necessary to buy a ship. Now all he had to do was find a seller. With the outbreak of war, the shipping market had become very quiet. Most countries had called up their ships for one kind of duty or another; only essential voyages were permitted by the naval authorities of many governments in order to reduce the danger of mishaps and accidents that might lead to retaliation and bring about dangerous clashes. The few ships still available with crews ready to take great risks had much better opportunities in the black market than in carrying clandestine Jewish immigrants. The prospects of ships being sequestered by the British Navy on the coast of Palestine deterred captains and owners of these few ships from becoming involved in our kind of trade. Agami saw one faint hope after another dissolve.

Since the spring of 1939 a new man was working in Athens, picking up where Yehieli had left off when he moved to Geneva. The new arrival was Shmariah Zamereth, an American citizen and a member of Kibbutz Beth Hashitah, who might be described as a well-balanced fanatic. The Mossad hoped that with his American passport Shmariah would be able to hold out in Europe longer than any holder of a Palestinian passport. He used his considerable charm in trying to revive the Verenikos brothers' interest in our endeavours. But they had lost three of their ships to the British Navy because of their illegal work and were so downcast that they could not be moved to assume new risks.

The Jewish Agency demanded of the mandatory government a quota of immigration certificates for Jews from the Balkans in view of the imminent fall of the Balkan countries to Nazi Germany. The High Commissioner was good enough to receive the Chief Rabbi of Palestine, Rabbi Herzog, but he remained unmoved by the Rabbi's eloquent plea for the Balkan Jews. There were at the moment, as far as His Majesty's Government was able to ascertain, seven illegal boats *en route* to Palestine, the High Commissioner informed the Chief Rabbi. The government, bound by the restriction of the White Paper of May 1939, was obliged to keep in reserve a certain number of certificates for the rehabilitation of the survivors of the war. At present there was nothing His Majesty's Government could do to alleviate the situation.

As soon as the snow had melted sufficiently, Agami took a train from Geneva to Belgrade and reviewed the arrangements that the Jewish community had made for the stranded convoy. Szime Spitzer and Agami, who took to one another warmly, decided to visit the Cladovo refugees. It was a dreary trip, first in a slow Yugoslav train, then in a derelict cab and finally when all roads ended, in an oxen-drawn cart.

Agami was appalled by the sight of the people. He had last seen them about a year before in Austria, when he visited the farms where they had found shelter. They had looked healthy and hopeful. Now they looked exhausted and their eyes showed the despair that was in their hearts. But they appreciated his coming and did not ask whether he had good news for them. Not a single one complained about his fate.

Agami spoke to the leadership at length, giving a detailed report about the attempts of the Mossad to obtain a ship for the continuation of their voyage. They understood that Agami was not holding out much hope for them. When Agami and Spitzer took leave of the refugees to return to Belgrade, Agami knew that he would never see them again.

Spitzer, however, visited the camp once more. The Jewish Agency had been able to scrape together 207 certificates for youngsters from within the convoy stranded on the Danube. Residues from former immigration quotas were made available to the refugees of Cladovo in spite of British indifference. The lucky ones were taken out of the camp and, with their little bundles in hand, marched off to the old bus that was to take them to the railway station. As Jukel watched the boys and girls – not one more than sixteen years old – walk towards an unknown destination, he thought that at least one adult should be placed at the head of that group on their adventurous voyage. As he looked around he saw a young man, his face drawn, waving to a lovely girl who was sadly walking away from him to join the others.

'Eide,' Jukel called out, using Serbian idiom, to the youngster, 'you go with them. I hereby appoint you the commander of this group.' Before he understood what had happened, Ernest Loehner was walking at the head of the column that was to be the only group of survivors from Cladovo.

On 18 September 1940 the Yugoslav authorities transferred the refugees from Cladovo to the tiny port of Sabac, nearer Belgrade. Huts and tents were put up there for the refugees, and camp life was organized on a more permanent basis. The refugees accepted the hardship and the hopelessness, believing that the day would come when they would be able to go to Palestine. But the day never came.

With a bombardment of the open city of Belgrade, the Nazi armies smashed Yugoslavia. One of the first operations of the victorious Nazis was the extermination of the inmates of the camp at Sabac. A memorial was erected by the Yugoslav authorities in 1965. On the marble statue there is an inscription that reads: '1,100 Jewish refugees were massacred here by the Nazi fascists on 7 April 1941.'

(9)

Interlude in Palestine

OUR FRIENDS of the doomed Cladovo group were still alive when Zvi and I realized that our mission in Vienna had come to an end. In December 1939, when the Cladovo transport was moved from Slovakia to Yugoslavia, the two of us went to the Vienna railroad station for the last time and boarded the train for Trieste. Our regular passports, complete with legal Palestinian visas, were, we thought, in perfect order. But as the train came to a halt at the Italian border and the guards went through the compartments to check papers, some error was found in Zvi's visa. I was allowed to continue to Trieste; Zvi was detained and required to check with the Italian Consul.

Not only did Zvi turn up on schedule the next day at the Trieste railway station, where we had optimistically agreed to meet when we were parted at the border, but he brought along a group of about ten other Jews detained at the passport control for similar reasons. He had bluffed the Italian Consul into letting all of them continue. When we met again as he got off the train at Trieste, we were only mildly surprised to see each other: Zvi was sure I would be there to meet him, and I was sure he would be there to be met. Each had complete confidence in the other.

From the railroad station, with about ten marks between us, we suddenly emerged from the world of Nazi Germany into an atmosphere that seemed to us miraculously peaceful, free and open: fascist Italy! A great many soldiers in uniform walked the streets, but without managing to create a military air. There was no blackout at night; there was plenty of food. Italian Fascism was far from German Nazism, and while anti-Semitism was, in theory, official policy, in fact it had no roots among the people.

The most striking expression of this new-found freedom, starting with our first moments at the railway station news-stands and lasting through what was to be nearly a month's stay in Trieste, were the uncensored newspapers freely available from neutral Switzerland. This was the rediscovery of a world we had almost forgotten. The German press, as a matter of course, reported facts by turning them upside down. Now we suddenly returned to a world we had once known: the world of doubt, of divided opinion, of leisurely analysis; a world composed of choices, of grey rather than black and white. The rediscovery of this world was the most profound element in the feeling that enveloped both of us — the sense of having been saved.

Besides the luxury of these feelings, we also happened to be staying at one of Trieste's most exclusive hotels. The two of us went straight there from the railway station with our very limited funds, secure in the belief that Zvi Yehieli, the Mossad's financial man in Geneva, would arrive soon to debrief us, as the last people from our organization to have seen conditions in Vienna, and to provide us with money for the rest of the trip. We had a three-week wait until the first available boat — the regular Italian passenger ship, which still plied its normal route between Haifa and Trieste — was due back.

So Zvi and I, practically penniless, stayed at the Grande Imperial Hotel – Yehieli's abode on his frequent visits to Trieste – on the Trieste seafront, while the other *émigrés* whom Zvi had brought with him were cared for by the Palestine Office in town. For reasons of security and caution, we were not to appear there. Trieste was swarming with British spies – including even one or two Palestinian Jews who had taken up this work – and because of our involvement in underground activities, the head of the Palestine Office in Trieste simply did not want us to come near his premises.

Yehieli was a long time in coming. Alone in Geneva as the co-ordinator of the Cladovo transport, he had difficulty finding time for a trip to Trieste. Meanwhile, Zvi and I continued to lead our strange double life in our beautifully appointed room (which was nevertheless cold, as the wind blew in from the sea and this was hardly the resort season). The other guests included a few Jews, among whom it was hard to distinguish between the genuine and the spies, and a handful of Italian businessmen. The food was excellent, but we could not afford to eat it. We consumed coffee and rolls at cheap cafés, avoiding the moment of truth each time our weekly bill was presented. Zvi was especially good at this. At such times he would produce our one remaining note of paper money (and Italian currency then was nearly the size of a pillow-case) and finger it absent-mindedly in front of the *concierge,* after which we would escape for another endless session at our café.

Finally Yehieli arrived. We reported on the situation in Vienna, received funds to pay our bills and boarded the steamer for Haifa exactly on schedule. It was a macabre four-day trip. The world was at war and there were rumours of dangers to shipping, but everything passed uneventfully. The other passengers played cards and danced to music at the bar – which Zvi and I avoided out of ignorance. On our first night out we conducted a solemn burial at sea for my

German Army paybook, the document which had taken me to Slovakia with Ceipek: we tied it to a piece of metal and threw it overboard, an act I have often regretted. At the time, however, it was a gesture to mark, with full ceremonial honour, what we considered the formal end of that chapter of our lives. During most of the trip we talked about how much more we could have done in our rescue efforts if only we had had more resources.

Hanna could not get away to meet the ship when it docked; she was at a girls' agricultural-training school and passes were rarely given. I went straight to Jerusalem to report to my superiors and make plans for what I was sure would be my new life as a farmer. Hanna and I wrote to each other constantly during the next few months – peculiar love-letters, now that I look back on them – largely heated exchanges concerning the 1939 White Paper and the partition of Palestine.

The plan of our group was to establish a new kibbutz whose members would be Austrian Jews – the handful of us already in Palestine plus our friends in the Cladovo transport still waiting in Yugoslavia. Our first step was to form a nucleus and spend a year's training at an established kibbutz in order to learn farming and to adjust to communal living. This we did at Kinneret, on the shores of the Sea of Galilee, where the lake's waters flow into the Jordan River. Shaul Avigur, the Chief of the Mossad, was a founding member of this kibbutz, and there I spent the year 1940. It was a year of manual labour in a setting of palm trees. Our reactions to the news of events abroad were composed almost equally of total helplessness and total involvement, and we lived out our peaceful personal lives against a distant backdrop of disaster.

Kinneret was an austere, tense place in spite of the cloudless blue sky and bright sunshine. Some members of the kibbutz had decided to give up even margarine (nobody was eating butter in Palestine) out of solidarity with their brothers in Europe, and contacts with the Haganah under-lined every aspect of the pastoral setting. Whenever some-body from the outside turned up – some young man in shorts walking through the fields, approaching a member and asking by name for someone else – there was unspoken awareness of what was happening: the Haganah was giving out an assignment. When one of our members would disappear for a while, it was all understood, in silence.

News of the occasional arrival of an illegal ship also spread quickly among members of the underground. In the summer and autumn of 1939, every organization involved in illegal immigration activities took desperate measures to step up its work. It was painfully clear that the days were num-bered. The Revisionist equivalent of the Mossad dispatched a number of ships from Rumania. An enterprising individual in Bulgaria scraped a few old boats together and sent them on their way.

On the day the war broke out, the *Tiger-Hill* arrived off the coast of Tel Aviv from Rumania with 1,400 Polish refu-gees on board. It was the boat Ruth Aliav had organized. Under British pressure the convoy was held up at the Ru-manian border, and for a dreadful forty-eight hours its fate hung in the balance. Ruth obtained an audience with the King of Rumania and, impelled by the terrible danger to her charges, managed to hypnotize the Monarch into counter-manding the strict orders his government had issued. The convoy moved towards the Black Sea and redemption.

The shots that welcomed *Tiger-Hill* to the coast of Tel Aviv were the first shots fired by British arms after the decla-ration of war on Germany. The three women and one man who were felled by these shots were the first casualties of the war between the Allies and the Nazis.

Another Mossad ship from Central Europe, the *Hilda* – which had begun its odyssey in October 1939 – arrived in January 1940. Travelling from Berlin through Vienna, its passengers had passed the unhappy Cladovo transport on their long way to the sea. The *Hilda* was seized by British warships off the coast of Istanbul and escorted to Haifa. There the British took an unprecedented step: they prepared to expel the new arrivals to Paraguay, the country officially designated as their destination. The entire country was seized by fury. Protests, strikes, threats of sabotage and of rebellion against the British finally forced the mandatory government to allow the passengers to disembark in Haifa. For over three months, they had been kept crowded in their little ship right there in Haifa harbour.

The largest Revisionist ship ever, the *Zacharia,* arrived with flying colours just after this macabre experience, and the refugees were allowed to disembark but were placed in a detention camp to wait for regular immigration certificates to be taken off the official schedule.

One of the ships that never reached the shores of Palestine was the *Salvador.* She foundered outside Istanbul in a gale and went under, taking with her 107 refugees, including sixty-six children and the hapless Turkish officials who had been posted on her deck to prevent her return to Turkish waters while the British blocked her progress towards Palestine.

In the first week of April, Germany invaded Norway and Denmark. The war which had been 'phoney' for so many now became as real as it had long been for us. At Kibbutz Kinneret we worked not only in the banana groves, but also in the construction of cement tank-traps, on order of the British Army, in the event of an invasion from the north, through Syria. Indeed, relations with the British became a major subject of debate for the Jews of Palestine for the next two years, with British policy taking alternate turns and the Jewish Agency and the underground organizations fluctuating accordingly, with rising and falling hopes.

The debate among us was whether the Jews should join the British Army or concentrate on independent underground

operations. Those who said that we should enlist as individuals in the British forces (British reaction to our request
for the formation of Palestinian units within the British
Army took a series of twists and turns during this period)
argued that we must create the 'political fact' of having participated in an Allied victory and use our participation to
bargain with the British. This position was influenced by
factors in the First World War, when T. E. Lawrence, on the
one hand, and the good account of the Zion Mule Corps at
Gallipoli, on the other, had acquired certain political capital.
Those opposed to joining the British Army argued that any
Jew who did so would be effectively neutralized by the
British; that he would not be permitted to gain any worth-
while military training and would be kept from any position
in which he could aid the Haganah.

The Jewish Agency demanded mass mobilization for the
war against Hitler, but the British turned down the idea because of their wish to be 'even-handed' with respect to the
Arabs – and few Arabs cared to enlist in the war against the
Nazis. In fact, many of their leaders openly supported the
Axis, which at that time seemed to be winning the war. Eventually the British did permit the formation of Jewish service
companies within the Engineers and Transport Corps, but no
satisfactory development took place until the formation of
a symbolic 'Jewish Brigade' in 1944.

On 5 May 1940 Hanna and I were married in Jerusalem.
We went for the day to the Dead Sea, where the atmosphere of
eternal stillness is like no other place on earth. That evening
we returned to my parents' home in Jerusalem and the next
day travelled together to Kinneret. We made the trip via
Jericho – on top of a truck bringing supplies to the kibbutz –
and settled down to our new home, which was in one of the
twelve tents set up by the members of Kinneret for our
group. Four days later Germany invaded Belgium and the
Netherlands and on 28 May the British evacuated Dunkirk.

The news of Italy's declaration of war against France and Britain on 10 June came to us during a night shift, as we were working under floodlights building cement tank-traps. David Nameri, our foreman and a man with a reputation for seeing that work went forward as speedily as possible, appeared out of the darkness.

'The Italians have come into the war,' he said. 'I'm taking over now.' There was an audible rush among us under the glaring lights, and the pace of work suddenly quickened; for us, at the eastern end of the Mediterranean, Italy's declaration meant that we were now cut off from the rest of the world. That same 10 June, the Allies withdrew from Norway and King Haakon VII went into exile in London.

Paris was evacuated three days later, and the Germans entered the city unopposed on 14 June. The news reached us as we were sitting in a hut in the middle of the kibbutz banana plantation, eating lunch after a morning's work. We were discussing the distressing developments overseas – a common pastime. One old farmer in our group, who had come from Russia years earlier and still remembered talk of the fall of Paris in 1871, solemnly declared, 'If Churchill doesn't take the necessary steps now, England is lost.' Just then someone came to our hut with the news that Paris was in enemy hands. It seemed the beginning of the end.

Black events followed, one after another, as 1940 drew on: fifty-six German planes were downed over bombed-out London on 15 September; Greece was invaded by Italian planes later in October; and Hungary joined the Axis on 20 November (Hungary was a staunch ally of the Nazis, but to a lesser degree than Rumania, which waited three days to join the Axis formally).

On that same 20 November, we in Palestine heard news that dealt another blow to illegal immigration – the one remaining link connecting us with those suffering in Europe. This was the announcement by the British mandatory gov-

ernment of a new policy to combat the trickle of those still
managing to arrive. From now on, all who attempted to enter
illegally would be deported to a British colony. 'Their ultimate disposal,' the announcement stated, 'will be a matter
for consideration at the end of the war; but it is not proposed
that they shall remain in the colony to which they are sent, or
that they should go to Palestine. Similar action will be taken
in the case of any further parties who may succeed in reaching Palestine with a view to illegal entry.'

This announcement had been preceded by the interception
on 11 November of two broken-down ships, the *Pacific* and
the *Milos*, together carrying nearly 1,800 refugees. Their two-
month trip had been one of the worst ever. Into the *Pacific,*
with a normal capacity of sixty passengers, about 1,000 had
been jammed, with only one paraffin cooking-stove and no
drinking water. When the ships were not permitted to land on
arrival, there were protests throughout Palestine, and the
Jewish Agency declared a general strike. The response was
the government declaration of 20 November.

On 23 November Rumania joined the Axis; on 24 November, Slovakia followed. On that day in Palestine, the hulk
of a third ship filled with refugees was brought into Haifa port;
its passengers were to be transferred to a French ship called
the *Patria,* abandoned in Haifa port by her crew (to which
the people from the *Pacific* and the *Milos* had already been
transferred) for shipment to the island of Mauritius in the
Indian Ocean.

The Haganah decided to scuttle the *Patria* as a warning
against the policy of deportation. But the quantity of explosives was incorrectly calculated and, before the advance
warning to the passengers could be heeded by all, the ship
exploded. The 240 refugees and about fifty of the crew and
Palestine police aboard at the time fell victims to this operation.

Soon after, we joined forces with a group of young people
who had come from Czechoslovakia and formed a new

kibbutz. We moved from our tents in the palm-fringed settlement of Kinneret to the town of Nahariya, on the seacoast north of Haifa. There we worked a small plot of land and took outside jobs to support our commune (which remained in Nahariya from 1941 to 1946). There were about fifty of us at the start and about eighty when we were finally allotted land for our own settlement in Upper Galilee – now the prosperous kibbutz of Neot Mordechai, which is my home today.

While the tragedy of Europe deepened, the tasks I performed were bucolic. My first job was growing alfalfa for a dairy farmer. I sowed the field properly and to my amazement and delight the grain sprouted in eight days, exactly as scheduled. But a few mornings later, I found the seedlings had vanished and the field denuded. It turned out to be caterpillars, but at first we did not believe this simple agricultural explanation and were sure it was sabotage. I was fired from my job (I should have sprayed the field) and went to work driving a pair of mules.

On 10 May 1941 London suffered the worst air raid of the war, and 1,436 people lost their lives. On 22 June Russia was invaded by Germany and Rumania.

One beautifully clear and still summer morning, I found myself in Jerusalem, just outside 'the last house on Gaza Road' where, in those days, the pavement stopped and the stony Jerusalem hillside began. (Today, that house is very much in the centre of town.) I had been asked to come there from Nahariya by a young man I had met just once before and who was beginning to rise in Haganah circles. His name was Moshe Dayan. He had lost an eye earlier in June of that year on a mission in Syria fighting the pro-Nazi Vichy-French and was in Jerusalem recuperating from the wound. At the same time, he was involved in a number of plans then being worked out by the Jewish Agency's Political Department in cooperation with certain British authorities.

Dayan apologized for having arranged our meeting so

early in the morning. At six, he said, he was due to meet with 'The Killer' – an anonymous British officer who was training Haganah men in close-combat techniques. We walked back and forth along the street, up to the last house on Gaza Road and back again, our footsteps echoing on the pavement, and Moshe questioning me sharply. He wanted to master a whole series of details about life in occupied Europe, and he had decided to put the questions to me, as one of the latest Mossad men to come out of there.

I knew that Reuven Shiloah of the Jewish Agency's Political Department had approached the British with a plan to use Jews who had recently escaped from Europe as operatives back in their native lands. With luck, these people, who had ideal 'cover', could return undetected to their communities in Slovakia, Hungary and Rumania and bolster the Jewish underground. Dayan told me that our plan was to parachute about 1,000 people into their countries of origin. We had the men but lacked the means to get them to their destinations. The problem, therefore, was finding a way of making this scheme appear useful to the British.

Fortunately, Shiloah discovered the Secret Service department concerned with the liberation of Allied airmen from enemy prison camps and soon worked out a solution that could serve British needs as well as our own. Given the opportunity to get our men into Europe, they would work with the Jewish underground and simultaneously as co-ordinators of a network to spirit escaped Allied prisoners of war out of enemy-occupied territory. It was for this reason that my talk with Dayan centred around penetrating questions about life in Europe – how people dressed, what they were likely to carry in their pockets, how the changing seasons affected daily life – and he suggested that I send him a fuller report in writing.

Throughout our brief talk, I was amazed by the analytic powers of this *sabra* who had been out of Palestine only once in his life (I was two years younger, but I thought I had seen far more of the world) and by his purposefulness and determination to defend Jews without compromise. He had complete confidence that we would be successful, if only we operated with skill.

'When you give me your full written report,' he said, 'take into account that the lives of our agents must not be unnecessarily sacrificed.' Then, after his discussion with me on the rescue of Jews from Europe, he went off to his meeting with 'The Killer' to learn improved techniques for defending the Jews of Palestine.

Our conversation that morning was only the beginning of a long and frustrating process to bring the plan into operation. Ever-new pretexts for delay prolonged negotiations at headquarters in Cairo. At every stage, opponents of Jewish participation in the war effort introduced obstacles. While we were eager to send at least 1,000 of our men behind enemy lines, their major concern appeared to be obviating any mark of a significant Jewish contribution to victory. The exasperating negotiations dragged on over four years, and only in 1944 did twenty-odd men and women see their audacious dream come true. Seven lost their lives either in enemy hands or on the battlefield with partisan units; the others succeeded in carrying out their double mission of rescue.

Meanwhile, another joint plan – this for the systematic interrogation of refugees arriving from Europe who might provide information useful to the Allied cause – was worked out between the British Secret Service and the men of the Jewish Agency's Political Department, Reuven Shiloah, David HaCohen, Eliahu Elath and Teddy Kollek. One such interrogation centre was set up in Haifa under Manulla Wilenski, and it was decided to establish a second in Istanbul, in cooperation with a British officer, Major Arthur Whittal. This arrangement in Istanbul was the brilliant idea of Teddy Kollek, who wanted to build a cover for our illegal operations in Turkey.

In our complex relations with the British, paralleling these events were other decisions taken in this same year: to intensify the White Paper measures by enacting laws prohibiting Jews from owning land and to demand that the Haganah turn over its arms (claiming that the British arms supply was insufficient). This demand naturally was refused by the Haganah High Command, and the claim that the British lacked rifles was yet another reason for us to keep ours. At about the same time, the terrorist organizations consented to a form of unilateral 'truce' with the British and agreed not to attack British targets for the duration of the war.

The Japanese attack on Pearl Harbor in December 1941 and America's entry into the war directly affected German actions against the Jews. Prior to this, the Nazis were somewhat inhibited by concern for American public opinion, but once America became an active enemy there was no longer any reason for such inhibitions, and the 'Final Solution' of the Jewish problem could proceed swiftly and efficiently. At the same time, it became increasingly harder to locate ships for the rescue of refugees, and the limited number of neutral vessels available commanded exorbitant prices. Against this background, the often-described story of the *Struma* played itself out.

A ramshackle boat, organized by the Revisionists, arrived in Istanbul with 769 refugees from Rumania. Because she was not seaworthy in her overloaded condition, and because the passengers had no legal destination, the Turkish authorities refused to let her land. For two months the *Struma* remained off shore, a floating prison, waiting for someone to make a move. It came on 23 February 1942, when eighty Turkish policemen forced their way aboard, tied the *Struma* to a tug and, without providing fuel, food or water, towed her through the Bosporus and into the Black Sea. A few hours later the *Struma* sank. The citizens of Istanbul and the Allied nations disregarded the SOS of the stranded ship and so were spared the spectacle of the drowning passengers. What's more, their problem was solved; only one man survived the disaster.

A message arrived in Nahariya from the Chief of the Mossad, asking me to come to see him at Kibbutz Kinneret. We sat on the sloping lawn, under a palm tree, looking down over the Sea of Galilee.

'I understand that you received a letter from a friend of yours not long ago,' said the Chief.

I had indeed. A few days earlier a non-committal note had come to me, by way of Istanbul, from Ferdinand Ceipek, the mysterious and foolhardy Pimpernel who helped our rescue operations to relieve his own conscience. Ceipek had addressed the letter to the offices of the Jewish Agency in Jerusalem, as he was unaware of my whereabouts. The Jewish Agency had forwarded the letter, realizing that this was something to do with clandestine contacts maintained by the Mossad.

Ferdinand Ceipek inquired after my health. His own, he wrote, was good as ever 'in spite of prevailing circumstances'. He was feeling strong and vigorous and capable of almost anything – a clear hint, as I understood it, that he was still in a position to help save Jews.

Showing no emotion, eyes half-closed, the Chief very quietly asked me whether I thought it might be wise – and convenient – for me to go to Istanbul to try to re-establish contact with our old ally; or perhaps it might be more prudent for me to forward a note to Ceipek and suggest that he get in touch with the Istanbul representative of the Mossad, Dani Shind.

I was in a dilemma. Dani could probably get the same help from Ceipek that I could, yet my heart was throbbing as I realized that here was perhaps a faint opportunity that I might be selected to continue the work I had interrupted when I left Vienna. As was his manner, the Chief brought the conversation to an end without indicating his own preference. We shall have to think about it for a while, was all he would venture.

It was Teddy Kollek's specific request for me that helped the Chief make up his mind. A few days after my talk with him I received word to report to the Mossad's headquarters in Tel Aviv. 'Go to the main building of the Trade Union's Secretariat,' I was advised, 'and ask for Moishele.'

Moshe Carmil, as I learned, was the Chief's factotum, a little fellow with a sceptical look in his sad eyes. His strength in the midst of this community of conspirators and guardians of secrets was that he always had a kind word, a warm smile, an encouraging remark and held the Mossad workers together. Perhaps more than any other single person in our small company, he was welding them into a team of reliable friends – not just conspirators on an exciting mission.

He explained to me that I was to go to Istanbul on behalf of both the Political Department of the Jewish Agency and the Mossad. He also cautioned me that my way to the exclusive and desirable mission for which I had been selected was paved with hard and tedious work. First of all, I had to spend a few weeks in Manulla's office in Haifa to learn the methods used in interrogating 'sources' and the techniques of cataloguing, editing and reporting the information so received. It also had been decided that I should undergo training as a radio operator before going to Istanbul. It might become possible, Carmil told me, to establish a secret radio post in Istanbul. Then we could make our communications independent of the favours of 'The Friends' – the name by which we called, with an ironic inflection, our new allies, the British Secret Service.

The Haganah had established secret radio posts in the

homes of reliable Haganah veterans in Tel Aviv. I was directed to one such post in the north of the city and was given a special instructor, as there was not, at that moment, a course intensive enough to teach me the complicated work of an independent radio operator in the brief time I had. Finally I received a regular Palestine passport. My occupation was given as 'correspondent', and I was issued a press-card by *Davar,* the labour daily.

Tense and excited, I went to the Mossad's branch office in Haifa. There, hidden away in the busy offices of the National Labour Federation's Construction Company, was the operations room of the Mossad where Shlomo Zimmerman received me unceremoniously as if I were on a routine errand. He took me across the street, where an Arab cab company operated a commuter service between Haifa and Beirut. With his friendliness and warmth, Zimmerman bought me all that morning's newspapers and a box of candy. He must have felt how jittery I was. He gave me a long embrace, patted me on the shoulder and said, 'You'll do all right. And we shall keep in touch with Hanna.'

The Arab driver forced his way through the narrow side streets of the Haifa port area. The passengers were a gay and noisy group, and I was the only Jew among them, but I did my best to hide my awkward mood and join in their banter. As we entered Lebanon, although I could not have known it then, I glanced around at the last I would see of Palestine for years.

PART TWO

THE BOSPORUS

(10)

Tea with the British

I ARRIVED IN ISTANBUL on a sweltering morning in August 1943, after a two-day rail trip through Syria and Turkey, and went straight to a flat that was shared by Dani Shind and Teddy Kollek and was now to be my home as well. It was a pleasant place on a quiet side-street on the hill of Taxim overlooking the Bosporus, and from the window we would one day watch our ships arriving and departing. Teddy (whom I was to replace in his work for the Political Department of the Jewish Agency) and Dani (whom I was joining for the Mossad side of my new work) had tried hotels but found that a private flat had its advantages. Hotels teemed with spies, agents, informers and black-marketeers. There was more privacy in a rented flat, and it was also less expensive – a major consideration.

Soon after my arrival, my two colleagues had to leave for a pre-arranged luncheon meeting with a Greek banker who also was the financial wizard of the British Secret Service. They gave me some general advice on behaviour ('Speak French rather than English – it's more neutral – and avoid strangers!'), the address of a place to eat and some Turkish money and went off on their business. I was glad to be alone.

I wanted to savour the feeling of being in Istanbul disguised as a journalist, but in fact preparing to take part in a desperate rescue effort. I wanted to absorb the incredible atmosphere and complacent coziness of this buffer of neutrality between two war-torn continents: Nazi-occupied Europe, where the ovens of Auschwitz smoked night and day; and the burning sands of the Middle East, where our political future was in balance.

With these thoughts in mind, I walked through the peacefully exotic streets of Istanbul and came to the restaurant that Teddy had recommended – the 'Abdullah', frequented largely by foreigners and their influential Turkish contacts. At the table next to mine sat a group of nondescript young men, quite athletic-looking, talking German in low voices. I assumed they were German officers on some secret mission in Turkey. At the table opposite sat a party of Americans who joked uninhibitedly in their unmistakable accents and sounded as if the war were on another planet. I let my eyes wander from one table to the next. Each group was concentrating on schemes to harm the other, and both were living on a standard infinitely higher and less dangerous than that of any of the countrymen on whose behalf they were enjoying Abdullah's delicious specialties. I realized that I also had joined that crowd.

Meanwhile, Teddy and Dani were lunching at another good restaurant with Polos Mestides, the Greek who had spent most of his sixty years in Istanbul as a 'Private Banker' and performed illegal currency operations for the British Secret Service. I heard about him when the three of us were back at the flat and I was unpacking my bags. My colleagues introduced me to their activities by telling me about this important new acquisition in their growing network of contacts. I myself was soon to work with Polos Mestides – the inevitably black-suited man with a prominent forehead and rosy cheeks set in a wrinkled face, his penetrating dark-brown eyes reminiscent of a country parson rather than a clandestine foreign-exchange broker on an extended black-market operation – and would come to know him well. We were using ever-larger amounts of money for two main purposes: to send local currency (or gold) to the centres of rescue activities in occupied Europe and to buy ships in Bulgaria (and later in Rumania) that were to bring refugees to Turkey on their way to Palestine. Mestides and the other agents were paid with the funds we received from voluntary contributions in Palestine and from the Jewish community of America.

The meeting between Dani, Teddy and Mestides was in itself a sign of the deep and unconventional understanding that the local head of British Intelligence, Major Whittal, had for our work. He had suggested that we use the services of his own man and warned us against exposing ourselves to the double risk inherent in large-scale black-market dealings: if you dealt with the wrong person you might get cheated, and the Turkish Government took a particularly tough view of infringements of its stringent currency restrictions. Private dealers sometimes took advantage of the utter illegality of such transactions, but there was no recourse to law if you found yourself without any recompense for the amounts you had entrusted to them. With 'Mercury' – as Mestides was code-named by us – there was no such danger. There was no risk of detection, as we were covered by the immunity of the British Secret Service; as for fraud, we had Major Whittal's word that Mestides could be trusted.

'You'll meet Major Whittal soon,' Teddy said as I finished unpacking. 'He's coming to tea at five.' Teddy was in a particular hurry to hand things over to me and to have Major Whittal meet his replacement. He had been promised quite some time before that he would be relieved of his duties in Istanbul. He felt that he had done his share in establishing contacts with British Intelligence in Istanbul, in breaking in the spirit of cooperation between two strange bed-fellows, and that the time had come for him to hand things over to someone else and to be free for new challenges.

Teddy had achieved the special status we were aiming for in our collaboration with the British: our representative was the head of an independent team of one of Britain's allies in the war against Hitler, not an employee of British Intelligence. We received neither payment nor orders from the much more powerful British. We consulted one another and worked out a common project, clearly stating our own interests with regard to the rescue of Jews and giving these interests preference if we suspected there might be a clash between the general Allied interest and our particular concern for the victims of the 'Final Solution'. Teddy's personal charm and tireless work made up for much of the imbalance between two unequal partners. His brilliant inventiveness and initiative cultivated a fast-growing relationship between the Jewish Agency's Political Department and the British Secret Service.

Promptly at five, Major Whittal arrived for tea, accompanied by his assistant, Sergeant Parkes. Arthur Whittal was a slim, tall Englishman, the son of a wealthy business family who had lived in the Levant for generations. He had an oblong face with a prominent nose and enigmatic green eyes, which could break into a whimsical smile of their own without moving so much as a facial muscle. Parkes was heavy-built and a little awkward in the refined presence of his superior. He continuously cleaned his rimless glasses and was used to answering only when addressed. Parkes could not know that he would finish the war as a major in the British Army – partly because of the kudos he received as a result of the cooperation that was planned at tea that afternoon.

I felt a bit at sea listening to the unrestricted and easy conversation among Teddy and the two Englishmen. I was presented as an expert in gathering information from new arrivals from occupied Europe. The proficiency of the office where I had received my training enhanced the professional authority Teddy advertised so warmly. Although I knew that these two Secret Service men were fully aware of all we were doing in addition to interrogating new immigrants, I felt nervous when Teddy, with complete aplomb, informed our counterparts that I was also to be Dani's junior assistant in the efforts to rescue Jews – something the mandatory government of Palestine looked upon with annoyance.

'We shall help you get the sources,' Major Whittal said to me as they took leave. 'Do your best to get us their information.'

'Don't be misled by Arthur Whittal's gentleness,' Teddy commented when our guests had gone. 'We are still living under the White Paper. Harold MacMichael is the High Commissioner, and he – not Whittal – typifies the British attitude to Jewish Palestine and to the rescue operation in Europe. But we have found a narrow crack in an otherwise impenetrable wall, and we must treasure it and work on it.'

Arthur Whittal did his job under the guise of a Passport Control Officer in the Visa Section of the British Embassy. This was useful, Teddy was quick to point out, as he was in a direct position to help us. And indeed he did, rather than just holding out promises for the great reckoning after the victory.

My introduction to our British partners on the very afternoon of my arrival confirmed my status as a member of the team. My feeling of belonging to this select group was further strengthened when Dani, the oldest among us, helped me to get settled in my room and, after tea, invited me for a walk, the first of many we took together in the streets of Istanbul.

'Our most recent acquisition is an elderly Bulgarian by the name of Jordan Spassoff,' Dani explained as we walked. 'He is a merchant who has lived in Greece part of his life and was always attracted by the smell of the sea and the sweet smell of money so many Greeks make through the sea. He has decided that the time has come for him to go into the shipping business, and I was lucky to have been chosen as the financier of his ambition.'

Spassoff had been recommended by an Italian friend. Dani had first written to him more than a year before, taking care to be extremely cautious: letters from Istanbul to Sofia – where Spassoff had lived since the war – were undoubtedly censored by the Turks, the Germans, the Bulgarians and who knows who else. He had nothing to rely upon but his instincts when it came to judging whether Spassoff was a trustworthy businessman who wanted a healthy profit, or an irresponsible adventurer who planned to make off with the Mossad's money. Dani had spoken to Spassoff several times on the telephone. The man sounded serious enough, but it was impossible to conclude a deal of this kind on a telephone tapped by all the secret services imaginable, and in a language Dani spoke with difficulty.

In March 1943 Dani decided to ask Spassoff to come to neutral Istanbul. He wanted to meet him personally, and he wanted Teddy to help him size up the man with whom he was to work. When Spassoff arrived, Dani and Teddy conducted a 'ten-day seminar' for the aspiring shipowner. Spassoff seemed to be a competent trader. There was no doubt that he wanted to get rich; it was even conceivable that he wanted to make his money decently and gradually. But he was hopelessly unfamiliar with the specific problems of shipping. He would have bought, without much concern, the first boat offered – and the choice at that time was hardly varied – and he had carefully let Dani know that all his money was blocked in Greece. In short, he had little beyond his good reputation. In return for the advance he would get from Dani to purchase a ship and register her under his name, Spassoff could only give a promissory note – a poor guarantee for what he was getting in return, considering that he was an enemy subject, that the transaction was illegal and that Dani could never sue him if he defaulted. At the end of Spassoff's ten-day visit, a contract was drawn up and duly signed. Spassoff was to have his ship. Now what remained to be seen was whether we would have on board the Jews we wanted to rescue.

The unbelievable happened. In June Spassoff happily informed Dani that the Bulgarian authorities had granted permission for the emigration of 1,000 Jews. He had acquired a small boat, the *Maritza,* which could carry approximately 300 passengers on the short run from a Bulgarian port to Turkey. His plan was solid, but it never materialized.

Under pressure from the Germans to agree to the deportation of Bulgaria's Jews, the King of Bulgaria and his government, wholeheartedly supported by the people of Bulgaria, decided on a course of subterfuge. Rather than hand Bulgaria's Jews over to the Nazis, they would transfer them from the capital to provincial towns; but they would not allow the Germans to take hold of the Jews.

The resettlement of all Bulgarian Jews in ghettos was a terrible shock to the small, closely knit Jewish community. They could not know that only the most humanitarian motives were behind the decision of a weakened government opposing its overlord, and they inevitably regarded their dispersal as the first step on the road to the German extermination camps. All Jewish activities came to a standstill; the organs of the community were completely disrupted. When Spassoff set out to search for the former heads of the Sofia community in their new places of residence, he was received with suspicion by some and with utter despair by others.

Dani received frequent reports of Spassoff's efforts and tried to imbue Spassoff with his own sense of urgency despite the censored telephone. In broken Russian Spassoff implored Dani to believe that he understood the situation very well, but it was the fault of the authorities and frightened Jews that nothing progressed. At this point the conversation would abruptly come to an end: the censor permitted no comments critical of the authorities. Dani knew the motives behind the expulsion of Sofia's Jews. He was ready to believe in the good intentions of the Bulgarian Government and people, but he also knew the meaning of German might and brutality.

Yet he had to make a decision. While the exit permit from Bulgaria was expiring, the *Maritza,* on which the survival of several hundred Jews depended, was idle in the Bulgarian port of Varna. Dani decided not to wait any longer. If the situation in Bulgaria improved, she would return there, but for now the *Maritza* would go to Rumania.

'Rumania,' Dani continued, 'is regarded as one of the safer places for Jews under Hitler. But this assumption is only partly correct.' The first major blood-bath of the war had taken place under Rumanian auspices. In the autumn of 1941, after Odessa had been occupied by Rumanian troops, the Jews of the city were accused by their Rumanian captors of having directed anti-Nazi activities from the main synagogue. As punishment for these imagined crimes, the Rumanian Nazis copied the example of their German masters: 26,000 Jews were massed into an abandoned army camp, pits were dug and the victims were machine-gunned.

In 1942, by agreement between Germany and Russia, the territory between the Dniester and Bug rivers became a dumping-ground for the Jews of the Rumanian provinces of Bukovina and Bessarabia. Until the Russian conquest of this area, Transdnistria served as a death zone: Jews were transported there and left to starve to death or succumb to disease and the cruelty of the elements. As these Jews were forced to take on strenuous work in an area governed by a stalwart anti-Semite (the notorious Alexianu, a Professor of Law at Czernowitz University who had organized pogroms on his own initiative as early as 1938), Transdnistria became the scene of the gradual, cold-blooded extermination of part of Rumanian Jewry. It seemed to Dani that Antonescu was playing a despicable double game: he had abandoned the venerable Jewish communities of Bessarabia and Bukovina – seats of age-old traditions of learning and of Jewish family life – to the fate demanded by the Nazis; yet he was preserving the Jews of central Rumania as a sort of alibi for himself in case the Allies won the war and he had to make a last-minute reversal of political affiliation.

Dani told me that before the war broke out and the representatives of the Mossad were forced to leave Rumania, they had had an extraordinary contact in Bucharest by the name of Pandelis. An Oxford graduate, unscrupulous extortioner and a man of affable charm and grandiose dynamism, Yanaki Pandelis (nicknamed 'the Fat One') was a Greek who pretended to be a shipowner. All he could show for it, however, was an uncanny knowledge of shipping – just as he excelled in many other fields – and a constant readiness to try (with other people's money) to obtain ships for the transport of Jews. He had done so before the war started and, Dani was happy to say, he was still in a position to help.

Pandelis had worked with the Mossad before the outbreak of war, but he had given them no monopoly over his priceless contacts and dynamic initiatives. He had also worked with other groups that organized illegal emigration from Rumania to Palestine. Foremost among these was the Revisionist team under the leadership of Eugene Meissner, a man with keen political sense, great courage and integrity.

At the beginning of the war, when the Rumanian Jewish community suddenly felt completely cut off and abandoned to its own devices, Meissner made a bold decision. Despite the Rumanian authorities' edict that all organizations had to disband, Meissner decided not to liquidate his group, the Emigration Committee of the Revisionist Zionists. Instead, he went underground, but maintained contact with Pandelis and channelled help to members of his organization. With broad-minded loyalty to the entire Jewish community, and despite his political position as a member of the opposition, Meissner also kept in touch with the official representatives of the Zionist Organization as well. Leo Enzer was the head of the Palestine Office of Rumania, but he was unable to operate, since the Rumanian authorities kept a particularly sharp eye on him and on anyone who tried to contact him. Enzer was known to them as the chief official of the Zionist Organization and of the Jewish Agency for Palestine, which, as far as the Rumanians were concerned, now belonged to the Allied, enemy camp.

Yet, despite the constant surveillance on Enzer, Meissner succeeded in making his hopes and expectations known to him. And now, in the summer of 1943, Pandelis instinctively began to stir and a triangle of clandestine cooperation was established between the Oxonian Greek, the underground Revisionist and the head of the Palestine Office.

At this point, Dani took up another thread of the narrative and began to describe the strange affair of the *Darian*, an episode which had taken place in the spring of 1941 while I was in Palestine.

Shmariah Zamereth, the 'American' of the Mossad, was in Greece then, still searching for some ship to take the doomed Cladovo transport from the Black Sea to Palestine. He finally found a sturdy tug-steamer, the *Darian* – small but reliable – and bought her at once.

At the same time, the Political Department of the Jewish Agency was trying to cultivate influential contacts in the British military establishment, for the British authorities refused to let the Jews of Palestine participate in the war against the Nazis lest they accumulate bargaining capacity for the inevitable showdown after the war. These efforts to find a crack in the British opposition were most helpfully complemented by a man who, at a later stage, was to become one of the legendary leaders of the Mossad: Yehudah Arazi.

Ruth Aliav and Yulik Braginski were the Mossad's emissaries in Istanbul at the time that the Political Department of the Jewish Agency needed the *Darian* for some top-secret special operation. To thwart this threatening diversion to their activities, Ruth instructed Shmariah Zamereth to dispatch the boat post-haste to Bulgaria, fill her with whatever refugees were available, and then send her on to the nearest Rumanian port. She was to wait there, no matter what happened, for the people from Cladovo. But the people from Cladovo were no longer able to move. In that extraordinarily cold winter of 1941, the Danube had already frozen and there was no way of reaching the last available ship in time. Dani left Palestine for Bulgaria, arriving there virtually together with the invading German troops, in order to add more refugees to the 160 already on board the *Darian*.

In Ruth's room in the Park Hotel in Istanbul, a heated debate took place. David HaCohen and Yehudah Arazi pleaded for cooperation with the British. They regarded our help as a major contribution in the war and were prepared to buy the *Darian* from the Mossad for the enormous sum of £10,000 if we agreed to take her to the estuary of the Danube in Rumania and to sink her there in order to close the route to enemy shipping. The advocates of this scheme promised great advantages for the continued rescue of Jews in the form of cooperation with a high-powered department in the British Secret Service.

But the people of the Mossad remained adamant. The ship had been acquired with the greatest difficulty in a practically nonexistent market, and it had been paid for with the Mossad's last reserves just to save the Cladovo transport. If that proved temporarily unfeasible, she would carry other refugees and return to take the Cladovo transport later.

The *Darian* finally sailed from Bulgaria with 750 people on board. She never made her suicide trip to Rumania; but neither did she save the Cladovo transport. On her way back to the Black Sea, without passengers, she struck a mine and sank. The crew was saved.

Dani had one last piece of background information to complete the picture of the situation up to date. Six months before my arrival, in February 1943, two brothers, Alfred and Dolfi Ebner, and their wives, had arrived from Bucharest by train. Through them we were introduced to contacts who opened up yet another avenue of escape.

Like so many other Rumanian Jews, the Ebners had received letters from Joseph Goldin, the assistant to the Jewish Agency's representative in Turkey, Chaim Barlass, certifying that on their arrival in Turkey they would be granted entry permits to Palestine on the grounds that such certificates were available to the Jewish Agency.

These letters, Barlass and Goldin hoped, would protect their bearers while in enemy countries, as proof that they were seriously planning to emigrate. But the letters were similar to those we had issued in 1938 to stateless persons in Austria, giving them the only protection we could produce ourselves – an affidavit without backing, a guarantee without collateral. In the first place, there were very few certificates; secondly, incredible as it seems today, Jewish refugees who succeeded in escaping from Nazi Europe were considered by the British as enemy citizens when they arrived in neutral Turkey.

The Ebners belonged to the thin uppercrust of the very rich and well-connected that topped the mass of Rumanian Jewry, and they wanted to be doubly reinsured. Through the Rumanian Central Bank they engineered a deal between a leading Rumanian textile firm and a group of Turkish investors to establish a spinnery in Turkey with Rumanian know-how. Two directors – the brothers Ebner – and three technicians – *bona fide* textile experts – would be allowed to travel to Turkey. Of the five, only the Ebners needed

Turkish visas: the others were not Jewish, and non-Jews could enter Turkey without hindrance in the spring of 1943. The enormous sum of £ 10,000 changed hands (many hands, some of them sticky), and the visas were granted.

Meticulous and thorough as they were in both their business and their private affairs, the new arrivals contacted a British undercover agent, to whom they brought an introduction from a pre-war friend in Rumania. They consequently proved to be most useful in evaluating intelligence from Nazi-occupied Rumania, and they soon became friendly with the British in Istanbul. But as far as their entry permits to Palestine were concerned, they were still considered enemy citizens.

Joseph Goldin suggested to them that they ask their newly won friends in British Intelligence to intercede on their behalf with the one man who was strong, imaginative and broadminded enough to realize that they were Jews who wanted to go to Palestine and not enemy agents in disguise – something the Jewish Agency had incessantly, but unsuccessfully, pleaded ever since the war had started.

A few weeks later the British Embassy in Ankara received clear instructions exactly to this effect from the Foreign Office, at the direction of the Prime Minister himself – Winston Churchill. This intervention became a precedent, and late as it was in the course of Hitler's war against the Jews, the definition of Jewish refugees as enemy aliens became a notion of the past.

(11)

Lord Cranborne's Letter

WHEN DANI FIRST DESCRIBED Simon Brod to me, I found it difficult to visualize this faithful friend of our network. Indeed, until I came to know the little man with the chubby, rosy face crowned with silvery hair, I could not have imagined eyes quite like his – they were like the heads of steel-blue pins that darted around to take in every new situation; they could be angelic one moment and scornful the next.

The son of a prosperous tailor who had fled from Russia to Turkey fifty years earlier, Simon had turned his father's shop into an enormous textile enterprise. But in 1933, with the flow of refugees to Turkey, he turned the keys of the business over to his younger brother and began looking for people to help. His home was in the same elegant building in which Major Whittal lived; but his work took him not to the policy-makers, but to the lower ranks of clerks in the police and the municipality. With them he would work out the details of individual cases.

He remained the refugees' full-time patron even after the Rescue Committee and other professional organizations became active in Istanbul. He was always the first to learn, through his innumerable friends in the Turkish bureaucracy, of the arrival of new groups or individuals, and he was always the last to give up when we came up against a particularly complicated case.

Brod had a remarkable way of keeping his accounts: he always listed his expenses on the cover of a pack of inexpensive Turkish cigarettes. A chain-smoker, he went through four or five packs a day, tossing away the used one as soon as he opened the new pack. In this way, he threw away his accounts for thousands of pounds, spent out of his own pocket to help refugees coming through Istanbul from the time Hitler took power in 1933 until some time after the formal end of the war in 1945.

One day at the end of August 1943, Major Whittal sent for Dani and me to come to Simon Brod's for an urgent meeting. We entered and found the Major already waiting. I had seen Whittal only once, on the day of my arrival when he had come to tea at our place. Whittal was the picture of eagerness and energy, sitting in one of Brod's comfortable easy chairs, looking like a hawk prepared to fall on his prey.

Before our conversation could begin we had to go through the inevitable ritual of Turkish hospitality: Brod's servant placed before each of us a small cup of coffee and the obligatory glass of cold water to be swallowed first in order to prepare one's palate for the delight of the exquisite drink. As soon as the servant withdrew, Whittal came directly to the point.

'The British Embassy in Ankara has received secret instructions from Lord Cranborne, the Minister of State in the Foreign Office, which concern all of us. For you they may well be a new version of the Balfour Declaration and may spell deliverance for your people behind enemy lines. For me, they may represent a decisive turn in the flow of information.'

Major Whittal took a slim book bound in expensive crocodile-skin out of his breast pocket. As we tensely waited for an elaboration of his enigmatic statement, he slowly and gracefully unfolded a small chart. Evidently quoting from it without reading the exact wording of the secret instructions, he said: 'The British Embassy in Ankara was advised by the Minister of State that from now on every Jew who is able to reach the shores of Turkey under his own steam – repeat: under his own steam . . .' – the Major rested his eyes on each one of us as he read out the words, emphasized by the coded command 'repeat' – 'is to be issued a visa to Palestine and to be sent on his way by the British authorities.'

This was indeed the charter for which we had been waiting. Thousands of Jews might have been saved had these instructions been given sooner. It had taken the disaster of the *Struma,* the extermination camps and the incessant pressure of the Jewish Agency and other Jewish organizations to squeeze out of the British Government the order that was to snatch human beings from the threshold of destruction.

Elated, we assured Major Whittal that we would use this secret information with discretion; under no circumstances would we cause him embarrassment by disclosing the source of our knowledge. We would, of course, immediately advise our people in occupied Europe of the new legal situation, and we would encourage Jews to come to Turkey 'under their own steam' – or any other steam. And once the first contingent arrived and was processed to Palestine, the new instructions would no longer be secret. Information about saving lives travelled very fast.

Whittal was visibly gratified by our reaction. He was obviously doing a bit more than merely organizing the flow of information about wartime conditions in occupied Europe, and he seemed happy to have been instrumental in conveying the message that would help human beings stay alive.

Unknown to us at that moment, however, was a catch. The British Government had carefully abstained from communicating this important policy decision to the authority most concerned: the Government of Turkey, for whom Jewish refugees were an undesirable category of applicants for visas. Turkey refused to be flooded by the victims of other people's hostilities. The attitude of the wartime Turkish Government towards its *own* national minorities, including Turkish Jews, was negative. They were not ready to be used as a haven, and certainly not by desperate Jews. The tragedy of the *Struma* was still on everybody's mind. With their own eyes, the Turks had seen the agony of the rejected, wringing their hands in dreadful hopelessness, begging to be let in to a city they could practically touch from the boat which was their prison. The final disaster of the *Struma* was laid virtually on the Turks' doorstep.

We left Brod's apartment and made our way to Chaim Barlass in the Jewish Agency office to tell him the news. We knew that we were bringing only half a message of redemption, but Barlass had known all along that such a British promise was essential in order to obtain Turkish cooperation. He, therefore, received our information with great pleasure, for now he had material with which to work.

'The difficulties are not over,' he said. 'As a matter of fact, they will remain with us as long as the Turkish Government does not change its outlook. But make no mistake. We shall only be able to create new procedures once a boat with Jews from Nazi-occupied Europe reaches the shores of Turkey . . . under its own steam,' he added as an ironic afterthought.

The first test of the new legal situation would come with Jews from Rumania. In Bucharest, the trio of Pandelis, Enzer and Meissner was active. In the autumn of 1943 an obscure travel agency in Bucharest, which had lost most of its business because of the war, was approached by a fat Greek with an offer to purchase the dying enterprise. To the surprise of the Rumanian owner, the deal went through and he recovered an astronomic sum, compared to the losses he had suffered since the outbreak of war. The agency bore the uninspiring name of Office Roumaine, Agence de Tourisme; Pandelis called it ORAT for short.

The Zionist youth organizations set up shop in Pandelis' travel agency, and the opening of ORAT provided the Zionist underground with semi-legality under the big and slippery hand of 'the Fat One'. With the help of the magic black box and the infinite patience necessary for the establishment of telephone connections, Dani informed ORAT of the availability of two ships: the *Milka* and the *Maritza*. He was extremely gratified that he had re-established his pre-war contacts with 'the Fat One', the proven and reliable authority on illegal machinations. In Bucharest, Pandelis, Enzer and Meissner, working under the cover of ORAT, went about the complicated work of preparing passengers for departure on the *Milka*. Any sort of publicity had to be avoided, as some German department might intervene at the last moment if attention were drawn to the imminent rescue of several hundred prospective victims.

The telephone on the mantelpiece in our living-room again became the centre of our life as we waited to hear Pandelis' voice, or that of one of his men, announcing that the *Milka* had left port. When the unbelievable message came through, we began studying a snapshot of the boat so that we would be able to make her out from the distance the moment she appeared on the horizon. A naval map was spread out on our dining-room table, and Dani and the Chief (Shaul Avigur, who had come to Istanbul as soon as the prospect of a departure from Rumania began to materialize) were constantly measuring distances and calculating where the ship might be. We had visions of torpedo boats and enemy submarines tracking the small vessel. Every time the telephone rang we all froze. Dani always reached for it; he was the senior member of the local team and was to receive messages and give instructions as the case might demand.

Chaim Barlass had to forgo the pleasure of being present when the boat arrived. As soon as we received word of the *Milka*'s departure from Constantsa we informed Barlass, who immediately left Istanbul for Ankara. For months he had been negotiating with the Turkish Government in preparation for the eventuality that, for the first time since the disaster of the *Struma,* another ship would appear in Turkish waters carrying refugees from enemy-held territory who lacked entry permits to either Turkey or Palestine. The matter was a delicate one, for the Turkish authorities still had not received formal notification of the change in British policy outlined in Lord Cranborne's instructions. So besides Barlass' word, the authorities had no reason to believe that the refugees would be allowed to continue and legally enter Palestine.

Kemal Aziz Payman, the Turkish Foreign Office official with whom Barlass had endlessly discussed the eventuality of a ship's arrival, was now to be put to the test. No one was less surprised than Barlass – the greatest realist – when Kemal Aziz reacted coolly to the news of the *Milka*'s impending arrival. Alone in Ankara, Barlass feared a new disaster, as he was kept waiting for Foreign Minister Numan Menemenciogulu's decision. After all, the passage of a few hundred Rumanian Jews through Turkey was such an extraordinarily important affair of state that only His Excellency himself could make the fateful decision. As Barlass instinctively foresaw, the decision was negative, in the first instance at least.

The representative of the Jewish Agency had enjoyed no official status in wartime Ankara, and so he was not allowed to see the Turkish Foreign Minister personally. He had to carry on his dealings with cautious subordinates. But there were other ways to reach Menemenciogulu. Barlass went to see the American Ambassador, Laurence Steinhardt. The Ambassador was already under instructions to assist the rescue of Jews and he did his duty immediately. Steinhardt had a long talk with Menemencioglu, but his plea was refused.

The British Embassy was obviously the decisive factor. Barlass mobilized all the influence that he had patiently built up during the last years. He had been criticized more than once for being too lenient with the British, for not giving them a good piece of his mind; but he knew that he had to build up a reserve of goodwill in anticipation of a crucial moment. As the *Milka* moved closer and closer to Turkish shores, Barlass knew that that moment had come.

The combined pressures of the various diplomatic channels that Barlass activated brought results. But it was the definite commitment of the British Embassy to issue Palestine entry visas to the 240 on board the *Milka* that pushed Menemencioglu to a final decision. He phoned the American Ambassador personally to say that he had decided to make an exception with this one ship. He would not, however, permit any of the refugees to remain in Turkey. He would provide a special train with Turkish police supervision to transport the refugees directly from the ship to the railway station. From there a train would take them to Allied-occupied Syria. Barlass was alone in his hotel room when the American Ambassador phoned the news. Overcome by joy and exhausted by the tension of the last thirty-six hours, the ambassador of a people who had no embassy broke down and wept.

We in Istanbul received the news in a different fashion. The phone woke me up long before dawn. As I groped for the receiver, I felt the tension growing in me. Was this *the* message?

'You lazy bums,' I heard Simon Brod's gruff voice. 'You sleep comfortably in your soft beds while I slave here in Terapia on your behalf.' Brod hung up before I could answer.

The Chief, Agami (who had also come to Istanbul) and Dani were already awake when I put down the receiver. It was not necessary to relate what I had heard. Minutes after Brod's call we were sitting in a cab, and within what seemed like seconds, we reached the seaside restaurant that Brod had chosen as his base. To our great surprise, Arthur Whittal and two or three of his clerks were there too. Brod had alerted them even before speaking to us. He wanted the Palestine visa to be affixed to whatever travel documents the refugees might produce, to prevent the Turks from using any excuse whatever for complicating the transit of the first group of refugees.

We were not allowed to go near the boat, which was anchored at some distance from shore. Police and health officials surrounded her in small barges. A police officer – obviously on more than just official terms with Simon Brod – was standing by as Arthur Whittal ceremoniously set His Majesty's seal on the wrinkled paper that was the passenger list and that served as the collective passport. Then the officer grabbed the list and rushed back to the *Milka*.

With her whistle blowing joyously – or so it sounded to us – the *Milka,* now fully legal, continued her voyage on the short trip to Haydarpaşa, the railway station on the Asian shore of Istanbul.

'These will be Manulla's sources,' Whittal said whimsically pointing to the 'sources' as they departed in the direction of the opposite shore. 'But never mind, it was a privilege to have set the seal to their deliverance.'

Brod, practical as always and concealing his emotion better than anyone else, conducted us to a table laid with an early breakfast. 'To the safe arrival of all the boats to come!' He lifted a glass of red wine, and all of us – members of Haganah, of the British Secret Service, the Turkish waiters and policemen – drank the toast to the rescued. Then we rushed to Haydarpaşa in our cab. Barlass was scheduled to

arrive from Ankara on the early-morning train. We wanted
to be there to greet him, and we hoped to get near the refugees while they were boarding the train to Palestine.

The train from Ankara arrived just as we were filing into
the station. Barlass was overwhelmed with emotion when we
told him that at that very moment the rescued were in the
same station with us. Brod led the way. We found the Orient
Express waiting for the signal to go, but the train – usually
quite punctual – was delayed. Four non-passenger cars had
been detached and replaced by four passenger cars. On these
cars we noticed a sign saying: 'Reserved for passengers to
Palestine.' A dream? Or were these signs actually put there
by the Turkish Railways!

And then they came. We stood at a distance, and at Brod's
advice we refrained from making contact with the refugees as
they were conducted gently and with much attention by
Turkish policemen into the waiting cars. 'Do nothing to give
the authorities an excuse to discontinue their helpful attitude,' Brod warned.

But here they were filing past us in the flesh, people saved
from the other side of freedom still not believing that they
were no longer in enemy territory, exhausted from years of
anguish and from the nerve-racking trip on an overcrowded
boat through mine-infested waters to an uncertain destination. Their eyes lit up, as ours had before, when they noticed
the signs 'Reserved for passengers to Palestine.' They began
to believe that they were near.

The Chief, clearly moved by the spectacle, suggested that
we return to our flat for an urgent consultation on further
work. Had he not been there, it is quite probable that in the
euphoria of victory we would have taken the day off for a
trip to Principo and celebrate on the luscious island facing
the glorious city of Istanbul. As it happened, we returned
dutifully to our flat, and Dani composed the following letter
to the Mossad in Tel Aviv.

We have been privileged to see with our own eyes the *Milka* entering the Bosporus with refugees from Czernowitz on board. Our feelings were mixed: we were overjoyed by the arrival of the ship, yet fearful of what lay ahead and thoroughly disgusted with our 'well wishers' who had left the remnant of our people to fend for themselves. We shall never forget the proud entry of the ship filled with Jews saved by the efforts of Jews after our 'sympathizers' had announced that all possible steps had been taken to advance the rescue effort. Let the *Milka* bear witness to the sin of neglect on the part of the enlightened world. We have often met with setbacks, but our work has not been in vain after all. We only hope that we shall have time to save greater and greater numbers.

A few days later, back in our office, the telephone rang and the party at the other end spoke French so rapidly that, without giving me an opportunity to get a word in edgewise, the voice said, 'I have come from Bucharest with important news from Pandelis, "the Fat One", and with orders to come and see you at once.'

The speaker was Stefano D'Andria, a commander in the Italian Navy who bore a startling resemblance to Peter Lorre. According to his own description, D'Andria was Pandelis' right-hand man. He had been deeply involved in the preparations for the departure of the *Milka,* and now he brought us detailed accounts of the imminent departure of the *Maritza* with 244 survivors from Transdniestria – 'the Jewish God willing,' he added, piously turning his frog eyes to heaven.

Pandelis was Greek and therefore unable to move around at will. But as an Italian, D'Andria was considered a friendly foreigner by the pro-Nazi Rumanian régime and so had freedom to travel. Besides, Pandelis' continued presence in Bucharest was essential. So he sent D'Andria to Istanbul to be near the representatives of the Mossad – a kind of apostolic nuncio, D'Andria said modestly, at the court of a friendly sovereign. With his uncanny intuition, Pandelis realized that there had been a basic shift in the policy governing rescue work. He could not afford to be absent from the scene, and he would not rely on garbled telephone communications, so he sent his own man to be where the action was.

We code-named D'Andria 'The Gnome'. Hardly a day went by without long conferences with him about schemes and plans to buy boats and bring people out of occupied Europe. Very early in our friendship, he disclosed to me that he had a practical philosophy based on three tenets: first and foremost, there was a Jewish God in heaven who specially and specifically cared for the Jewish people. Although the Jews were going through indescribable hardships, there was no room for despair – the Jewish God was with us. Secondly, obstacles in the way of achievement were there for one purpose only – to be removed or circumvented and overcome – and he, the chosen instrument for redeeming some few Jews from their doom, was the vehicle for the implementation of this magic formula. Finally, and with a gaze that reflected both astute shrewdness and the innocence of a new-born babe, he admitted frankly that he loved money.

As D'Andria had presented himself as Pandelis' liaison man, it was assumed that he would be taking orders from us – the initiative would be ours, while he would responsible for the implementation – but it never worked out that way. Stefano D'Andria's perception was infinitely quicker than our ability to elaborate on complicated situations. I doubt whether he was aware of any of the intricate considerations – with which even the most junior functionary of the Zionist Organization was familiar – surrounding the 'Palestine problem'. Yet as soon as he set foot in Turkey, he somehow sensed that the entire constellation of our work had changed as a result of what we called 'Lord Cranborne's Letter'. The limitation Lord Cranborne had prescribed – that refugees arrive under their own steam – meant nothing to D'Andria. The Jewish God would see to it that they arrived, and once here, they would proceed, *basta* (end of discussion).

D'Andria made contact with Turkish shipowners who were ready to talk business: he was able to tell them that the Turkish authorities no longer objected to the use of their boats for the shuttle traffic from Rumanian ports; he was able to promise them that the refugees would be taken by rail to Palestine; he offered them the most profitable business imaginable; no wonder he was flooded with offers of everything from kayaks to small motor vessels and medium-sized ships.

D'Andria was an experienced businessman. He acquired the services of an elderly Turkish notable, Naim Bey, who acted as his contact man with the shipowners. He himself was very discriminating in the selection of those considered worthy of a personal interview and discarded offers that seemed shady. He had an unerring intuition for serious offers, as opposed to fly-by-night dealers after an easy dollar. Within weeks after D'Andria's arrival, we had signed contracts for five ships – each larger and more seaworthy than the two Bulgarian boats we had acquired with such difficulty. What for years had appeared only as a fantasy suddenly became reality.

'If only the Jewish God had sent you sooner,' Dani joked one day on the way to the docks just outside Istanbul where we proposed to fit the ships for the trip to Rumania.

'Let's face it,' D'Andria said matter-of-factly. 'The Jewish God was a bit late dispatching those secret orders to the British Embassy in Ankara. Had they come sooner, we could have saved tens of thousands.'

(12)

Postcards and Smugglers

THE APARTMENT shared by Venya Hadari and Menachem Bader was the nerve-centre of our contacts with Jewish communities, youth organizations and Zionist federations in occupied Europe. When bad news arrived, it normally came to this place first: and gradually archives of incredible horror were built up in this apartment.

Menachem Bader was much older than the rest of us. As an emissary of the kibbutz movement of Hashomer Hatzair, he had established a name as a practical man with a flair for economic matters and a logical mind that permitted no illusions. I was to find that he also had great compassion and the soul of a poet.

Venya Hadari was a member of Ramat Rachel, a kibbutz just south of Jerusalem. He was born in Poland and brought up in the Zionist-Socialist youth movement there. To him the names of ghettos and camps were not mere geographical terms; he lived the reality of doom.

'Our first task was to establish an address,' Bader explained as he began to describe to me the work he and Venya had been doing for nearly a year before I arrived in Istanbul. 'Quite simply an address, so that people in occupied Europe would be able to write to someone they trust and know to be genuine.'

It was not easy. From Palestine they had brought mailing lists of political organizations of Zionist youth movements and subscribers to Palestinian newspapers living in what had become the Nazi empire. They began by writing thousands of postcards containing a concealed hint of the senders' identity. Their secretary, Sarka Mandelblatt, a Jewess living in Turkey and holding Turkish citizenship, allowed them to use her name and address for the correspondence they were trying to develop.

But many of the addressees had been forced to change their addresses; others had died – or had been exterminated. Letters or postcards bearing Jewish-sounding names were severely scrutinized by the Nazi censors. Venya and Bader were flashing signs with tenacity into a distant and still night. Was there anyone at all who received the message?

The answers started to come slowly, haltingly, sporadically. Venya had written: 'Please let me know how you are. Eretz [the land (of Israel) in Hebrew] is longing for you.' Some weeks later Sarka Mandelblatt received a postcard that said: 'Encouraged by your interest in my situation. *Rahamim maher* [quick relief] is much needed. Please keep in touch.'

Contact had been established. When an address had been verified it was passed from one person to another, from one centre to another. With the address they were able to send warnings to those who still did not understand the terrible writing on the wall and encouragement to those who were falling into despair.

Now Venya and Menachem were working on schemes to transfer money to Jewish communities that had become utterly destitute – money that could buy documents, food, shelter: the raw materials of survival. Now that they knew where to address the money, the great question was how to transfer it to neutral Turkey and then to forward it to enemy territory. Even in peacetime, foreign-exchange deals were supervised. To export currency from Mandated Palestine was definitely prohibited. In situations of this sort, however, we thought of ourselves not as law-abiding citizens of the British Mandate but as representatives of an independent people, and we acted in accordance with what we regarded as our moral obligation to defend our national interest.

The correspondence developed by Venya and Bader branched out into each and every country under Nazi rule. As more and more letters and postcards were mailed from Istanbul, more and more messages returned acknowledging the contact. Organizations wrecked by the Nazis began to take shape again. From letters carefully camouflaged as innocuous family communications, it was learned that there still remained groups of Jews who were able to keep in touch with one another and co-ordinate action.

'If only one of us could go there and talk to them,' Venya moaned, tormenting himself while he tried to find a way to make this possible. He was soon to learn that at the very time he was spinning schemes – and discarding them – practical steps were being prepared for exactly this purpose.

At the same time, Menachem Bader became aware of the need to co-ordinate the rescue work of all the emissaries who were already in Istanbul – Barlass and his assistant, Joseph Goldin, from the Jewish Agency; Venya, who represented the United Kibbutz Movement and the Histadrut; Dani Shind, who worked for the Mossad; and Teddy Kollek, representing the Political Department of the Jewish Agency. At the outbreak of the war, Bader had been in Central Europe on behalf of the kibbutz movement of Hashomer Hatzair and remembered well how much harm had been done by the political fragmentation of the Jewish communities, how much more might have been achieved had there been more co-ordination and less competition. The Jewish Agency Executive in Jerusalem also began to adopt this line of thought, and so under the leadership of the veteran Zionist leader Yitzhak Grünbaum, and with the concurrence of all groups and parties, a central rescue committee began to take shape.

Parties outside the framework of the Zionist Organization, and not represented in the Jewish Agency, were also invited to participate.

Bader's initiative in Istanbul bore fruit. Rather than fall back into the unforgiveable mistakes of the pre-war days, we were now going to operate as one comprehensive body. He suggested to the Histadrut that the representatives of the kibbutz movements and the Mossad – all members of the Haganah – form one committee. As our number in Istanbul grew, and as the Central Rescue Committee came into operation in Jerusalem, a branch was established under the chairmanship of Chaim Barlass, with Bader as his deputy-chairman. In the interest of complete harmony we invited Joseph Klarman, the eminent Revisionist leader, Jakob Griffel, a representative of the ultra-orthodox, and Dr. Meir Tuval, formerly of the Yugoslav Jewish community to join the committee.

The Istanbul community of Palestinian representatives now had the status needed to act effectively. It also took the initiative to induce organizations in Nazi-occupied Europe to follow its example. Central rescue committees now came into existence in Budapest and Bucharest. The committee in Budapest was to occupy a special place. Compared to other countries in Europe, Hungary was a haven for refugees – until the complete take-over by the Nazis in March 1944. Although the first deportations of Jews had taken place from Hungarian soil, the Government of Admiral Horty, Hitler's unflinching ally, relented for a time with regard to Hungary's Jews. Between 1941 and 1944, Hungary, compared to her neighbours, seemed a safe place, and therefore the committee there was able to play a key role.

At the end of 1942, the essence of the Istanbul Rescue Committee's work changed radically as the result of a chance meeting of two men in Budapest. One was working in the cause of his own people; the other was a secret agent. Both were leading double lives. Samu Springman was one of the recipients of a postcard from Istanbul signed 'Sarka Mandel-blatt'; Bandi Grosz was a master smuggler. Although a Jew, Bandi worked for the Hungarian counter-espionage service, but he continued to pursue his smuggling profession as well. In the Central European underworld on the eve of war, he was known as 'the king of Persian carpets'. When the war broke out, he decided that in order to continue making a profit on smuggled merchandise one had to be in with one of the secret services. He would become a double agent.

Samu Springman, born in Poland, had been brought to Budapest during the First World War. The Springmans were poor and lived in a proletarian neighbourhood crowded with Polish refugees. When Samu's father returned from the war as an invalid, it fell to ten-year-old Samu and to his younger brother to support the family. From childhood he had to use his wits to evade the anti-Semitic police and earn money to keep the family from starvation.

Samu became an apprentice to a watchmaker and later graduated to a silversmith. He also developed a keen sense of inventiveness in dealing with the police. The Hungarians often reminded the Polish refugees of their temporary status and of the fact that they were in Hungary on sufferance, rather than by right. With his charm and sharp mind, before the age of sixteen Samu became the liaison man between the Polish Jewish refugees in the ghetto and the Hungarian police. He also discovered how to win leniency for the ghetto's Jews by buying the favours of the police inspector in charge of the area with the lawman's special delight in life – rare books.

Samu was aware, however, that his makeshift solution to the tensions in Budapest could only be a temporary one. There was but one wholesome solution: the Jewish refugees had to go to Palestine, the land for which Jews had prayed for generations. Samu the watchmaker, the supplier of rare books to the police inspector, the intermediary between the refugees and the brutal authorities, now became the founder of the Zionist-Socialist youth club in the ghetto. The first tangible activities he started were to give Hebrew classes.

When Hitler took over Germany in 1933, the necessity for concrete action increased, and so did Samu's proficiency. He befriended the Polish Consul in Budapest and together they established a flourishing business of supplying Polish papers to refugees who otherwise would be regarded as stateless. Samu's apprenticeship in rescue work and in the shrewd machinations of consular affairs stood him in good stead when the war began, and the difficult situation in which he and his fellow refugees had found themselves for so many years became outright desperate. It was just this feel for rescue work and political undertones that made him read the postcard he received from Istanbul several times.

The text sounded innocuous enough – greetings from a cousin. But since he had no cousin in Istanbul and he did not expect any business communication in code from outside Hungary, he soon resolved that this must be a signal from people who wanted to establish contact with him. It was clear from the text that one who would write 'Eretz [the Land] is longing for you,' was a Jew from Palestine. Samu repeated this phrase over and over again in his mind and reached a decision: he had to find someone who could travel to Istanbul and establish contact with the mysterious sender of the enigmatic message.

On the Diamond Exchange he met a fellow who was just preparing to go to Istanbul. The man was Erich Popescu, a dashing young Rumanian who, Samu knew, worked for Hungarian espionage. He also smuggled diamonds – partly to cover up for his treasonable activities in Turkey and partly to supplement his salary. Samu spoke to Popescu with complete frankness. The 'Final Solution' had not yet reached Budapest, but the Jews were already outcasts, especially if they were poor and particularly when they were not even Hungarian subjects. Samu knew that Popescu was a cold-blooded man interested only in money, and that he was not concerned with the source of his income as long as it was constant. He offered Popescu £ 50 to be paid to him on his return to Budapest with delivery of a note from the person who signed his (or her?) name Sarka Mandelblatt.

A few days after the meeting on the Budapest Diamond Exchange, the bell rang at an apartment in Istanbul. A blond woman opened the door. Yes, she was Sarka Mandelblatt. What could she do for the caller? Popescu produced a handwritten note from Samu Springman. Sarka Mandelblatt excused herself for a few minutes, and rushed to the adjoining room where Venya and Bader sat.

The first response had come! Setting all conspiratorial prudence aside, both men entered the room where the stranger was waiting. He had come! He had been in touch with Jews in Nazi-occupied Europe; he had actually spoken to them; and he was prepared to be the go-between they had been praying for. Venya uttered the benediction that the Jewish rite prescribes on the occasion of some extraordinary event. Bader, no less moved but better able to control his feelings, discussed with the 'courier' when he would be prepared to come and fetch an envelope with letters addressed to Samu Springman. Having assured himself of another £ 50, Popescu promised to be back the next evening before his journey to Budapest.

Popescu was still away. Samu, unable to wait passively for his return, went to 'La Parisette', one of Budapest's popular coffee-houses, the meeting place for the 'active people' – the glorified smugglers and spies who abounded in the peaceful island of the Hungarian capital. He sat sipping his 'Cup of Gold', the Hungarian version of cappuccino, and watched. Sooner or later someone with the proper qualifications would pass by.

'Why are you unshaven and so distraught?' Samu asked

the man who winked at him as he passed his table. As he sat down with Samu, he exuded the sickening odour of cheap perfume mixed with strong tobacco.

'My dear Mamma has died and I am in a state of shock.' The man's suave voice was clouded by the predicament in which he found himself; Samu understood better when he went on.

The man was Bandi Grosz. Although they had been in primary school together, Samu – like most other people he knew – had always shunned Grosz. A disreputable character, he had been jailed for criminal offences before he was of age. At twenty-one he already owned one of the shadier coffee-houses, which attracted the special attention of the police even in the pleasure-loving Budapest of pre-war days. As everybody who frequented La Parisette knew, Grosz was smuggling Persian carpets from Iran to the prosperous markets of the *nouveau riche* under the pro-Nazi Hungarian régime. What no one knew was that in order to protect his movements and gain immunity from the Hungarian security services, Bandi Grosz had sold himself to those whose suspicion he feared.

'I must make an urgent business trip to Istanbul,' Bandi told Samu. 'You, as a good Jew, must advise me: Is it proper for me to travel during the seven days of mourning for my dead mother?'

'I am not a rabbi,' Samu hedged. 'If it is an urgent trip – go. But if you want to do honour to the deceased – work for me.'

Grosz listened carefully. He saw no reason to refuse his help on a humanitarian matter that one day might, as he put it, 'whitewash part of his soul'. If nothing more was involved than the smuggling of letters, he would be glad to oblige an old friend.

Replies to the urgent inquiries that Popescu brought back from Istanbul were sent barely forty-eight hours after they had arrived. Grosz was on his first trip as a courier for the Jewish underground. He could not know that he was to become involved in matters quite different from the mere smuggling of letters.

One day, soon after my arrival in Istanbul, I knocked on the door of Venya and Bader's place and Sarka Mandelblatt let me in. She motioned me to Venya's room and in sign language explained to me to keep quiet. I found Venya on his bed, writhing with pain, exhausted from crying. Letters and documents lay on the floor: Joszi Wieninger, another regular courier, had arrived that morning and Venya had been reading the mail he brought. I tiptoed to Venya's bed, where he lay breathing heavily and sighing from time to time, and took the letter lying next to him. Then, returning silently to the hall, I stood and read the following lines from Nazi-occupied Poland:

Bendin, 17/7/1943.
Dear Friends,
    After a long wait, today we received your courier and the letter he brought from you. Unfortunately he came a little too late. For years we dreamt about an opportunity to report about our life and our struggle. During the first year and a half of the war, we established an immense network of training farms and a strong youth movement, much larger and stronger than in normal times. But then, suddenly, all regular work was disrupted, the ovens were installed, and the systematic extermination began.
    The operation began in the Warthegau and in the districts of Posen and Lodz. About 80,000 Jews were gassed. The official term for this procedure was '*Aussiedlung*' [population transfer]. In the town of Lodz there remains a small, hermetically closed community: they are doomed to die of hunger and consumption. At the moment we have no news from there. The place of extermination is called Chelmno, the death camp at Kulmhof.
    For the past few months we simply have had no news from Lithuania. Most probably, it is '*Judenrein*'. We have prepared ourselves for self-defence measures to no avail. In the *General Gouvernement* of Warsaw, Lublin, Czenstochau and Cracow, there are no Jews left. They were gassed, mostly in Treblinka.

This is a notorious camp, where not only Jews from Poland but also from Belgium, Holland, and other Western countries have died.

The most beautiful chapter in our struggle was the uprising in Warsaw. Zivia and Yosef organized the defence together with many youngsters. There were terrible battles in the ghetto. To our sorrow only about 800 of the enemy fell. The result: all the Jews and the ghetto utterly annihilated.

There seem to be no more Jews in the *General Gouvernement,* once called Poland, except for about 30,000 in three forced-labour camps. In a few weeks they, too, will be gone.

In Warsaw several thousand Jews went into hiding on the other side of the ghetto among the Poles. Zivia, Gishak and Gehler are among them! Mordechai Anilewitz and all of our dearest comrades are dead.

The Ukraine is *'Judenrein'.* In Bialistok there still remain some 20,000 Jews living under relatively better conditions. The district of Lublin was entirely liquidated. East Upper Silesia was the last Jewish community where something resembling human conditions prevailed. But three weeks ago, 7,000 Jews were 'transferred' from there. They are being exterminated in Auschwitz: some are shot, others gassed.

In the near future the district from which we write to you will also be *'Judenrein'.* When you receive this letter, none of us will be alive. Many of those who received *Schutzpässe* [*laisser-passer*] from abroad simply vanished. At first we thought they were safe; but some of them turned up in Auschwitz. You must intervene immediately with the protecting power that issued these passes (Switzerland). We look for an escape route to Hungary. Please advise us if you can! Do all you can. But it is doubtful that your help will reach us. We expect these are our very last days. Our hope to reach Palestine will unfortunately never be realised. Please greet all our friends. We write in great haste, as the courier is in a hurry to leave. We have neither strength nor patience to write more detailed reports at this time. We greet you warmly.

Aranka, Hershl, Zvi, Koziak, Shlomo.

(13)

'All in a Day's Work'

AFTER THE ARRIVAL of the *Milka,* the Chief returned to
Palestine and resumed his duties as the head of the entire
Mossad operation, but Agami stayed in Istanbul and joined
our team. It was because of Agami that our activities
branched out into rescuing Jews from Greece, which had
been occupied by the Nazis since 1941. This operation began
with a trip he made to Izmir, the Turkish port at the mouth
of the Dardanelles. The ostensible reason for his trip was to
make contact with the head of the city's Jewish community,
Rafael Baki, but the truth of the matter was that Agami was
drawn to Izmir by curiosity. The port city had long been a
frequent destination of Commander Wulfson, the Naval Attaché of the British Embassy in Istanbul, with whom we were
cooperating on a scheme to parachute Palestinians behind
enemy lines in order to aid the escape of British prisoners of
war (mostly RAF pilots who had been shot down). Wulfson's
repeated appearance in Izmir prompted Agami to think there
might be something of interest in the town for the Mossad as
well, and so he went to scout out Izmir for himself. But once
Agami met Baki, all other interests besides the swift rescue
of Greek Jews faded from the scene.

The man in charge of implementing the 'Final Solution' in Greece was the fat, pink-cheeked Dieter von Wisliceny, a man who had once been Adolf Eichmann's superior in the Nazi hierarchy, but who had been succeeded by his pale, pedantic and tireless underling. By the time Agami arrived in Izmir in the spring of 1944, the Jewish community of Salonika had already been exterminated by the Nazis, but the Jews of Athens and of some of the small towns in southern Greece were still permitted to survive under dismal conditions.

Rafael Baki, a prosperous businessman, was all too familiar with the details of the extermination of most of Greece's small Jewish community and was eager to work with Agami. He had already established contact with some of the Greek sailors, fishermen and smugglers who plied the network of islands between the mainland of Greece and Turkey. His initiative had a concrete purpose: Baki's elder brother was still living in Athens. Although he was likewise one of the wealthy and respected members of the Jewish community there, he refused to exploit his position and flee Greece while his fellow-Jews were in such mortal danger. He had decided to stay in Athens and help his community as best he could. From the safety of his Izmir home, Baki provided his brother – and through him the Jewish community – with medicine and food smuggled with the generous help of certain fishermen. These were goods no money could buy in wartime Athens; and Baki had found that every one of his consignments had safely reached the hands of his brother. He had only words of great praise for the Greek fishermen who engaged – for a negligible return – in this dangerous traffic.

When Agami asked to meet the leader of these fishermen, Baki made the necessary arrangements and soon after introduced him to Thomas, a sturdy young man with burning eyes and the manner of an experienced smuggler. Because he trusted Baki, Thomas took Agami into his confidence and disclosed that he was not just a private smuggler. He was a member of the Greek underground, ELAS, the Freedom Fighters for democratic rule in Greece, and he had deep sympathy for the Jewish victims of Nazi atrocities in his country. Agami explained that he, too, was the emissary of a clandestine militant organization, the Haganah, and proposed to Thomas that the two organizations work together: Thomas would bring Jews from Greece to Turkey; the Haganah would send ELAS medicine, food, blankets and clothing.

Messages reporting on the agreement between the two resistance organizations were sent through Thomas to Baki's brother in Athens. Without delay he hired cabs to transport small groups of Jews from Athens to the coast of Euboea, where illegal transports of Jews had departed before the war and where they now were met by Thomas and his fellow-conspirators. The tiny fishing boats took on small groups of Jewish families with their children and carried them through the mine-infested routes to the salvation of the Turkish coast. Covered by Lord Cranborne's letter, the Turkish authorities not only did not obstruct the arrivals, but did all they could to expedite their transfer from the uncomfortable boats to a camp near Izmir, where they were given hot food and allowed to rest before they continued, on Turkish trains, southwards through Syria to Palestine.

We insisted that only Jews were to be transported by Thomas and his companions. This was not because we objected in any way to the rescue of anti-Fascist Greeks: they were our allies, and we naturally would have liked to do more for them than merely sending supplies. But we were afraid of the revival of the British pretext against the rescue of Jews, the implication that the Nazis might use our transports to smuggle agents disguised as Jews into Allied territory.

One day, as Agami was settling accounts with Thomas in Baki's living-room in Izmir (we paid one gold sovereign for every person brought out of Greece), Thomas acted uneasy, and Agami had the feeling that he was about to announce the end of our satisfactory partnership.

'I have a confession to make,' Thomas said finally. 'I acted against your orders. On this last shipment I brought one person who is not a Jew. But nobody will ever be able to claim that he is an agent of any side. I brought a Greek who has a brilliant future and who one day will be a leader of my people. He comes from my home town, and I was unable to refuse his plea to rescue him. His name is Papandreou. I know you will be angry with me for disobeying your orders, but in the future you will be proud to have contributed to his rescue.'

He insisted on paying for the Greek leader's transport but Agami refused. He was convinced of Thomas' sincerity and, after all, he had been on a trip financed by Agami. Thomas proved to be right; we never did regret having contributed to the rescue of this one non-Jew – the future Prime Minister of liberated Greece – in the face of British suspicions.

At about the same time, late in the spring of 1944, a cable in our usual code arrived from Samu Springman in Budapest, announcing that 'Wieninger and a friend' were coming to see us in Istanbul. We were expecting Wieninger – he had taken payment orders for huge sums on his last trip from Turkey to Budapest and was now due to bring the receipts for reimbursement – but we had no idea who the friend might be.

Whenever a courier was expected, Venya and Bader remained in their flat and Dani and I in ours; the man might come to either place, and we could not risk his finding the door closed. This time the bell rang at our flat, and when I opened the door I looked into Wieninger's vulgar, greedy face. The man standing beside him was entirely different: handsome, elegantly dressed and looking very much like a James Bond type – long before the time of the movie hero. He introduced himself as Rudi Schulz.

We had been curious to meet Rudi Schulz, who was

working for us behind enemy lines for some time now. He had originally been brought into our network of couriers through his girl friend in Budapest, a Jewish girl who had fallen in love with this Austrian businessman. She was aware of Springman's work, for she had been a secretary-typist for the Rescue Committee in Budapest. When she told Rudi about the couriers who risked taking money to ghettos in Poland against tremendous odds, he offered to participate. He was not, however, interested in the pay.

At present, Rudi Schulz was an agent for the 'Gestapo-Leitstelle-Stuttgart in the fight against resistance movements'. In this capacity he often went to France, where his main task was to prevent gold coins and gold bullion from falling into the hands of the French underground. His superiors supplied him with the capital to make 'preventive purchases' of the prohibited gold and to bring it to the safety of the Gestapo vaults.

Rudi was well chosen for this job. In his youth he had practised the art of safe-cracking in his native Vienna. In 1936, with the police on his heels, he made a narrow escape and disappeared to Paris, where he was received by professional acquaintances. Rudi led a more-or-less quiet life in France. He learned the language and the customs of the land, and when 'Greater Germany caught up with him,' as he put it, he suddenly realized that the good times were over. As an Austrian he had become German by virtue of the *Anschluss,* and as a German in Nazi-occupied France he was eligible for service in the German Army. He succeeded in talking himself into a soft job and was sent to Stuttgart for duty with the department that fought against underground movements. With his knowledge of French and his excellent connections in the French underworld, it was obvious that his assignment would be Paris. He had achieved exactly what he wanted.

Rudi looked more like a distinguished scholar than a former criminal and present criminal agent. He talked well and generously. He had looked death in the eye (on his own behalf and on behalf of his present employers) so often that he was no longer aware of 'what people call fear'. He had the best cover for travel in Europe, for he could always claim to be on a mission for a Gestapo department that was regarded with special awe. Rudi disliked the Nazis intensely. He loved the girl in Budapest. He wanted to do something 'out of the ordinary'; he decided to work for us.

Wieninger went on to Bader and Venya's to deliver the mail and to settle his accounts with them. Rudi agreed to stay for tea. He in fact had come to meet us, for he was interested in who was behind this operation of the Jewish underground and he wanted to meet the type of people who directed it.

Dani and I assumed that there was more to Rudi's visit than mere curiosity. Perhaps he wanted us to put him in touch with the British, in order to create an alibi for himself for the future. Gently, we steered the discussion in this direction. But Rudi became angry when he understood our intention. He was not in politics; he had no political opinions whatsoever; for him both sides were exactly the same. True, he disliked the Germans and he hated the Nazis, but that still did not make him a lover of the Allies. We dropped the subject. Rudi apparently held a sufficiently strong position in his department to be able to indulge in his whims and leisurely pursuits. More definite proof of this came that same evening.

Venya and Bader came to dinner at our place. They, too, wanted to meet Rudi. Fortunately, they came without Wieninger, who had another appointment in town. Venya excitedly produced a letter which had come in the mail that Wieninger brought from Budapest. It was from Springman, and it explained a great deal about Rudi. In the subject's embarrassed presence, Venya now read us this report, complete with details provided by eyewitnesses to the story.

Springman's letter began by relating that a few weeks earlier, when our last payment orders had arrived in Budapest, they included one for a considerable sum to an address in Kolomea, Poland. At that time no one could travel to Poland without a special permit, and as Polish bank-notes were in small denominations, it was practically impossible to smuggle in the quantity of Polish currency we had indicated. Springman approached Rudi for the job. He explained the special difficulties, and the challenge appealed to the daredevil.

Rudi bought several new suits and used them to cover the pile of Polish bank-notes in his suitcase. At the frontier control he sat reading calmly in his compartment, and when the guards came in he brandished his impressive credentials. Nevertheless, he was asked to open his suitcase. The guards were shocked to see the expensive new suits – a most severely prohibited commodity, as tailor-made suits were sold for exorbitant prices on the Polish black market. Just as Rudi had calculated, the suits were respectfully confiscated, and it did not occur to the guards to search further in the suitcase of the high-powered Gestapo envoy who, no doubt, had been unaware of the prohibition.

When Rudi reached Kolomea, he found the town exceptionally still; there was no movement in the streets. He soon learned that a general curfew was in force: the final 'Resettlement Action' (the German euphemism for the deportation of the entire Jewish population to a death camp) was in full swing. Here was Rudi Schulz of the Leitstelle-Stuttgart, with no authority to be in Poland at all, in Kolomea during an *Aktion*. He could have returned to the station and taken the next train to another city. He did not; he stayed and went directly to the address we had given him. He entered the house only to find that it was a kind of headquarters of the Zionist youth movement of the ghetto of Kolomea. In a room of the first-floor flat, he found a number of people lined up by the SS detachment that had come to take them away. The SS corporal in charge of the operation held a list from which he read out the names of those present. In a split-second, Rudi took in the scene. He glared at the SS men, who were stupefied by the unexpected arrival of a very self-assured civilian carrying a suitcase and sporting a brilliant swastika in the lapel of his black coat.

'Stop your idiotic proceedings this minute,' Rudi shouted at the SS man. 'I have travelled all the way from Stuttgart to have this bunch of criminals arrested, and here you are quite prepared to snatch them from justice and send them to the anonymous ovens of Auschwitz. These people will lead us to the arrest of some of the most dangerous subversive elements in the entire Reich!'

Rudi tore the list from the SS corporal's hand and glanced at the names (which he was seeing for the first time in his life) with sarcastic irony. 'The main thing in life is timing,' he said to the trembling SS men and ordered the arrest 'of the whole bunch of traitors'. He commanded the SS guard to bring them to the railway station in their truck and requisitioned two compartments on the train to Budapest for them. Then Rudi assured the three SS men that he would not even report them: after all it was not their personal fault that they were about to deprive the Gestapo of this important booty. Some idiot higher up had probably omitted to read his orders properly. 'Let's keep this amongst the four of us . . .'

Rudi had listened to Venya's account of his bravery with complete *aplomb*. When Venya finished, the rest of us stared at our guest, unable to speak. Obviously feeling awkward at having become the centre of attention, Rudi said: 'I'll admit to you that I felt somewhat uncomfortable on the long ride to Budapest.'

'Why didn't you tell us about this during the afternoon?' Dani asked, perplexed.

'Well,' Rudi said, 'it's all in a day's work.'

Rudi's bravery in this incident was only one aspect of the

multitude of activities carried on by the far-reaching arms of the Mossad. And while the Mossad, representing the Palestinian Jewish community, had been involved in rescue activities since before the outbreak of the war, now that the conflagration was in full swing – indeed, the die of the final downfall of the Nazis already cast – other countries also began to take heed of the horrendous situation of European Jewry and slowly and painfully began to take steps to alleviate it.

It is likely that the event which caused the tide of concern to flow occurred in Warsaw. On 19 April 1943 the armoured cars of Major-General (of the Police) Jürgen Stroop entered the ghetto of Warsaw, and for the first time since Bar Kokhba, 2,000 years earlier, armed Jews rose in revolt against their executioners.

It took the German Army thirty-three days to crush the insurrection. In addition to conventional military methods, they were forced to seal the sewers of the area and blow up whole streets in order to squelch the last resistants.

It was, of course, only the merest coincidence that on exactly the same day a very different set of people met to deal with the same issues through completely different means. On the tropical island of Bermuda, representatives of the British and American governments met to see what could be done in the face of growing restlessness over continued Allied equanimity towards the ruthless progress of the 'Final Solution'.

The conference became meaningless before it opened, as the heads of the two Allied delegations made opening statements in which they promised that nothing would come of their deliberations. 'The persecuted people should not be betrayed into a belief that aid is coming to them when in fact we are unable to give them immediate succor,' said Lord Coleraine, the British chief delegate. The American chief representative, Dr Dodd of Columbia University, supported this line of sober realism: 'The problem is too great for solution by the two governments here represented.'

Yet, because of increasingly uneasy public opinion in the Allied countries, it was impossible to evade the issue of the 'Final Solution' completely, and those governments therefore tried to satisfy by diplomatic niceties demands that could have been met only with great courage and straightforward support for the victims of Nazi persecution. While the extermination of Europe's Jews continued unabated, the Allied governments shied away from openly identifying with their plight. Such identification, some of the policy-makers believed, would only give strength to the Nazi accusation that the Allies were fighting the war for the sake of the Jews. In order to remain completely objective, the tragedy of Nazi persecution was discussed without so much as naming the main victims in the meaningless resolutions that were the sole results of the conference.

The Rescue Committee in Istanbul, the representatives of the Jewish Agency and the Jewish Congress in Switzerland and in Sweden continued to feed their American colleagues detailed reports on the extermination. Under the leadership of Chaim Weizmann, the President of the Zionist Organization, public meetings, attended by tens of thousands of both Jews and Gentiles, were organized in the United States. In innumerable private meetings with congressmen, senators, members of President Roosevelt's administration, journalists, writers and the leadership of voluntary humanitarian organizations, the true facts about the Holocaust were divulged. And while the diplomats carefully sifted innocuous statements for possibly offensive words, public pressure for action grew.

On 22 January 1944, as the war was entering its fifth year, the President of the United States announced the formation of the War Refugee Board. Several officials with a reputation for integrity and concern met in Washington to plan an operation that was tragically overdue. The first instruction issued by the acting head of the new organization, John Pehle, ordered all American diplomatic missions abroad 'that action be taken to forestall the plot of the Nazis to exterminate the Jews and other persecuted minorities in Europe'. It seemed that the time of even-handed prudence had come to an end.

Ira Hirschmann, the representative of the hastily established American War Refugee Board, came to Istanbul with somewhat overrated ideas about the importance of his mission and the unlimited possibilities that his late appearance on the scene heralded for the disjointed and futile attempts of inferior forces. In his haste, he nearly stifled our efforts by engaging in a logical but utterly hopeless programme. Hirschmann wanted the Red Cross to guarantee the safe arrival of refugees from behind enemy lines by issuing certificates of safe conduct to seaworthy ships large enough to conduct evacuation on a meaningful scale.

The Executive Vice-President of Bloomingdale's department stores, fortified with a generous scope of reference from no less than the President of the United States, regarded his own arrival almost as a form of salvation. As we, the Mossad 'boys', were doing 'illegal' work, and as Hirschmann was the envoy of the supreme power, he refused at first to recognize our existence. He dealt directly with the Red Cross and the Turkish Government, but condescended to meet with Barlass, who at least represented the Jewish Agency. It took Hirschmann weeks to find out that the Red Cross was deeply interested in such matters as the issuance of certificates of safe conduct, but that their freedom of activity within Nazi Germany would be impeded if they sided too openly with efforts to rescue Jews. Likewise, it took weeks to convince the representative that he was day-dreaming when he thought it possible to charter large, well-built Turkish ships for the transport of refugees from Black Sea ports to Istanbul; these ships were needed elsewhere at no less exorbitant prices.

Ira Hirschmann went through his formative stages with *brio* and optimism; but he took his defeats, one after the other, with growing alarm. Yet his disillusionment did not lead him to despair; he acted on the one logical option left to him – he practically joined the underground.

Dani was the first to have a persuasive talk with him. He explained that we were indeed fighting the British and the restrictions of their White Paper, but he also impressed upon Hirschmann that at present our overriding interest was to rescue the Jews from Nazi Europe rather than to have it out with the British.

Hirschmann's final conversion occurred when he met with our entire group of Mossad and Haganah 'boys'. During that meeting, Menachem Bader finally convinced the American official to adopt our ways. He discarded Hirschmann's plans for correct high-level cooperation with the appropriate institutions of a well-ordered world and pleaded with him not to rely on big words and big wheels. His face white as chalk, Bader turned to the American envoy and said slowly and emphatically: 'We prefer to expose the refugees to danger on their way to life, rather than to abandon them to death without having tried to leave no stone unturned.' After that conversation Ira Hirschmann became a trusted and valued ally of the Mossad. The extent of Hirschmann's power and connections were tested more than once, but the incident that remains clearest in my mind was his part in helping us trace the tragic voyage of the *Mefkure.*

We were now in possession of several boats. The *Milka* and *Maritza* flew the Bulgarian flag, and we directed them by telephone to Bucharest. In Istanbul the *Morina,* a sturdy 325-ton boat; the *Mefkure,* a little smaller than the *Morina;* and the *Bulbul* (Turkish for nightingale), the 'flagship' of the three, formed our small fleet.

The *Morina,* the *Mefkure* and the *Bulbul* left for Constantsa, and when Dani lifted the receiver he knew that this was the word he had been waiting for: our little armada was

on its way. There had been a last moment hitch. It seemed
that the German Navy had attempted to stop their departure,
but the attempt had been foiled. The regular Nazi Navy
routine was slower and more involved than Pandelis' efficient,
well-oiled apparatus. The three ships had cleared the port
and were sailing to Istanbul.

The scene in our apartment overlooking the Bosporus was
very similar to the one when we had waited for the *Milka,*
months before. The Chief and Dani spread a detailed navy
map (generously supplied by Commander Wulfson) on the
dining-room table and, working with nautical instruments,
followed the progress of our convoy, trying to overcome their
anxiety through rational, professional calculations. Venya
and Bader joined us for the long wait, and we indulged in
delightful fantasies of ever-increasing convoys, in the wake of
the one presently on its way. Agami passed the time with the
most effective work of all: he sat alone in the studio, im-
mersed in an activity as old as the troubles of the Jewish
people – the reading of Psalms in praise of the Lord who
now held the fate of His children in His hands.

On Saturday, 5 August 1944, the Turkish border-police
sighted the *Morina* with 308 passengers on board, as the
little ship sailed serenely into Istanbul harbour. But there was
no word from the *Bulbul* or the *Mefkure.* Barlass alerted the
Turkish authorities, who did all they could to locate the two
ships. Hirschmann frantically phoned his own contacts in the
American Embassy in Ankara and mobilized an American
plane, which happened to be in neutral Turkey on courier
duty. But aeronautics were still quite primitive, and the plane
was driven back by the same gale that had churned the Black
Sea into a battlefield for our two small boats.

Our anxiety grew, and our forebodings became certainty
when we learned that the *Bulbul* had reached a remote bay
on the Asiatic coast of Turkey in the early hours of the next
day. Her passengers immediately disembarked. The Turkish

frontier patrol stationed on the spot was ingenious and help-ful. With mules and asses, they ferried the stranded pas-sengers to shore and provided them with all the warmth, food and shelter they could.

Simon Brod also looked after the refugees from the two ships. Generous and efficient as always, he provided them with food and warm clothing and sped them off to a special train waiting to take them to Palestine.

But the *Mefkure* was lost. She was torpedoed by a German warship off the Turkish coast barely 40 miles from Istanbul. Except for five survivors, all the passengers, including ninety-six children, drowned. The Turkish crew used the single life-boat to save themselves, rowing directly to the attacking German ship, which picked them up. Two of the Jewish survivors are now in Israel – then they were newly married, and the young wife was eight months pregnant. They have always believed that the crew was forewarned of the attack and acted in collusion with the Germans.

These two survivors (of the other three, one was a woman who became demented as a result of the experience; the other two were men whose present whereabouts are not known) told me about the last night of the *Mefkure,* nearly thirty years after the event. Lesley Fulop was a young man of twenty-two at the time, and this is his description of his family's escape from Hungary to Palestine:

When the Germans occupied Hungary in March 1944, my father was there on business; he was a wealthy man with interests in both Rumania and Hungary and high-placed friends in both countries. There was complete chaos and confusion in both Budapest and Bucharest. At first my father did not believe the news about the German invasion. He telephoned the head of the Hungarian police, who was a personal friend of his, but the man had been arrested. Father saw how other friends tried – and failed – to buy entry permits to Portugal from the Gestapo. I myself managed to cross the Hungarian-Rumanian border: once in a Hungarian army uniform which a friend got for me and on orders I wrote myself, and once through a friend of my father's who was a colonel. Finally, again through friends – including the Rumanian Minister of the Interior – and through the payment of a huge sum of money, our family was put on one of the first transports to Palestine. I was the one who really wanted to come. My mother felt that the heartland of Rumania was safe and that 'it won't happen here'; my father also was more optimistic than I regarding Rumanian reliability. In the end, my wife, her mother, brother and I were put on the *Mefkure*. A friend in the Secret Service warned us that something might happen to the boat, and we knew that the Germans had photographed the *Mefkure* in port.

We sailed on 2 August. Rumanian battleships accompanied us for a day and a half, until we reached Bulgarian waters. Then, on the evening of 4 August, the sky suddenly lit up. My wife and I were standing on deck, together with my wife's family and some other passengers. We saw the outlines of three dark objects at a distance, but we took them to be ships. Suddenly, fire opened up from these objects. My wife's mother and brother died instantly, their bodies torn by machine-gun fire.

Seeing that her mother and brother had been killed and grasping the situation in general, my wife decided that in spite of her physical condition we should jump into the water. We took off our shoes and jumped. I should tell you that we were both good swimmers – my wife held a championship for the backstroke, and I had been a member of our national water-polo team. Just before we jumped, a man who had been seriously injured – and later drowned – offered my wife a knife so that she might kill herself. But she told him that she wanted to live – for her child's sake.

In the water, we tried to avoid searchlights and the glare from the ship, which had caught fire. We heard horrible cries of terror and anguish, and the sound of shots pinging across the water after those who had decided to swim. My wife took hold of a little boy, about three years old, and put him on a plank from the disintegrating ship, which she had found floating near us.

We heard voices, in German, from the attacking ships – I think they were small patrol vessels, not submarines. There had been just one lifeboat on the *Mefkure*, and the moment the first salvo was fired, the captain and crew took to it and saved themselves.

With the first light of day, my wife distinguished a moving point in the distance; it grew into a ship which, we were sure, must be either the *Morina* or the *Bulbul*. It came near, but as the waves were very high, we were unable to get close to it. But we shouted, and in spite of the very heavy seas our cries were heard and one of the passengers threw me a rope. I motioned in sign-language that my wife was still in the water and couldn't get into a lifeboat because of her advanced pregnancy. She was completely exhausted, and had long since lost hold of the plank with the little boy.

This is how Vera herself described the closing moments of the long ordeal: 'The *Bulbul* moved in very near to where I was staying afloat with my last bit of strength. Someone threw me a rope, and then – when I sensed what felt like a thousand hands pulling at the other end – I lost consciousness.'

The *Bulbul* took more than a day to reach the nearby shore, because of the raging storm that swept the decks. From the village on the seashore, the refugees travelled by foot, mule and finally by freight train to Istanbul. On the train, Vera Fulop noticed barrels labelled 'Intercontinental, Bucharest', which ironically was the large export firm of which her father had been a director.

We took turns visiting the Fulops in the hospital in Istanbul. Both recovered quickly, and exactly one month after the disaster Vera Fulop gave birth to a healthy baby boy. He was called Thomas – after Vera's brother who died on the *Mefkure*.

Today, Lesley Fulop is well known in the elegant circles of Europe and America as the originator and developer of one of Israel's most famous fashion firms, 'Beged Or', whose distinctive designs in leather are featured in exclusive shops everywhere. 'Beged Or' fashions are made in a town near Nazareth called Migdal Haemek, which is made up almost entirely of new immigrants.

(14)

Yoel Brand

THE FIRST CLUE of things to come was a telegram from Budapest, signed by Rejô Kastner, the chairman of the Budapest Rescue Committee, and received by Chaim Barlass' office at the Pera Palace Hotel. It advised that 'Engineer Eugen Band and Bandi Grosz' were about to arrive in Istanbul and requested that they be received by 'Chaim' to discuss important proposals.

Hungary, until recently an island of relative security, had suddenly become the focal point of the continuing extermination of European Jewry. Just two months before this telegram arrived, at the end of March 1944, the Germans had occupied their ally's territory and established a radically aggressive Nazi régime. Eichmann and the Gestapo immediately opened their own offices and – thanks to previous experience – efficiently set about the task of exterminating the 600,000 Jews of Hungary before the now foreseeable Allied victory thwarted their 'Final Solution'.

We had no idea who Engineer Band might be, but Kastner was our representative in Hungary, and this was no time for hesitation. After consulting with members of the Istanbul rescue team, Barlass replied to the telegram in the affirmative.

It was Bandi Grosz's squeaky voice which informed us that the two had just landed in Istanbul. Even more sullen than usual, he bewailed the fact that we had again failed him: 'Here I am with Yoel Brand. We have just arrived in the plane that carries the German diplomatic pouch and the courier. We have no visas, and you are not here to meet us properly!' But how were we to know that Band was Yoel Brand? What's more, how had he escaped from Germany in a German courier's plane?

Simon Brod got busy on the 'messy' side of the business at once. Through his not-so-official contacts, he arranged for the two unusual passengers to come into town for the twenty-four-hour period that the courier plane was expected to remain at the airport. Then they would have to leave exactly as they had come.

We were all gathered in Barlass' office when, later in the afternoon, Bandi Grosz's awkward form entered the crowded room. He was followed by Yoel Brand. The difference between the two could not have been more pronounced. Brand was neatly dressed, he walked with the gait of a sailor – carefully placing one heavy foot before another – and his blue eyes were full of sincerity and wonder. Reddish hair gave him a healthy, youthful air, and his rosy cheeks made him look not like the bearer of messages from the dead and the dying, but like the harbinger of good news. From our correspondence with Budapest, we knew that Brand was one of the reliable dare-devils in the Budapest underground. We could hardly wait to hear what had brought him to Istanbul under an assumed name, with a German diplomatic passport and in the company of Bandi Grosz, the brute.

The latter took me aside and drew me into the far corner of the room. As he bent over me to whisper into my ear, I was overpowered by the mixture of bad breath and loud *eau-de-Cologne*.

'Don't believe a word of what this fool is going to tell you. I am the one who put it all on. I was arrested when the Nazis

took Hungary. To save myself from certain death, I invented
the greatest stunt of my career. This fool, Brand, is only the
tool of my own salvation. Pay no attention to the fairy-tales
he will feed you – as if he were some envoy of supreme
power over life and death.'

I broke away as quickly as I could from his sickening
whispered confidences and took a seat in the circle of chairs
that had formed around Yoel Brand. I listened – struck, like
everybody else in the room, with the unbelievable spectacle
of sitting with this 'visitor' from the prison of Hungary. In a
monotonous voice, and with a hypnotized stare fixed on a
point on the wall opposite him, Yoel Brand began his
account.

Since the occupation of Hungary in March, Eichmann had
been deporting about 12,000 Jews a day in sealed box-cars
from the provinces to the extermination camp of Auschwitz.
But the ovens there did not suffice, so a special camp was
established in Birkenau. There the Jews were gunned down
with machine-guns, their bodies piled on huge pyres and
cremated. The Jews of Budapest had not yet been seized, but
thousands of them had been sought out in hospitals, lunatic
asylums, orphanages and old-age homes and were carted
away for burning.

Kastner and Brand opened negotiations with Dieter Wisliceny. As in the case of Slovakia, where Wisliceny had put
off deportations against huge payments, they tried to interest
him in buying Hungary's Jews as well. The end of the war
seemed near, the outcome certain. If only they could get
Wisliceny to negotiate *and* to stop deportations while talks
went on! Then, suddenly, the rescue committee was ordered
to send a representative to Eichmann's office. Yoel was
chosen for the task, he said, mainly because he was the
only one on the committee who spoke flawless German.

Brand appeared before Eichmann on 8 May. The *Hauptsturmführer* spoke slowly, pondering every word: 'If you
can get me a military truck for each 100 Jews and, in addi-

tion, soap, coffee and tea – 1,000 tons of them – I may consider selling you some of the remaining Jews.'

He had offered a million Jews in all. As proof of his good intentions, he was prepared to stop deportation briefly in order to give Brand a chance to meet with representatives of the 'Jewish Internationale' in Istanbul. 'Blood for merchandise,' Eichmann had said, visibly enjoying his formula, 'merchandise for blood.' He sat down slowly, swinging back and forth in his swivel chair, lovingly caressing the leather whip he held, as always, in his hands.

There was complete silence when Brand reached this point. He stopped talking for a moment, concentrating, as it were, on the scene he was reliving, and it seemed that for the first time since his arrival he realized that he was no longer in Budapest but among his own people – perhaps even in reach of the salvation he had been sent to achieve. Then we started to fire questions at him. As Bandi Grosz had quietly slipped out of the room while we had hung in fascination on Brand's words, we first interrogated him about Grosz's role in the mission. (I had had no occasion to reveal Grosz's confession – or whatever it was – to my colleagues.)

Brand told us that Grosz was attached to him as a kind of supervisor, a collaborator with the Nazi officials who had sent him. Brand believed that Grosz's role was to watch him doing his job, report home if he failed and see to it that they returned quickly. Brand was certain that high-level Nazis were just as interested in getting their own names whitewashed at this late hour as they were in getting the commodities Eichmann had stipulated. Absurd as it sounded to us, Himmler seemed to believe that he, of all people, would be acceptable to the Allies as an alternative to Hitler for purposes of negotiating peace.

As we were considering the subtle complexities of Brand's message, Brand made it clear to us that the problem was out of our league.

'What about Chaim Weizmann? What about our visas and

permission to stay in Turkey until we finish negotiations?' he asked.

Only then did we realize that the 'Chaim' in the original telegram from Budapest referred to Weizmann, the President of the Zionist Organization – who was in England at that time – and not, as we had assumed, Chaim Barlass, a mere representative of the Jewish Agency in Istanbul. What a disappointment it must have been for Yoel Brand to discover that we believed his mission was negotiable on our level; that we had not grasped the immense importance attached to his meeting with internationally known personalities by the men who had sent him; that nothing was to come of his presence here unless the Nazis learned that he was in touch with people who might be able to move the world. He was even more shocked when we explained that it was not so easy to obtain Turkish visas.

'We get thousands of people over Nazi-controlled borders,' he shouted angrily as we explained our predicament. 'Do you mean to say that you, the big bosses in neutral Turkey, must stand in line at British passport control and beg favours for them to intervene on your behalf with the Turks?'

We were worlds apart in our approach to the situation. Brand could not understand that we were here on sufferance; that we led a thinly disguised existence between enemy camps, trying to make use of the Allies, whose war we supported with all our resources. But our resources were, after all, meagre crumbs, and our reward was offered with condescension, rather than with gratitude or a sense of duty. Before we parted that night, Brand had worked up a terrible anger against what seemed to him our hesitation, cowardice and lack of resolution.

As Dani and I entered our flat, the telephone rang. Grosz was at the other end.

'Has my fool companion told you his fairy-tales?' he asked in his creaking voice, now audibly greased with liquor. 'Don't believe a word he says. I invented the whole escapade. I was in very hot water there after they took Hungary and I had to get out at all costs. So I instilled some of the high-ups with the childish dream of being able to create an alibi for themselves by making an offer to let Jews go free, late as it is. All they want is to get in touch with Allied officers and make an impression on them. The people Brand quotes, Eichmann included, have as much power to stop the ovens – or the trains – as I have to stop the world. And even if they could stop them, they would never have the courage to propose it to a beast like Himmler. Don't be children! Don't believe a word!'

He hung up. Dani and I spent the rest of the night reconstructing the events of the day. We could not visualize Grosz thinking up a practical joke like this. We believed Brand's story about his talk with Eichmann. There must be something in the whole affair that we had no right to denigrate. We had to act – and to be seen acting – as if we were totally convinced of the authenticity of this devilish project.

Early the next morning we met again at Barlass' office. Bader suggested that Venya go to Jerusalem immediately and report to the Jewish Agency in person. Meanwhile, we would send confidential messages through the British Embassy to the High Commissioner's Office in Palestine for Moshe Shertok (Sharett), head of the Political Department of the Jewish Agency, although no one could be sure when and in what state these messages would reach him. First, however, we had to see about prolonging Brand's and Grosz's Turkish visas. If the Gestapo really shadowed our every step, they must not know that we were unable to keep their emissaries with us until the 'internationally known personality' arrived for talks. But where, indeed, was Grosz?

Dani and I went to Whittal's office and had a rare conference with him in the presence of Colonel Harold Gibson, his superior. We gave them an account of Brand's report, explaining that we knew of Brand and were convinced of his integrity now that we had met him: he was not an enemy agent. It was not necessary to introduce Grosz to them: they knew what he was. But despite our testimonial regarding Brand, we felt they regarded both men as equally untrustworthy.

Dani and I left the office with great forebodings. It was clear we had not convinced our British contact that perhaps this was a slight chance to save Jews – provided we had Allied help in staging 'negotiations' with Eichmann or his henchmen. Gibson's reaction was correct, but cold as ice. He was not in favour of recommending to London that we be allowed to go through the motions of negotiations with the Germans. His argument was that the Russians might get wind of the goings-on and suspect the British – and the Americans – of negotiating, not the release of 'several Jews', but a separate peace.

We were caught in a net of international intrigue and high-level politics, so we confined ourselves to requesting that the British transmit our report to Shertok and arrange for Turkish permission for him to come to Istanbul at once. Both requests were registered with much reserve.

When Dani and I returned to Barlass' office, where our whole group, including Brand, sat waiting for our report, we learned that Grosz had absconded. He had taken refuge at the Embassy of the Polish Government-in-exile and was not going to return to Budapest.

We activated all our contacts to extend Brand's visa, in the hope that it would be easier now that we were dealing only with an honest man, rather than with a multiple agent of ill repute. Simon Brod was again most useful, but even he was able to obtain an extension of Brand's visa on a twenty-four-hour basis only. Brod's main argument was that we were waiting for another Turkish department to issue a visa to Shertok, who was coming all the way just to meet Brand. The

Turks that Brod approached must have known that Shertok could only come if the British insisted, but they procrastinated; in this way, one day after another went by.

The news from Budapest was also bad: deportations were continuing at the rate of 12,000 per day travelling east in sealed freight wagons.

The next day Brand was arrested and taken to a police prison, where he was reunited with Grosz. The Polish Embassy enjoyed no extra-territorial status and was not immune to the law of the land. Both men were given three days to decide how they preferred to leave Turkey: north, through the frontier between Nazi-occupied Europe and neutral Turkey; or south to Syria, held by the Allies.

Grosz spared no time for reflection; he immediately chose to give himself up to the Allies and never return to Hungary, after all the trouble he had taken to engineer his escape from there. Yoel, on the other hand, went into a state of depression. To him, it appeared that all was lost. He could not dare to return without Grosz – the Nazis had told him not to; he was betraying friends who had entrusted him with a crucial, albeit grim, mission; and he was abandoning his family to their certain fate. His mission had been wrecked.

To further add to our despair, we received a cable from Shertok: under the influence of 'certain factors', the Turkish Consul in Jerusalem refuses to issue to the head of the Political Department of the Jewish Agency a visitor's visa to Turkey. He advised Brand to return to Budapest and tell Eichmann that he had relayed his offer, and the Jewish Agency was busy obtaining the necessary approval from appropriate quarters.

Another cable – this one from Budapest – also reached us on that day: 'Deportations continue.'

With the help of Joe Levy, a *New York Times* correspondent and a trusted friend, Brod obtained another concession from the Turkish police: the two prisoners would be allowed to spend their nights at the Pera Palace Hotel. They were released from prison after dark and had to report back early in the morning before the daily parade. It fell to Menachem Bader to convince Brand to return to Budapest. Every night Bader would struggle with him. Brand protested that he could not return empty-handed and without his escort. Finally, Bader suggested that we draw up an official-looking document in legalistic language that we would call the 'interim agreement'. It would constitute a kind of protocol of the talks he had had after delivering Eichmann's message and plan. But Brand remained firm: although he might gain time by this device, he had lost confidence in our ability to accomplish the task. He suspected that we would lose interest in him and in his mission as soon as he was out of our way. 'You condemn me to death,' he told Bader. 'You ask of me what you would not be prepared to do yourself.'

At the end of the third long night, Brand gave in and agreed to return to Budapest. Bader drew up the interim agreement and signed it, along with Brand, but he had a miserable feeling that rather than strengthening his courage he had merely weakened Brand's senses.

Then Dani and I were summoned urgently to Whittal. When we arrived at his office we were told that the British had decided to let Brand go to Jerusalem and meet Shertok and his colleagues there, as the Turks refused to let Shertok come to Istanbul. This message was received with deep suspicion; we could think of no other motive except a British plan to eliminate Brand altogether. Once he was in Jerusalem, British Security would surely obstruct his return to enemy territory. We therefore suggested to Whittal that the meeting with Shertok take place in Aleppo, on the Turkish border with Syria, rather than in Jerusalem. Then it could not be claimed that Brand had seen secret British Army installations or had learned other secrets, which might serve as an excuse to forbid his return to Budapest. Whittal agreed and promised to have confirmation in the morning.

Dutifully, we reported our talk with British Intelligence to our colleagues and to Brand. We still suspected a British trap insofar as they might allow the meeting to take place but nonetheless refuse to let Brand return to enemy soil. But as soon as he heard the news, Brand's mind was made up. Even the so-called interim agreement would gain in value if it were delivered by him or by anyone else after a face-to-face talk with the head of the Political Department. If he returned directly from Istanbul – in effect from a Turkish prison from which the united strength of the Jews and their Allies had not been able to save him – he would be a lost man the moment he crossed the German border at Svilengrad. He would never reach Budapest alive.

As a precaution of sorts, we dispatched the 'interim agreement' on the same night Brand would have left had he returned directly to Budapest. For a minimal consideration, a Swiss courier took the document to Budapest and delivered it safely into the hands of Rejô Kastner. It was also decided that I should accompany Brand to Aleppo, and Simon Brod volunteered to go with us as far as the Turkish border. We left that evening on the Taurus Express from Haydarpaşa.

Formalities at the Turkish frontier were negligible: the frontier control had evidently been advised of our arrival. Most passengers left the train at stations still on Turkish soil, but we moved on through no-man's-land into Syria. There, too, passport formalities were perfunctory. Had I merely imagined the sly twinkle in the British official's eye?

I knew that Selim, our man in Aleppo, had been advised by cable of our arrival and the exact location of our compartment, so I was surprised not to see his familiar face as the train moved slowly into the terminal. Brand, however, was excited. He was in Allied territory now, and he believed that his mission was again coming to life.

Each of us took his suitcase down from the rack in preparation for leaving as soon as Selim appeared. After waiting a
few more minutes, I decided to get off and look for him
myself, as I was familiar with the Aleppo terminal from
previous trips. I warned Brand to stay put and wait for me
and, above all, not to talk to strangers.

It turned out that for once the trains had been early, and I
met Selim walking in the direction of our compartment. He
had good news: Shertok was in Aleppo, accompanied by
Reuven Shiloah and the Chief, and he was waiting for Brand
at the Hotel Baron.

We walked back to our compartment, but I did not see
Brand from the platform. My heart sank. We boarded the
train and entered the compartment. I spotted my suitcase on
the unmade bed, where I had left it a few minutes ago, but
Brand's suitcase was gone – and so was he. Frantically, we
looked into every compartment, but they were all deserted
and Brand was nowhere in sight. The façade of British
cooperation had been a trap!

We jumped into Selim's car to the Hotel Baron. Without
recriminations or preliminaries, we took stock of the situation. I gave Shertok and his colleagues a brief report, filling
them in on those aspects of the situation not covered in our
cables. Shiloah took it upon himself to locate Brand by getting in touch with friends in British Security. After a few
phone calls he reached the man who seemed to know all
about our case. It was agreed that Shertok should see Brand
the next day. The pretext for the delay was that Brand
needed rest. We assumed, however, that the British wanted
to grill him before they allowed us to contact him.

I had an irrepressible feeling of guilt: had I stayed with
Brand, he might not have been taken away. Rationally, I
knew that the British Empire would not have been shaken
into immobility by my presence, but it was difficult for me to
calm my emotions. Only much later, when he arrived in

Israel after many tribulations, did I learn from Brand what had happened to him that day. Two men in civilian dress, but acting with the authority of policemen, entered the compartment and took Brand's suitcase. Then the senior one, with a commanding voice, said in German, 'You come with us.' They led him down the corridor of the vacant sleeping-car and alighted from the train using the door on the wrong side of the platform. The small column made its way between our train and another packed next to it. At some point, they boarded one of the cars of the other train, passed through it and alighted on the platform parallel to the one on which I was desperately searching for Brand. From there he was led to a waiting cab outside the terminal and taken to some unknown destination.

Brand's arrest by British Security organs had been well prepared. It had been timed so that he was snatched from Shertok and his team even though the delegation had come to Aleppo on the express promise of the High Commissioner that they would be able to talk with Brand upon his arrival.

Shertok, Shiloah and I spent several hours talking to Brand. He repeated, word by word, the story he had told us in Istanbul. During much of the interview, a member of British Security was present. When we were alone, Shertok was more intimate and cordial with Brand, strengthening his spirit without creating false hopes for success. He promised Brand that he would go to London immediately and do all he could to follow up the 'interim agreement' by tangible diplomatic activity. He implored Brand to bear his lot with resignation. We were at the mercy of our friends, and we had no power to compel them to do what we wanted – except by persuasion and insistence on the justice of our cause.

Brand was then transferred under detention to Cairo (where he again met Grosz, this time in a British jail), and the diplomatic manoeuvres in London went their predictable way. With great courtesy and a sudden awareness of the urgency, the British authorities gave Shertok the necessary priority for travel to England on a military aircraft. He reported first to Chaim Weizmann, who had been kept informed of developments from Istanbul.

Even before Shertok met Anthony Eden, the Foreign Secretary, he had learned that Winston Churchill was against negotiating with Himmler. No good could come from any compromise. Victory was the only salvation for the Jews – as for the world. Furthermore, Churchill was most anxious to avoid Russian suspicion of a separate deal between the Allies and the Nazis. Nevertheless, Shertok pleaded with Eden to help play for time by agreeing to and going through the motions of preparing for negotiations. The end of the war was near; Germany was embattled on all fronts; but the danger was acute that the last remnants of Europe's Jews would be destroyed before an armistice.

The British established contact with the American Government. Ambassador Steinhardt, alerted by Barlass, had kept his government informed ever since Brand's arrival in Istanbul, but it was for the British, still a major power and directly concerned with Jewish matters in Palestine, to take the initiative. The Americans, as often before, proved to be more broadminded. Ira Hirschmann, who was in Washington for consultations, was sent to Cairo post-haste with orders to interview Brand and the British and to see what could be done. There was enough activity – and smoke-screen – for us in Istanbul to cable Budapest daily, building up a picture that more meaningful contacts would ensue. All we received in reply from Hungary was: 'Deportations continue.'

Both the British and the Americans were adamant on the main issue: no Allied or neutral person was going to negotiate with Himmler and Eichmann's representatives. Only victory, not compromise, could save the remnants of European Jewry. And naturally, all barter of strategic commodities was completely out of the question, particularly since the Nazis had tried to tempt the Allies by their promise to use these vehicles only on the Eastern front. We wanted to gain time by making it appear that there was a chance for negotiations. The Allies wanted to convince us that they were frantically searching for a constructive move, but that there was no possibility of satisfying our demands.

On 9 July 1944, Bader received a cable from Kastner in Budapest asking him to proceed to Hungary for urgent negotiations. As a gesture of 'goodwill' the 'authorities' were prepared to send 1,500 Jews to neutral Switzerland. As our baffled group was discussing how to react to the cable, Sarka Mandelblatt received a call from the German Embassy. The German Foreign Office had instructed them to prepare a flight to Vienna for Bader, for reasons best known to him. The plane would be at his disposal at the Istanbul airport in case he required some time to prepare his trip and to obtain the necessary travel documents.

At the Embassy's request, Bader returned the call, mainly to find out whether this was a genuine offer or a hoax. He agreed to meet the German who spoke to him on the phone in a well-known bookstore. There the two of them stood a little while later, browsing among unsuspecting customers. The message first phoned to Sarka Mandelblatt was now repeated by the mysterious German.

Bader was all ready to go. He was fully aware of what was at stake but never doubted for a minute that it was his duty to accept the invitation, regardless of the outcome. But his orders from the Jewish Agency were strict: he was *not to go*. As a Palestinian, he was a citizen of an Allied nation, and he had to respect the authority of the Government whose passport he carried.

Shertok was promised a considered reply by Eden's deputy, the Minister of State at the Foreign Office. It was clear that the reply would be negative. Shertok tried in vain to convince the junior minister of what he had obviously failed to convey to his superior: the fate of tens of thousands of human beings depended on the tactics they discussed, and Britain and her allies were accepting a responsibility too heavy to bear if she did not cooperate.

Junior though he was, the Minister of State let the truth slip. 'The proposal you defend,' he told Shertok, 'is not meant to save Jews. It is intended to sow distrust between us Western Allies and our Russian friends. But assume for a moment – just for the sake of argument – that you are right and I am wrong. Where, Mr Shertok, shall we put these Jews if Eichmann keeps his word and sends them to the border?'

With these words, Shertok was unequivocally informed that Brand's mission had died. There is an epilogue to this sad story. Four years after the event, with the proclamation of Israeli independence, I was appointed Ambassador to Czechoslovakia. One day, to my great surprise, I received a call from the British Embassy in Prague. The British had not recognized Israel yet, and their diplomatic personnel avoided us. My caller was Harold Gibson, the former Chief of Intelligence in Turkey and now – as before the war – the First Secretary of the British Embassy in Prague.

Humbly, as befits a First Secretary talking to an Ambassador, he asked me to have lunch with him. When I came to his modest home, I realized that his humility was motivated by more than protocol.

'When you gave us information concerning the enemy in Istanbul, we believed your reports and passed them on with the highest marks for reliability. I must admit, however, that every time you brought us news about the extermination of Jews, we thought there was a grain of truth in your reporting, but we were convinced you had greatly exaggerated that grain of truth for purposes of Zionist propaganda, in order to elicit concessions from our side regarding Palestine after the war.

'Now, having returned to Prague, and being able to gauge

the magnitude of the Jewish catastrophe for myself, I must confess to you that I was utterly and completely deluded by my preconceptions.'

How different, I thought after this talk, things would have been had we had a sovereign state of our own when Hitler ruled Europe.

(15)

The Mossad Moves On

IN THE SUMMER OF 1944, the Soviets advanced into Nazi-occupied Europe, and with unbelievable speed the liberating armies reached the borders of Rumania and Bulgaria. As they moved on, Jews in their communities and centres of deportation carefully dared to raise their heads and look around – the nightmare was over. Pessimists had always predicted that our rescue efforts could never save meaningful numbers of Jews, but we in Istanbul, and most Jews in Palestine, believed that the rescue of even a single life was enough to justify the greatest efforts, expenditures and risks.

On the last day of August 1944, Rumania unconditionally surrendered to the Allies, and the Red Army took Bucharest. About a week later it swept into Bulgaria, where the fascist régime collapsed on 9 September 1944. We in Istanbul had no special knowledge of what was happening with such lightning speed in our immediate neighbourhood, but our proximity imposed upon us the obligation to attempt making contact with the liberated Jewish communities. Communications became, if anything, even more complicated than during the Nazi epoch. Telephone lines broke down, overland traffic was interrupted and our network of couriers vanished overnight.

We realized that it was important to make use of the

turmoil and confusion of liberation to get our people into the countries that had just become accessible. Knowledge of Russian was now a great asset, and in the general clamour for transfer from Istanbul to Sofia and Bucharest, it determined who would go first.

Venya, aflame with energy, was the first to move. With the help of the Jewish Agency office in New York, he was appointed a correspondent of the Jewish Telegraphic Agency and received a Bulgarian entry permit. During the very first days of the liberation, the British element in the Four-Power Control Commission was still strong enough to arrange for its protégés to obtain the coveted entry permits to the newly liberated countries. And Major Whittal's switch from wartime alliance back to the hostility of anti-Zionist White Paper policies was slow enough for him to help with visas.

Venya had barely arrived in Bulgaria, and although in the hubbub of re-orientating himself to an entirely new situation, he already placed himself at the head of the non-Communist Jewish majority. Official Communist circles were most sympathetic to our projects: they felt that Bulgarian Jews had a right to emigrate, even though no one else would be allowed to leave the country; and they fully supported our programme to bring food and clothing to the Jews of Bulgaria as they began to return to their homes. (They had been evicted from their residences by the previous régime, as a measure to meet the German demand for their elimination halfway without having to abandon them to Nazi justice.)

Only a small band of vociferous Jewish Communists were more Stalinist than the official Stalinist Communist Party of Bulgaria. The Jewish Communist faction within the general Communist Party of Bulgaria fought against Zionism with a vengeance. They had to prove that their theory of participation in the dictatorship of the proletariat was more correct and more advanced than the 'retrograde, archaic, chauvinist nationalism of the Zionists'.

In this delicate and fluid situation, with people changing sides and constantly awaiting direction from stable forces and new complications continually arising in a game of ruthless tactics, Venya kept his head. He supported the reconstitution of the old Zionist parties from pre-war days, not because he thought they were the ideal solution for the needs of reconstruction of Jewish life after Hitler, but because he wanted to make use of every element of positive participation, alienating no one, and giving all a welcome feeling in the effort to revive the paralysed Jewish community.

Acting as a journalist and taking his duties perhaps more seriously than those journalists who had no other concerns, Venya obtained the right to use Sofia Radio for broadcasts to his 'Agency'. He meant the Jewish Agency for Palestine, while the press department that permitted him the use of their equipment had the Jewish Telegraphic Agency in mind. Soon after he took up residence in the first liberated capital of Eastern Europe, he began making his Friday-evening broadcasts in Hebrew from Communist Bulgaria. These were eagerly awaited by the public in Palestine and carefully monitored by the Mossad in Istanbul and Tel Aviv for hints and bits of information about the changing situation.

Then Agami and Joseph Klarmann, a leading Revisionist, went to Bucharest. Klarmann, who in his youth in Poland had been a genuine journalist, had no difficulty in establishing himself as the JTA man in Bucharest, as Venya was in Sofia. For Agami, the Mossad obtained an appointment as the Rumanian correspondent of the Palestine labour daily, *Davar*. They would be less demanding than the professional agency and more patient with Agami, who had more immediate tasks than press cables.

The spirit of cooperation that had prevailed in Istanbul during the war made it possible for Agami and Klarmann to go to Rumania as a team. Agami, the top representative of the Mossad, brought not only his experience from pre-war days, but came to Rumania with the status of a senior member of the Istanbul team. Klarmann, impressive looking, and experienced in public relations and journalism, took it upon himself to act as our delegation's foreign minister to the huge Jewish community of Rumania: 400,000 Jews had perished on Rumanian territory, yet another 400,000 had survived.

The Jews of the central province of Rumania, in which Bucharest was located, had somehow lived on the fringe of the war and had always felt a little safer than the Jews in the provinces. The resurrection of pre-war frameworks was more quickly achieved than in Bulgaria – and with them the old internal struggles and animosities.

As soon as they arrived in Bucharest, Agami and Klarmann were joined by some of the parachutists who had preceded them as emissaries to Rumania. The British demanded the return of the paratroopers for demobilization. But because of their very real need to recuperate from the experience of Nazi jails – and through a bit of subterfuge – they were able to prolong their stay in Rumania and help Agami – the unchallenged head of the Haganah in Rumania.

The Palestine Office in Sofia suggested to Venya that a leading personality from Palestine should come to Bulgaria, and perhaps also to Rumania, to meet with the liberated Jews. Venya immediately conveyed this suggestion to Istanbul, and we transmitted the invitation to Jerusalem. To our delighted surprise, Ben Gurion himself agreed to come. It was still necessary to obtain British consent for a Turkish visa and only grudgingly, and after much procrastination, was consent given. But Ben Gurion wanted to be sure that he would be welcome in both Bulgaria and Rumania before he began his voyage. Bulgarian consent to his visit was quick to come, but the Rumanian Allied Control Commission kept silent. Agami and Klarmann pressured all their contacts to bring about a favourable decision – or at least a clear and unambiguous 'no'. Klarmann had established a close working relationship with the most influential minister in the Rumanian Government, but, even so, it was impossible to obtain a reply. Finally, Ben Gurion decided to go only to Sofia, if possible, to talk to the Russians and then decide what to do next.

Ben Gurion's arrival in Istanbul in December 1944 was a sort of nostalgic return to the places of his youth. Prior to the British Mandate, Palestine had been a province of the Ottoman Empire, which crumbled in the First World War, and Ben Gurion had been a Palestinian student in Istanbul. He spoke Turkish fluently. In abrupt and rapid sentences, he addressed the crowd of Turkish Jews who had come to the railway station of Haydarpaşa. In honour of the Jewish leader from Palestine, the blue-and-white flag with the Star of David was unfurled on Turkish soil for the first time.

During his day in Istanbul, he met with most of those Turkish and British officials who had been helpful in our rescue work during the war. He thanked them for what they had done – often beyond the call of formal duty – and had an especially warm talk with Major Whittal, who had disclosed to us the secret instructions for the transport of Jews through Turkey. Ben Gurion assured him that it was thanks to him personally that a number of human beings had survived.

Ben Gurion told me, quite casually, that he wanted me to accompany him on the trip to Sofia. Naturally I was elated. We took the Orient Express and, for the first time, went to the railway station in the quarter of Istanbul that, unlike Haydarpaşa, is on European, not Asian, soil. For the first time too, we boarded the train with the sign Svilengrad-Sofia and so forth, names that only a few weeks before had spelt death and persecution.

We reached Bulgaria early in the morning. The feeling of

warmth for the Jews there – and for their leader – became immediately visible. A special car was attached to our train, and Ben Gurion was asked to transfer to it: it was the car reserved for the King of Bulgaria, and since the abolition of the monarchy a few weeks before, for dignitaries of the new People's Democracy. An official of the Bulgarian Government accompanied Ben Gurion and looked after his every need. A huge delegation of Jewish representatives from every community, from the Zionist Organization of Bulgaria and from the Palestine Office was on hand and entered the special coach for the trip to the provincial capital, where Anton Yugov, the Minister of the Interior, was waiting for the illustrious guest. The train had to stop at small stations it normally would have bypassed in order to allow delegations from distant places to see and greet Ben Gurion.

Venya's flat, where Ben Gurion stayed, was a veritable beehive with people constantly coming and going – cabinet ministers, members of the opposition (which still existed then in Bulgaria), local and foreign correspondents and, above all, delegations of Jews asking for immigration certificates. Each of the local papers carried banner headlines about the visit of the first foreign statesman to newly liberated Bulgaria. The Presidium, the Prime Minister, the Foreign Minister and other members of the government and of the Communist Party hierarchy received Ben Gurion. Only the Jewish Communists kept aloof, cold-shouldered Ben Gurion and spread unpleasant remarks, reminiscent of the recent past.

The public highlight of the visit was a mass demonstration in and around the 'Balkan', Sofia's largest cinema. The hall was filled with Jews of all ages from all parts of the country. Outside the building thousands thronged the narrow streets, benevolently kept under control by the Bulgarian police, who seemed to enjoy the spectacle. There was no false pretence in this friendliness: the brave Bulgarian people had saved most

of Bulgaria's Jews from the Nazis by sheer refusal to abandon them to brutality.

Ben Gurion spoke in Hebrew, a language many of those
present, particularly the younger ones, seemed to understand.
Those who did not were carried away, like the speaker himself, by the overflowing enthusiasm of the throngs who felt the
sweet sense of freedom and human dignity returned to them.
He called for the ingathering of the remnants of European
Jewry in an independent Jewish State; he spoke of the need
to begin life anew after the Holocaust; he explained how they
would be working as free people in their own land amongst
their brethren. His address was interrupted by loud applause
and by shouts of 'Aliyah, free immigration, no more bonds,
no more slavery!'

On the morning after the triumphant meeting at the 'Balkan', at his own insistence, Ben Gurion visited a quite
different crowd. He was taken to Yüç Bunar, the place of
assembly for those Jews of Sofia who had been expelled
during the war and on their return found their homes in the
hands of strangers, their property stolen and their resources
vanished.

In a building that looked like a mixture of an old bazaar
and a medieval prison, with narrow cells and oblong, ice-cold
halls, hundreds of hungry, shivering people sat squatting on
the floor. The enormous eyes in the children's pale faces
stupefied the visitors. They hardly uttered a word, although
they realized that someone from the outside world had come
to take interest in them. As we walked through the mass of
misery, one fact stood out: practically none of the refugees
had shoes, and the stone floor was so cold that they could not
put their bare feet on the ground.

Never before – or after – have I seen Ben Gurion so com-
passionately sympathetic. He tried, in vain, to encourage the
unhappy people of Yüç Bunar by a word, a smile, a gesture.
They remained apathetic to his advances. As we walked out

and back to less appalling conditions, Ben Gurion turned to me and said: 'The first thing I will do when I return is to send you 5,000 pairs of shoes for the children of Yüç Bunar.' Then suddenly he turned to us with that whimsical twinkle in his eyes and added: 'Or perhaps, should we not try to bring the feet to the shoes?'

Actually we did both: a consignment of shoes for the poor children of Yüç Bunar arrived shortly after Ben Gurion's return; and even before Israel declared her independence, the evacuation of Bulgaria's Jews began. With the splendid assistance of the Bulgarian authorities, virtually the entire Jewish population reached Israel during the first year of statehood.

With Venya in Bulgaria and Agami and Klarmann in Rumania, the Istanbul team began to break up. Bader returned to Palestine to impress the Financial Department of the Jewish Agency with the tremendous needs for the immediate post-war period. As ever-new death camps were discovered by the advancing Allied armies, the flow of refugees grew. People tried to get away from the scene of the slaughter and headed towards the sea, where they hoped to find boats to take them to Palestine.

Dani left Istanbul for Palestine but was soon pressed into new service for the Mossad. New Mossad emissaries came to Istanbul to replace those who had left and to stand in reserve as new countries in Europe became accessible to them. I requested to be released from my duties in Istanbul and asked the Chief to let me return to my kibbutz.

After many delays and postponements, Hanna – who had joined me in Istanbul during the winter – and I finally went to Haydarpaşa. We were on our way home. Hanna was expecting our first child and she wanted to be at home for the event. The voyage on the Orient Express seemed more tedious than on previous occasions. At every station we would eagerly inquire after the news: victory in Europe was expected momentarily.

We were having breakfast in the dining-car as the train moved out of a small station on the long stretch between Ankara and Adanan, near the Syrian border. A British colonel, meticulously dressed in khaki shorts, his brass emblems admirably blending with his greying temples, shared the table with us. Suddenly the door burst open, and the waiters and the train attendants stormed through the dining-car shouting at the top of their voices.

'Revolution?' Hanna inquired of the colonel, who spoke fluent Turkish.

Imperceptibly bowing towards her, and with the flicker of a smile, he replied, 'No, Madame. Victory. Surrender. Liberation.'

The dining-car head waiter appeared with a bottle of champagne and glasses. Turkey was no longer a neutral country. A few weeks earlier, like so many other previously neutral countries – some of them neutral on the side of the Axis – she had declared war on the doomed Third Reich to be eligible for founding-membership in the United Nations. The British colonel raised his glass of warm champagne toward Hanna and myself: 'To our common victory! The worst is over for your people, too.' I tried to explain to him that we had only partly been victorious. Nearly half of our people had perished in Hitler's war, and now we would have to care for the survivors – who had no wish to return to the graveyards of their former lives – faced by the stone wall of the White Paper.

The colonel was sympathetic, but unconvinced. Britain believed in fair play. 'Obviously, after the war, we will have to try to win back the friendship of the Arabs who had hoped for an Axis victory. Your demands in Palestine will have to be reasonable, but you may be sure of Britain's unlimited help in resettling survivors somewhere, somehow!'

The train rattled on, and in the optimistic glow of that champagne victory breakfast and the colonel's reassurance I remembered a conversation I had had with Dani not long before in Istanbul, when the Morgenthau Plan for the 'agrarianization' of Germany had been announced. At that time, I had innocently observed that with such a programme in view, security for the Jews would have serious support.

'Don't be such a fool,' Dani had said, with the far-sighted realism that typified his analyses. 'In just about a year, Germany will be the darling of America. There are basic reasons for that; and in any case, life must go on. There's no sense in revenge, or in fighting old wars. Don't forget that ultimately we have nowhere to look for security but to ourselves.' Dani had spoken without bitterness, but a phrase he used stuck in my mind. It simply formulated a fact of life: 'Most of the Jews have died. And most of the anti-Semites are still alive.'

As we passed from Turkish territory into Syria, still under British Military control, we had our last meeting with British frontier guards as comrades-in-arms. Twenty-four hours later the Arab cab from Beirut rattled to an abrupt stop at the gate of our kibbutz.

(16)

Interlude in Palestine

THIS TIME there was no peaceful farm work in green fields. After helping Hanna get settled at the kibbutz, I reported for work at the roof-top office of the Mossad in Tel Aviv. Debriefing was, as usual, a quick affair: Mossad headquarters were in such intensive contact with Mossad workers abroad, and interchange was so frequent, that we spoke a common language and had nearly complete community of thought. We were acting according to the biblical prescription: 'We shall act [first] and listen [to explanations] later.'

Our most urgent task was to dispatch as many emissaries as possible to the growing areas of Mossad activity in liberated Europe. But the struggle between us and the British had been renewed: the White Paper of 1939, with its strangulating restrictions, continued to be the basis for our relationship with the mandatory authorities. The British suspected, quite accurately, that the young men and women leaving Palestine so eagerly for war-ridden Europe had a common purpose and a specific task. As the Allied armies established military governments in the occupied areas, we were anxious to get our emissaries past the suspicious Palestine Police and passport authorities and penetrate these areas. The plausible pretext used for urgent trips to Europe was the desire to search out missing relatives who might have survived the Holocaust. Actually, this was not entirely untrue, although in most cases the relatives were not exactly the emissary's blood-relations.

Interviewing candidates for these vaguely defined and dangerous assignments became one of my jobs. As Europe was being liberated we expected to be called upon for urgent and daring rescue work among the survivors of the Holocaust. Moshe Carmil was quietly co-ordinating the stream of youngsters who had received, through their Haganah contacts or Palmach commanders, instructions to ascend to that mysterious roof on Tel Aviv's Allenby Street. Their response was, in most cases, enthusiastic. The anguish of the war years and the horror of hearing about the extermination of European Jewry had instilled in them a firm determination to rescue survivors and bring them to Palestine.

In the city and at the kibbutz, everybody was involved in the excitement of the early post-war days: people discussed our political relations with Britain, whether the Labour victory in Britain's first post-war election gave us reason for new hope, whether the central authorities of the Palestinian Jewish community were sufficiently united to stand up and fight against the restrictions of the White Paper and Britain's generally hostile policies.

The summer of 1945 reflected profound political changes brought about by the war's end. President Roosevelt had died in April and was succeeded by Harry S. Truman; that same month, the first United Nations Conference opened in San Francisco. In May, Winston Churchill's coalition government came to an end; and in the same week, Syria and Lebanon asserted their independence from France. In June, Czechoslovakia ceded a portion of her eastern territory to Russia. In August, Britain's Labour Party won an overwhelming victory, and Clement Attlee succeeded Churchill. Then Japan formally surrendered to the Allies, and everywhere in the world the war was finally over – except in Palestine, which was about to experience a new kind of war to be fought with renewed and concentrated effort.

One of the important lessons we had learned from the world war was the cold-blooded calculations of the stronger partner with respect to his weaker ally. Not only the Russians in Poland, but the British in Yugoslavia and Greece and France, on every pertinent occasion, had acted according to what they considered their own interests rather than according to high moral principles. The more sceptical among us feared that the British Government, faced with the need to reshape the Middle Eastern scene, would make greater concessions to the Arabs than to the Jews. The Arabs had given the Allies lukewarm support during the war – when they did not actually abandon the Allied side and go over to the enemy each time it seemed that the Axis was winning.

The predominant feeling at the war's end was that we were capable of living peacefully with an Arab minority in a Jewish Palestine. The majority did not conceive of a binational state: only a group of solitary intellectuals propounded such an idea, and it never received any noteworthy support. Most thought in terms of a Jewish Palestine, a haven for the survivors of the Holocaust, where Jews would determine who and how many would be admitted, when and how we could rebuild, to whatever degree possible what an indifferent world had allowed to be destroyed. We could not help assuming that some gesture towards the Jews was in order; that general support for assurances to the Jews that they would be allowed to return to the land to which they had clung during the generations of the Diaspora was more than coming to them.

After the hostilities ended, the Jewish Agency was eager to enter into negotiations with the British Government, so as to benefit from the momentum engendered by the fluid post-war situation. As early as May 1945, Chaim Weizmann, the President of the Zionist Organization, wrote to Winston Churchill and demanded the implementation of a new policy: the cancellation of the 1939 White Paper, the establishment of Palestine as a Jewish State, the transfer of responsibility for Jewish immigration to the Jewish Agency and the payment of reparations by Germany, beginning with all German property in Palestine.

After having sent this missile into orbit, the Agency addressed the British Government with a more limited demand for what seemed to be a more readily attainable goal and one that was more difficult to ignore: the immediate issue of 100,000 immigration certificates for survivors of the Holocaust.

The British Prime Minister replied to the first demand that the future of Palestine could not be settled before the victorious Allies were definitely seated at the peace table. Notice had been duly taken of our demands, and formal acknowledgment had arrived from the British side. The more pragmatic issue – and the more burning one – was to receive different treatment: our demand for 100,000 certificates was immediately termed 'ill-timed', and even before the British Government was able to formulate some coherent policy, the Jewish Agency was informed that this ill-timed memorandum was going to be 'of no effect'.

Soon after the demand for the 100,000 certificates, the British Labour Party was swept into office in the first post-war election, and Ernest Bevin became the new Foreign Secretary. The victory was greeted with joy in Palestine. The Labour Ministers – sons of light, like the socialist majority within the Zionist movement – would certainly be more forthcoming than their Conservative predecessors had been in regard to implementing the pledges of every British Government since the Balfour Declaration.

In June 1945, President Truman took a clear and affirmative stand on the Jewish demand for immigration certificates to Palestine for the survivors of the Holocaust. Truman decided 'to do something about Jews in occupied Germany [who were] not repatriable' to their former places of residence. The American Government computed 100,000 'Displaced Persons' – arriving, to our satisfaction, at the same figure the Jewish Agency had proposed – and recommended that these survivors be allowed to leave the camps in which they were still held, despite having been liberated, and proceed to Palestine.

It is characteristic of the circumstances of the time that the first personages asked by the Labour Government to comment on the recommendation of 100,000 certificates were the military chiefs. Considering the tension between the Western Allies and the Soviet Union, which began in 1945, the British Government believed that Palestine would become a key element in the defence of the British (and the Western) position in the Middle East in the event that the Egyptian base had to be abandoned. The military, therefore, strongly recommended against substantial immigration. According to their thinking, astronomical numbers of soldiers armed to their teeth were the minimal requirement to impose the immigration of 100,000 Jews upon the Arabs of Palestine.

The request for 100,000 certificates was not some political ruse. Hardened reporters and dignitaries from Allied countries who visited the camps were left stunned with disbelief at the unbearable conditions to which the survivors were fated. In Palestine, after the frustrations of the war years, tempers began to run short in view of the continuing procrastination. The Jewish Agency, in the face of all the evidence to the contrary, still counted on the moral decency of the British Government and dropped all other political demands in order to concentrate on the one overriding issue of the survivors' admission to Palestine. This was, without a doubt, the minimal requirement to alleviate an otherwise totally hopeless situation.

On 1 August 1945, Zionist leaders met for an emergency conference in London to take stock of the rapidly deteriorating situation, to work out a commonly acceptable formula for future negotiations and to decide on priorities. The most notable change in the attitude was expressed by Abba Hillel Silver, the American Zionist leader. While on the eve of the war he had fiercely fought against illegal immigration and subversive Haganah activities, his views had now undergone a complete reversal. The indifference and lack of active help during the disaster of Hitler's war against the Jews had turned him into a foremost 'activist'. At the London Conference, the erstwhile legalist and pacifist declared that there might be merit in violence and 'the height of statesmanship might be to be unstatesmanlike'. The President of the Zionist Organization, Chaim Weizmann, expressed his hopes for mutual understanding with the Labour Government. But Ben Gurion was sceptical: he warned against optimism and urged 'passive and active resistance to the White Paper policy in its present form and in modified shape'.

From the Zionist Conference Ben Gurion led a delegation to the Colonial Office, where he reiterated in the strongest terms the demands the Jewish Agency had formulated in its two memoranda: the immediate issue of 100,000 certificates and the establishment of a Jewish State. The Colonial Secretary was shocked. He confessed in a speech made in Parliament, still under the impact of Ben Gurion's demands, that 'the behaviour of my visitors was different from anything which I had ever experienced!'

Violent Arab statements followed this confession of weakness and, as usual, were taken at face value. Azzam Pasha, the Secretary of the Arab League, an experienced warrior of words, threatened that support of Zionism by the West might lead to a 'new Crusaders war' and placed himself at the head of the impassioned defenders of the true faith. The British Government retreated immediately in the face of these threats. The pre-war pattern of appeasement became evident again and the Colonial Secretary was adamantly against Ben Gurion's demands. He offered the Jewish Agency 2,000 certificates that had been left over from the White Paper, and he proposed that Arab agreement should then be sought to a further monthly immigration of 1,500.

The same period also brought serious changes in the political line-up within the Zionist movement in Palestine. The leading Labour Party was divided between those who accepted Ben Gurion's 'activist' approach and those who believed that moderation and negotiated compromise were all we could hope for.

The left-wing Socialist Party of Achdut Ha'avodah had split off from the Labour Party and created its own political entity. This group was against cooperation with the British in any way. They had opposed enlistment of Jewish soldiers in the British Army during the war, as it only weakened our own scarce defence resources without contributing decisively to the defeat of the Nazis. Achdut Ha'avodah sponsored the Palmach, supported the parachutists behind German lines and every imaginable rescue effort, but they looked upon military cooperation with Britain with disdain.

The right, too, had split. The General Zionists had an activist wing, now lead by the American Zionist leader Abba Hillel Silver; and the accommodating, more moderate one, led by Chaim Weizmann. And the Revisionist Party was torn between those who sympathized with the radical right wing but did not favour terrorism, and those who supported the two terrorist organizations of Revisionist parentage, the Irgun Zvai Le'umi (IZL) and the Freedom Fighters for Israel (known as the 'Lehi' or Stern Gang).

The Haganah, working in close cooperation with the Jewish Agency, had until now refrained from any sort of terrorism, sabotage or kindred military action against the British. Traditionally it believed in the 'creation of facts' rather than in demonstrative action, however dramatic and impressive. Now this policy also began to change, as hope for an agreement receded and British attitudes became more intransigent. Before there was any shift in the 'official underground' thinking, however, the Mossad had begun to plan new – and highly illegal – projects. Let the Jewish Agency and the politicians deal with the British Government; the Mossad was training candidates for rescue missions in Europe, and young men in new, ill-fitting suits and odd, too-loud ties were already on their way through the police check-point at Haifa port.

As the number of applicants for passports grew, it became clear that means other than official passports, which were issued most reluctantly, had to be developed in order to get our people to Europe as quickly as possible. The British Army unwittingly provided one way. Although demobilization was in full swing, there were still Palestinian soldiers returning from leave to their units in Europe; we decided to turn some of our emissaries into 'British soldiers'. Using information acquired from Haganah members serving in British units, the Mossad studied the routines and documents of British troop movements, and our little office on the Tel Aviv roof-top came to be as well-equipped with uniforms, movement orders and pay-books as any British military post. Our emissaries rather relished the idea of going to battle for the Mossad and for illegal immigration dressed as His Majesty's personnel.

During one of my interviewing sessions, a telephone call came from the kibbutz: Hanna had been taken to the maternity clinic in Haifa. Our first daughter, Dinah, was born on 15 August. The uncompromisingly dedicated men of the Mossad were nothing if not thoughtful in situations like this, and for the week that Hanna stayed at the clinic I was able to do my interviewing at the Haifa office of David Shaltiel, head of the Haganah's intelligence network. There I met with prospective emissaries living in the northern district; and I was even able to spend a few days at the kibbutz when Hanna brought Dinah home.

Another way of getting our men into Europe materialized with the arrival of the Mossad's first custom-built boat. This was one of the more outrageous of the many outrageously successful achievements of Yehudah Arazi, a man with a price on his head for smuggling arms. He had been hiding in Tel Aviv and had himself smuggled from Palestine via Cairo to Italy, where he began the boat-building adventure. His 'little' boats brought refugees from Europe to Palestine, but on the return trip they carried our operatives back to Europe, and with them, Haganah radio-operators, who were now being added to our underground network.

Yehudah's boats were so small that the British Navy, patrolling the coast of Palestine on the look-out for illegal arrivals, did not bother to stop them and check for illegal arrivals. But in each one of these tiny boats – built for three or four men on a fortnight's fishing expedition – were up to 80 refugees. They approached the coast at night, at pre-arranged spots. Nameri's landing teams were waiting as the boats came into the natural bay. The arrivals would jump into the water and, with the aid of the landing team, wade in single file through the shallow waters – or sometimes through the sky-high waves – to the shore. Trucks from kibbutzim would take the newcomers to the more densely populated inland region, where they were met by members of the kibbutz to which they were to be brought. When they changed into the more natural clothing of the kibbutznik, they were indistinguishable from their hosts. On the rare occasion that a British patrol ventured into a kibbutz shortly after a completed operation, they never spotted any new arrivals. Meanwhile, as soon as the newcomers had disembarked, a smaller and trained group would board the little boats: the Palmach team and the Haganah radio-operator were now on their way to Europe.

Painstakingly, a network of secret transmitters was established in every port earmarked by the Mossad for future activities. Every ship, even the smallest barge, had to carry a transmitter-receiver – for contact with the port they had left, with the shore they expected to reach and with other Mossad ships. More and more often there was more than one of our ships at sea at any one time.

The sets were assembled in clandestine workshops in Palestine; parts were bought systematically and without undue haste. On occasion, a radio-set and more spare parts than any single set could ever require were smuggled in from overseas. As the need for ever-more sophisticated radio-sets and for the operation of transmitters already on board grew, secret workshops were set up in Europe as well. The advantage was two-fold: spare parts and components were more readily available there, and there was no supervision and obstruction by hostile police authorities, as in Palestine.

The Jewish Agency could no longer restrain the Haganah, the Palmach and its own supporters, and the decision was made to engage in a tactic of 'related struggle' – related, in the sense of being linked to British opposition to immigration. The Haganah did not intend to wage terrorism *per se;* our main objective was the right to return to our homeland, but we were no longer satisfied with vacillating, diplomatic procrastination, and we were ready to support our rights – by military action if necessary.

In the first week of October 1945, the Haganah High Command approved plans, already worked out by the Palmach, for the forcible release of the inmates of the Athlit detention camp. This was a large military camp south of Haifa on the Mediterranean shore (originally a Crusader castle), facing the steep ascent to Mount Carmel. At the time it served as a detention camp for immigrants whose boats had been intercepted by the British Navy. In October 1945, 210 people were behind barbed wire at Athlit. The majority were refugees from Europe, but they also included thirty-seven Jews from Lebanon and Syria who, on their own initiative, had chartered a small fishing boat in Beirut in an attempt to escape from the Arab countries bordering Palestine. The Arab fishermen promptly pocketed their pay and took the Jews directly to the British Police post nearest the frontier. Once the green light had been given for the Athlit operation by the Haganah High Command, Nahum Sarig, the Palmach commander appointed to execute the action, a veteran of countless skirmishes against both the British and the Arabs and a fighter known for his resourcefulness and shrewd daring, swiftly set the plans in motion.

By sheer chance, I happened to be in the Haganah office during the suspense-filled day of the operation, and consequently I became the messenger who brought the report of the action to Tel Aviv headquarters. It all came about because, on 9 October, on my way north from the Mossad office in Tel Aviv to the kibbutz to see Hanna, I spontaneously decided to stop in at the Haifa office of the Mossad. Shlomo Zimmerman grinned conspiratorially: 'Don't go on just now. Stay here. You won't regret being in Haifa today.' Without further explanation, he hurried me into his medieval Ford, and we drove to Hadar Hacarmel, half-way up the hill of the enchanted city where I always feel like a tourist on holiday. We drove into the yard of the Haifa Fire Brigade (the headquarters of the voluntary fire fighters, with the constant movement of people and trucks and the noise of sirens, was the cover for the Northern District Command of the Haganah), and I noticed that something serious was going on.

Zimmerman gave the password and we were admitted to the little room that was the nerve-centre of the operations.

David Shaltiel, Commander of Intelligence, was in charge, but Shaul Avigur, the head of the Mossad, was also there – tense and quiet.

Radio messages reporting on the operation's progress arrived at intervals, and finally, the marvellous news of the successful coup reached the cramped room at the Fire Brigade. Shaul turned to me and said in his monotonic voice, untouched by the emotion that filled the whole room: 'Go to Tel Aviv. The Executive Council of the Histadrut is expecting a report on this action, and you're the only person we can spare.'

Sorry to miss the celebration, Zimmerman and I drove at the speed befitting a car that had been parked the whole day at the Fire Brigade, and we reached Tel Aviv at dark. I reported on the events at Athlit to the members of the Histadrut Executive Council, who were seated around a long table covered with overflowing ashtrays – evidence of a long day of tense waiting. I made the report brief, but later I heard a more detailed account of the encounter from Nahum Sarig:

On 6 October 1945 I received instructions from the Palmach General Staff to free by force the immigrants held prisoner in Athlit camp. The date fixed for the operation was the night of the 9th: I had only forty-eight hours in which to plan the attack.

Even before we had any detailed data about the detention camp itself, we began to think in general terms about the problem at hand. We would need more than one Palmach battalion, and at that time the Palmach was scattered among numerous kibbutzim. Assembling a large unit was a complicated matter. We alerted all units at once and began the selection of individual participants. Concentration of arms was even more complicated as these were hidden in different caches that could not be approached and opened by daylight.

The starting point of the operation had to be in a Jewish settlement nearest the camp: Kibbutz Beit Oren on Mount Carmel was our natural choice. We were also obliged to prepare a number of dispersal points for the prisoners after their release, preferably as far from the camp as possible.

Speed was a pre-condition for success. There was no hope for the fast evacuation of 210 imprisoned immigrants without having organized and alerted them in advance. Consequently, we had to infiltrate the camp with people who would make the necessary preparations inside. And for the sake of the speedy dispersal of the liberated prisoners, we had to provide a large number of guides to break up the group into small units that could escape in different directions.

We immediately dispatched scouts to discover the easiest approach roads to the camp and to determine which way the attacking force was to withdraw. They reconnoitered during the day, posing as civilians on an outing, and during the night in battle order. I appointed the commander of the unit that was to penetrate the camp and gave him instructions to gain entry to the camp by posing as a Hebrew teacher on behalf of the Jewish Agency and then to prepare the groundwork for another six who were to operate inside the camp with him.

The Haganah High Command sent us the following instructions: (1) Avoid bloodshed as far as possible. (2) Open fire only as a last resort, and only if, in your judgement, the very success of the operation hangs in the balance. (3) There is reason to believe that no units of the British Army will participate in search operations after the prisoners have been released. (4) The principal adversary is the Police Mobile Force.

British Army camps situated south of the road leading to Athlit and the Athlit Police Station at the crossroads prevented the withdrawal of the prisoners in a southerly direction. It was equally hopeless to move northwards: the nearest Jewish town was Haifa and any movement in this direction would require the use of the main highway, which was obviously out of the question because of a police check-post on the outskirts of Haifa. The only possible direction was, therefore, eastwards towards Mount Carmel. It was also considered essential that the detachment operating inside the camp would take control of the guards.

The attacking force consisted of four units: the assault force that was to take care of the sentries if the need arose and to prevent any attempt to bring in enemy reinforcements from outside the camp; a second detachment to surround the quarters of the British Police and prevent them from breaking out into the guardroom, where their arms were stored; a reserve force at the disposal of the commander of the operation; and finally the scouts, who were destined to guide the escaped prisoners to safety. I positioned a holding force opposite the police fortress on the main road in order to prevent reinforcements from that source from reaching the camp. This force was also directed to cut the telephone lines.

Zero-hour was set for 0100 on the morning of 9 October. I learned that the changing of the guards took place at midnight. It was my intention to give the guards a chance to doze off, yet leave sufficient time for withdrawal before the next shift came on duty.

The six Hebrew teachers – in fact, all instructors of judo – got into the camp safely and went to work. At 2300 hours, the main force moved into position. As part of the terrain had been plowed during the day, it was difficult to scramble over and valuable time was lost; it had to be made up on the last 2 kilometres, in order to keep to our time-table. Panting from the effort of running through the plowed soil, the men of the first unit took up positions near the fence, poised to break in. On the signal of a blue flare, the attack began. Within seconds, the entire force was in position inside the camp, having overpowered the lone sentry in the guard-house, who was bound and gagged.

With the help of our advance party, the prisoners had organized themselves in groups of ten, each under the command of one of their own men. Seven prisoners suspected by their fellow inmates of having been Nazi collaborators in Europe were tied and gagged and left behind in the camp infirmary. The column was on its way out of the camp minutes after we had penetrated it. My second-in-command stayed behind in the camp with the assault force in order to thwart any attempt to pursue the prisoners.

Our trouble started when we began the ascent of the hills facing the camp. The immigrants were less fit than the highly trained Palmach soldiers and were unprepared for the difficult climb. To our amazement, many of them had taken some of their baggage. One of the groups wandered off in the wrong direction and was met by the holding force, which was in the process of withdrawing. As soon as this was reported to me, I sent a truck to collect them.

Time was running out. I instructed my second-in-command to take care of the rear, pushing on with about 100 persons who were advancing at satisfactory speed. We entered Beit Oren after having taken the necessary military precautions. One of the holding forces encountered a police vehicle that happened by at the time and ordered it to stop. The police opened fire; it was returned. The police car overturned, a British officer was killed, and an Arab policeman was injured. A Jewish policeman who was with them in the car escaped – miraculously unharmed.

As dawn was breaking, I tried to speed the dispersal as much as possible. The first to disappear were the drivers of the trucks – civilians specially mobilized for this operation and devoid of normal Palmach discipline. Just as we had gathered them with enormous difficulties, we found that many of the immigrants had wandered off on a sightseeing tour of the first kibbutz they had ever visited. When we were finally ready to move – the hour was four o'clock in the morning – to my amazement I saw the headlights of an endless convoy of police vehicles approaching us from Haifa. Believing that all was lost and that the escape had already been discovered and reported, I had to make an immediate decision. With the headlights in my convoy glaring, I directed the lead driver to move in the direction from which we had just come: to Athlit detention camp. About 1 kilometre west of Beit Oren, at a curve that could not be observed from the more northerly road on which the policemen were travelling, I ordered my convoy to slow down. The escapees then jumped off the trucks, which continued freely on their way to Tel Aviv. The ruse succeeded. The Police Mobile Force continued to track down the now-empty convoy.

Not long after the Athlit action, Dani Shind appeared at my kibbutz. I thought he had come simply to see the new baby and to congratulate us, as indeed he did. But suddenly he took me aside.

'We must send someone to re-inforce our base in Greece,' he said in an urgent tone. 'The Mossad has two candidates for the job – you and me.' For serious personal reasons, Dani could not leave the country just then. With all possible sympathy for my responsibilities as a new father, he nevertheless told me that I had to go. I glanced at Hanna and our new child, but there was no choice.

Hanna understood; and once more I made preparations to leave my home. This time, I arranged to be appointed as a correspondent of *Davar,* the Histadrut daily newspaper; and just to be on the safe side, I also took with me a letter from the kibbutz secretariat appointing me correspondent of the weekly kibbutz news-sheet, *Yoman Ga'aton.* The exotic-sounding name suited my purpose and also freed me from the duties of a real reporter of a daily newspaper which, both for security appearances as well as for its readers, expected frequent cables.

This time I left from Haifa via Istanbul by ship: since the war was over sea travel was once more possible. On our first night at sea, 31 October, we received word of the 'serious single incident', known also as the 'Night of the Railways', the skillfully executed underground operation in which all the resistance movements, including the right-wing groups, combined to wreck railway lines, sink three small British naval craft and attack the Haifa oil refineries. In this period of mounting tension, I was one of a number of Palestinians travelling to liberated Europe on more or less false pretenses to engage in illegal efforts to bring to Palestine that remnant of European Jewry now beginning to surge out of Eastern Europe to the coastal areas, pressing for the forbidden voyage. Our war – against the British White Paper and for the freedom of unlimited immigration – was now concentrated on that one front.

PART THREE

THE SEINE

(17)

An Unfinished Drama
By Schiller . . .

IN ATHENS, I checked in at the Grande Bretagne Hotel, an old and fashionable establishment that, until recently, had catered primarily to Axis dignitaries. Now practically everybody at the Grande Bretagne was playing a part and disguising some second activity. In addition to my two newspaper appointments from Palestine, I also cabled the Jewish Agency in New York during my brief stopover in Istanbul asking to be appointed to some news agency with a neutral-sounding name. This was quickly arranged, and I was duly appointed European correspondent of the International News Service of New York. The Turkish Press Office issued me a press card – as they did to hundreds of other journalists, genuine and otherwise, who wanted to travel on to liberated Europe.

During the day, I was a journalist. Greece in the early months after liberation was a festival of internal political upheavals and tensions, and I was probably the most assiduous newspaperman of all. I interviewed every minister of every successive Greek cabinet, and after a while I could rattle off to them statistics about their departments that they themselves had not yet had time to examine before I turned up for an interview. Most of these ministers were ephemeral; consequently, they enjoyed meeting a reporter representing an 'American news service', for it gave them a sense of power and importance. And I actually did send cables to my New York office, for it was necessary that the censor have something to report about me to whatever security branch might be interested. Shortly after the civil war period Greece was no place for tourists, yet the air was generally relaxed: the worst was over; the war was won. The squabbles of the warring Greek factions were their own affair. We were supposed to report them, sipping ouzo and smoking light Greek cigarettes, but nobody was expected to become personally involved.

The reality was quite different. As soon as I arrived in Athens, I contacted Levi Schwartz, one of the Mossad's most experienced operatives and among the first to accompany the original illegal boats with refugees from Poland. Levi had arrived in Greece from his kibbutz in Palestine using false refugee papers. We met daily, after my regular performance of journalistic postures, but I never went to Levi's rented room, to avoid establishing any reportable contact between us; for not only we of the Mossad had left Istanbul to spread out through Europe; our contacts in British Intelligence were also dispersing in every direction. Just as we moved in the wake of the liberators into Rumania and Bulgaria – and now Greece – so did they; and we were bound to meet some of the men with whom we had enjoyed the *camaraderie* of war-time Istanbul and a common enemy. Now, however, we were to be at cross-purposes. The fact that I was known to British Security personnel did not in the least disturb Levi. On the contrary, he counted on me to function as a kind of decoy: security would watch me instead of him.

What concerned us most was the re-assessment of the political motives that determined our mission. The Mossad had been in Istanbul to save survivors from Nazi-occupied Europe, although that was during war-time and ours had been a mission of mercy, not politics. Now, in peacetime, we were again fighting a political battle. We had to bring Jews to Palestine not only because they had nowhere else to turn, but to increase the Jewish population of Palestine and prove to the British that the right of Jews to return to their own land was not negotiable. The period of 'fighting Hitler as if there were no White Paper and fighting the White Paper as if there were no war against Hitler' had come to an end. We now faced one single enemy: His Majesty's Government.

Levi had been lucky in locating the faithful Aristo Chorilos of pre-war days – 'the Attaché', as we called him – who had been such an asset to our operations in Greece in 1938. Chorilos put Levi in touch with a Greek shipowner willing to take risks: Spiro Gaganis, a man of about sixty with the paddling gait of an old sailor, which earned him the code name 'The Goose'. He had a small boat, which he put at Levi's disposal for a fairly reasonable price – one gold pound sterling per person. The first forty illegal passengers departed from Greece in September 1945. The *Gavriela* was able to get through the British blockade along the Palestine coast undetected: she was so small that nobody suspected her of running illegal immigrants. She returned safely to Greece and reported for further duty.

Encouraged by the *Gavriela*'s success, Levi and I decided to buy a larger boat and asked 'The Goose' to make us an offer. In the afternoons, when my fellow-reporters came down to the bar of the Grande Bretagne from their siestas, I, after one or two cocktails to make my presence felt, would steal away and join Levi at Gaganis' place – a charming little house surrounded by sturdy fig trees and a few goats and chickens running around unattended. There, in a mixture of

French and some Greek and much goodwill and mutual friendship, we discussed the various possibilities that 'The Goose' presented. Just before dusk, Gaganis would bring his derelict pre-war motorcar and we would set out for the little bay near Sounion, whose magic sunsets are watched by countless tourists from the nearby Temple of Poseidon. This was the appointed site of embarkation. With serious and professional movements, Gaganis would measure the depth of the water off the shore in order to determine where a boat might be fastened, so that passengers could be brought on board by row-boats. A friend of his, Nikos Kirinakis, had a small farm by the bay. We brought bottles of ouzo and retsina with us, Kirinakis would supply the grilled fish, and we all would indulge in boundless fantasies about how we were going to channel the remnants of the Holocaust through this little bay – whose promontory played a strategic part during the Greek wars of the third century BC.

The real problem was how to get the refugees there. Our theoretical calculations made in Istanbul at the end of the hostilities had proved impractical. We had failed to consider the strict supervision of both the Bulgarian frontier by Soviet security organs and the adjacent Greek territory by the British. Besides, the political situation in Greece was tense enough without the infiltration of refugees from Bulgaria – now a 'Soviet zone of influence'. And the Greeks had enough hungry mouths to feed without having to concern themselves with additional refugees.

Levi asked the President of the Union of Jewish Communities to organize some 200 young people who could stand the rough trip and prepare them for departure on the *Dimitrios*. The President, Rafael Baki's brother with whom we had worked in Izmir, gladly accepted our invitation and went to work discreetly and unobtrusively.

Gaganis, under Levi's supervision, had his workmen fix bedsteads for 200 passengers in the hold of the 200-ton ship. At first Gaganis thought he had misunderstood the figures: a little boat like that could not accommodate more than thirty, at the most forty people for a trip that was a minimum of five days and, even worse, five nights. But Levi was adamant: he wanted 200 berths. The inner hold of the little boat was opened and the divisions removed, allowing only for a narrow staircase. All available space was turned into narrow layers of berths, with barely 50 centimetres between layers.

The Greek carpenters worked without hesitation. They must have realized that they were preparing the ship for the transport of illegal immigrants: everybody was talking about the revival of a business that, on the eve of the Second World War, had been a golden opportunity for many an owner of small, old ships. But they could not care less about the political implications of their labours. Britain was the occupying power now, rather than the 'liberator', and had neither the popularity nor authority to impose its will on carpenters loyal to Gaganis.

One morning during the first week of November, I found Levi at Gaganis' place with two young men in the 'uniform' so familiar to us of the Mossad: the too-new-looking suits and the too-loud ties on boys who seemed entirely unused to this sort of elegance. The five of us drove to the ship at the secluded inlet of the Bay of Sounion, where the two Palestinians, who had just arrived by boat from Haifa, changed into work clothes and began to inspect the ship. They were both members of Palyam, the maritime branch of Palmach. One was a sailor who would take command of the *Dimitrios* as soon as her passengers embarked and would remain in command until the ship reached Palestine. The other was a radio-operator who would be in charge of the wireless we installed on the ship for contact with the Haganah in Palestine, which might include instructions for dealing with a possible clash with the British Navy when the ship entered coastal waters.

That evening, at Kirinakis' farm, turned out to be a long

but festive occasion. It began as a welcome party for the two Palyam boys, but it also became a farewell party, for that night we decided on the ship's departure date. Embarkation was set for the following Saturday night, when we thought curious policemen might be less alert than usual; the ship would sail at dusk on Sunday. By now we were calling her the *Berl Katznelson*, for we had received instructions from headquarters to re-name the ship and chose to name her after the teacher and philosopher of the Labour movement, who had died a few months earlier. Now the voyage of the *Berl Katznelson* would set off a chain of events that would spark a decisive change in the struggle going on in Palestine. The next morning I phoned the Palace, where Archbishop Damaskinos held court. An interview with the Regent of Greece was the plum of the local foreign correspondents' professional activities. I reminded the Regent's chief of Cabinet that I had been kept waiting for my audience for some time now. I hoped that both crowning achievements would occur simultaneously: the departure of our ship and a reception by the Regent, which would very nicely cover my other activities in the country he ruled.

Saturday was a sunny autumn day. Whoever could hire a cab or had his own car was on the way to some beach for a picnic and a swim. The cabs in which our passengers travelled from their camp to the bay were in no way distinct from all the others. Their rucksacks were hidden away in the back of the cab, and only the picnic baskets, with a day's provisions, were visible. As soon as one load reached the little bay, the passengers disappeared inside the ship and the cab returned to town. At the last count, after dusk, there were exactly 211 passengers on board. We had established our headquarters at Kirinakis' farm and gathered there after saying good-bye to the crew and waving for as long as we could see the outline of the slowly departing ship.

A foreign correspondent returning to the Grande Bretagne

in the early hours of the morning was not necessarily a reason to arouse suspicion of clandestine underground exploits. As I strode into the lobby, deeply satisfied with the immaculate departure of the *Berl Katznelson,* I returned the hall porter's ambiguous smile. He gave me my key in return for a rather large drachma note and in a mood approaching megalomania I said, 'And no calls until further notice! Except, of course, if the palace or British Headquarters rings.' And with this final message an on unimpeachable reputation well established, I went up to my room and fell into the soft bed and euphoric dreams.

Meanwhile, the *Berl Katznelson* had slipped out of the Bay of Sounion and was on her way home. For an eyewitness account of the events and their climax four days later, I spoke with the Palyam sailor who was in command when we met again in Greece the following year. We went over the story again many years later in Haifa, where today he is a publisher of children's books and actively involved with the collection of reproductions of old ships at the Naval Museum in Haifa. This is Kippi's story:

I let the passengers take turns on deck for some fresh air, though there was enough space below. They were in high spirits, because they were finally moving toward their goal. Our radio silence, imposed on all illegal ships nearing the coast, was interrupted only once, and even then just for a flash. That was when our radio-operator, anxiously waiting for a signal, finally heard what he had been waiting for: a coded message of barely two words. He rushed to me with a slip of paper; it was our landing instructions: 'At Shefayim'. [About 15 kilometres north of Tel Aviv, Shefayim was in 1945 little more than a secluded bay, with a kibbutz about 1 kilometre inland.] I knew that by the time we approached the spot a Palyam landing unit would already have arrived from its base in Caesarea, farther up the coast. It would include about 200 people, most trained in disembarking passengers, but also men to repair possible damage and a first aid team.

The landing area was enclosed by Palmach men who had

taken up positions on the dunes overlooking the bay, ready to obstruct British police, army or patrols, and to prevent them from coming into the area while the operation was in progress. The Palyam people lit two fairly large gas-lamps. I spotted their familiar light from the command bridge and ordered the captain to take course accordingly. The *Berl Katznelson* proceeded for another few minutes, and then the captain threw anchor. The ship had arrived.

As usual, disembarkment began at great speed in row-boats standing by for this purpose. Just as we were starting, three Arab fishing-boats were sighted in the immediate vicinity by the observation patrol. They were taken into custody to keep them out of the way and to prevent them from making trouble while the operation was progressing. But there had been a fourth fishing-boat – as we were to discover later – that got away. And the Arab fishermen did their civic duty: they reported to the nearby British police-station that something was going on in the little bay near Kibbutz Shefayim.

The British warship *Ajax* arrived as half of the passengers had safely disembarked. One hundred men, women and children had already reached land, were taken to Kibbutz Shefayim, served a hot drink, received a welcome hug and were already on their way by lorry to their next destination: a kibbutz farther inland, or perhaps a flat in Tel Aviv.

The *Ajax* drew near the *Berl Katznelson* and lowered several lifeboats with a detachment of sailors in each. By the time the first British sailors reached the rope-ladder of the *Berl Katznelson* and began to board her, all but eleven persons had disembarked and vanished in the dark of the night in the little row-boats of the landing team. The eleven remaining passengers were a fairly mixed group – some elderly people who had been kept waiting to last and seven youngsters. Three of them, including myself, were Palestinians and four – the captain and his mates – were Greeks, but nobody could have told them apart from me and my Palyam friends.

The British boarding-party approached us awkwardly and with hesitation, while the captain was ordered to float the *Berl Katznelson*. The rest of the prisoners were told to stand in line, surrounded by British sailors with submachine-guns on the ready, and wait for further orders. At that point, I felt the game was lost. They were going to arrest us sooner or later; I decided to get away before they took us on board the *Ajax* and into detention.

I was wearing my heavy winter clothing, a sweater and heavy boots, and I began to get out of them, as carefully and unobtrusively as possible under the watchful eyes of the British soldiers. I suggested that the rest try to get away with me, but they thought I was mad even to think of escaping – so closely were we being watched by the British soldiers, who outnumbered us about four to one. A soldier with a submachine-gun was following me as I walked towards the back of the ship, but I tried to show him that all I was doing was trying to help the Greek captain in complying with the British order to get the ship moving. I kept glancing sideways at my armed escort, and when he suddenly turned his head to hear an order shouted from the other end of the ship, I realized that my chance had come.

I jumped overboard, grabbed the anchor chain, and let myself down as fast as I dared. Just as I touched the water, the anchor came up out of the sea and the ship began to move. I felt the propellers of the boat dangerously close, but I began to swim towards the shore, blissfully aware of the fact that the foam of the propellers which had just about killed me had also hidden me from view. Against my skin I felt the heavy belt filled with gold coins that the Mossad had provided. They and the trousers of my uniform were so heavy that I had to get rid of them both.

The *Berl Katznelson* moved north, and I swam towards shore. Just as I reached shallow waters, I recognized Sara Jaffe of the Palmach landing team. She had remained to watch the departing ship as all the Palmach soldiers disappeared from the scene, and she looked at me now without recognizing who I was. But just seeing me standing there in my undershorts, shivering in the bitter cold of the autumn dawn, prompted her to take off her fur jacket and throw it at me. I am sorry to report that it was not long enough to cover my undershorts.

Sara took me to Davidka Nameri's command post, where I was received with no hint of surprise or emotion. I reported briefly to Davidka, and I remember being astonished that no one took the initiative to bring me any clothing. In my excitement I proposed to Davidka that the ship be attacked and taken as she passed near the Palyam base of Caesarea on her way to Haifa. Davidka brushed my suggestion aside without so much as a comment.

The remaining passengers, the few Greeks and the captain, were detained when they reached Haifa port and taken to the Athlit detention camp.

All the Greek sailors were repatriated except the captain. He stubbornly refused to answer any of his British interrogators' questions. He was afraid of giving away any information that may have been vital to our work. It is true that this brave Greek had worked for us for payment, but his loyalty far exceeded the call of duty: he identified completely with his passengers and their readiness to fight for their right to return to Palestine. For his stubborn loyalty, he was tried and sentenced to eight months in Acre jail before he too was repatriated to Greece. Upon his return, he reported to Gaganis and asked 'The Goose' to employ him again on the next illegal boat. He had learned the job so well that he wanted to make use of his skill. His request was granted.

In Palestine, news of the capture of the *Berl Katznelson* – the first illegal boat intercepted since the end of the war – and the refugees threatened with expulsion to their countries of origin – reached Haganah headquarters in Tel Aviv just before dawn on 23 November and was the marginal event that finally hardened an already hopeless situation. The Jewish population, disillusioned by the British Labour Party's policies, which completely negated pre-election promises, was far ahead of its cautious official leadership. But the Haganah had anticipated the development crystallized by the *Berl Katznelson* and had come to decisions in advance of the actual incident. As soon as an illegal ship was caught, the Haganah would strike. The British must be shown that immigration was not negotiable. But the Haganah would not employ terrorism for the sake of terrorism: every Haganah operation would be directly and indivisibly connected with the goal of free immigration, and its targets would be only those elements which interfered with immigration. There would be bloodshed and struggle, but only to remove British impediments. This became the principle of 'related struggle'.

The police fortresses at Sidni Ali and at Givat Olga and a radar station in Haifa were the targets of retaliatory action. The planning staff of the Palmach had quietly reconnoitred these and similar objectives for a few weeks. These coastal police stations, both near the bay in which the *Berl Katznelson* had been caught, were also bases for British naval patrols – part of the huge network consisting of battleships, cruisers, planes, speedboats and an army of detectives and undercover agents all over Europe. The *Berl Katznelson* had been intercepted from the Sidni Ali base.

Exactly two nights after the *Berl Katznelson* incident, on 25 November 1945, the two police bulwarks were attacked simultaneously by two units of the 4th Battalion and were blown up. The basic conditions of the two operations were identical, but the actual execution of the plan was different in each case.

One unit took up positions to cover the Sidni Ali attack; another unit secured the approaches to the target area. A unit of saboteurs penetrated the fence surrounding the police station and reached the building itself without resistance. They placed explosives timed to go off after fifteen minutes. Then the telephone operator of the Palmach unit connected a wire leading to his post with the telephone wire of the police station. He informed the police that the building was to be blown up in fifteen minutes and urged them to vacate the station.

While the saboteurs retreated, the covering unit remained behind to make sure that no policeman discovered and disconnected the fuse. After a few minutes of tense silence, there was a tremendous explosion as the fortress of Sidni Ali went up in the air. No life was lost on either side.

The Givat Olga incident, several kilometres farther north, unfortunately ended more tragically. The Palmach saboteurs were discovered after placing the explosives and shooting

broke out. The warning could not be issued as planned, and
although most of the policemen were still able to vacate the
building, seven could not, and they were killed in the explosion.

The third and most spectacular assault was on the main
radar station on Mount Carmel. The commander of the 1st
Battalion of the Palmach, then stationed in the vicinity of
Haifa, had received instructions in the beginning of November to prepare for the eventuality of the 'related struggle'. His
name was Dan Lanner, although once it had been Ernest
Loehner, the son of the exclusive Vienna shopkeeper, Rudolf
Loehner, who at the last moment and by pure chance had
been plucked from the doomed at Cladovo to accompany a
small, lucky group of youngsters to Palestine. Since then he
had served as a parachutist-liaison officer in Tito's headquarters during the Yugoslav partisans' war of liberation,
and from a Palmach commander he was to rise to the rank of
general in Israel's army. The young man who only a few
years earlier had been an 'illegal immigrant' himself was now
commanding an operation to help secure the arrival of what
was left of the victims of Nazi Europe.

The radar station, situated on a meadow overlooking
Haifa Bay, had been reconnoitred by young men and women
in the Intelligence branch of the battalion by observing activities from the conveniently placed office of a graphologist
facing the base or by posing as innocent lovers roaming
through the meadows. The plan finally decided upon was to
have a unit penetrate the station by night and place the
explosives underneath the radar tower, setting the timing
device to go off two hours later. When the plan was approved
and the date of the co-ordinated attack decided, everything
developed smoothly. The attacking unit infiltrated the camp
without resistance and deposited the explosives at the proper
spot. Then the commander of the station was telephoned and
warned that he had two hours to evacuate the installation

before it would blow up, a precaution taken to avoid bloodshed.

It appeared that the operation had worked perfectly, but as it turned out one factor had not been taken into consideration: the strong nerves and efficient operation of the British paratroopers. As soon as the saboteurs withdrew, the paratroopers went into action – cool and undisturbed by the danger confronting them – and searched the installation for the explosives. Well aware of the mechanics of the game, they quickly found and dismantled the charge, an act of bravery that prompted the commander of the Palmach, Yitzhak Sadeh, to address an expression of his admiration to the General Officer in Command of His Majesty's Palestine Forces, adding a warning:

> Please convey my respects to the brave soldier – or officer – who removed the explosive charges from the radar station. I must, however emphasize the following: should the radar station continue to hunt immigrants, we shall blow it up – this time without previous warning.

The British response was to remove the Jewish Supernumerary Police from guard duty at the base and replace them with the 6th Airborne Division.

Two weeks later, Dan Lanner, at his pressing request, received permission to make another try. In the fighting that broke out when the British realized the Palmach had penetrated into the area again, one member of the Palmach was killed; no British lives were lost. But this time the charge was not discovered, and with a blast that shook the windows in the city of Haifa, the radar installation was no longer.

On 28 November 1945 Ben Gurion made the following statement in an 'Open Letter to Ernest Bevin':

> We, the Jews of Palestine, do not want to die. We believe, contrary to the opinion of Hitler and his followers in different countries, that we, the Jews, have the same right to live – as individuals and as a people – as the English and others. But we

– like the British – have something that is dearer to us than life. And I want to say to Bevin and to his comrades that we are ready to die rather than to surrender the following three things: free Jewish immigration; our right to rebuild the wasteland of our country; the political independence of our people in its land.

While the fate of the *Berl Katznelson* was touching off repercussions of ever-mounting tension, my own activities were diverted by the same circumstances to a sudden change of scene. When the telephone woke me in my room at the Grande Bretagne, my first thought was that it must still be night – that same night of the *Berl Katznelson*'s departure, when I had gone to bed so full of optimism, with instructions to allow calls only from the loftiest quarters. Now the apologetic voice of the hotel's switchboard operator announced that there was indeed a call for me from the Royal Palace. By now, fully awake, I heard the Regent's ADC asking me to forgive the short notice, but would I be free for dinner at the Palace that same evening? Cheerfully, I accepted. Could there be a more appropriately distinguished celebration for our recent success?

I had barely dozed off again when the phone rang once more. This must be British headquarters, I thought, lifting the receiver. It was the hall-porter: 'There is a message for you, sir, from British headquarters, sir, and please forgive my waking you up, but it sounded urgent. Will you please, the message says, call at British headquarters, Room 201, immediately.'

My watch said half past ten. Half past ten on a Sunday morning! It must be a very urgent matter indeed. I dressed in a hurry and walked to the building next to the Grande Bretagne, where British headquarters was conveniently situated.

Room 201 was on the ground floor of the building. It took only my signature and the wave of the orderly's hand and I was knocking at the door of the room to which I had been urgently summoned. I was not really surprised to see Captain Parkes, Major Whittal's assistant from Istanbul days, facing me across the small room. With a whimsical smile, he opened our first talk since we had last met in neutral Istanbul. He came straight to the point.

'When you hear the name *"Dimitrios",*' he said, looking stern, 'what is the first thing that comes to your mind?'

'Dimitrios?' I repeated. 'Dimitrios? Well, what comes to my mind is the unfinished drama by Friedrich Schiller, the German poet . . .'

'Not such a bad definition, my boy,' said Parkes, 'because an unfinished drama is also what your stay in Greece will be. Your game was sharp, but now it's over. You did all you could for the International News Service and they must be quite flooded with your penetrating reports about Greek politics. Your other bosses will perhaps be less satisfied with your endeavours. But such is life, you can't have every-thing . . .'

It was clear that he knew something about the ship formerly called the *Dimitrios,* now the *Berl Katznelson.* But evidently the main fact had not reached his desk, for he did not act as if he knew that the ship had already left.

'Where will you go, now that we have orders to ask you to leave Greece at once?' This was once more my friend from the old days.

'I'll go home, of course.' Where else could I turn after such an unfortunate *contretemps*?

'Don't do that,' he warned. 'Don't go to Palestine. The CID there have had you on their black list for some time now. And they'll be glad to arrest you to keep you from making further mischief.'

He was now talking as if we were still Allies in a common cause.

'Look here,' said Parkes, 'after all, my only duty is to get you out of Greece. Nobody told me to hand you over to the

Palestine authorities so they can send you to jail. I'll arrange for priorities for you on the first plane leaving for Italy. I suppose that the Mossad will prefer to know that you are there rather than in the dark dungeons of the Palestine police.'

'I'm having dinner with the Regent tonight,' I protested feebly against Parkes' paternal precautions.

'My itinerary won't interfere with yours,' he said. 'There is no flight for Bari, Italy, before Monday morning.'

(18)

We Meet in Belgrade

WHEN THE MILITARY PLANE landed at Bari airport, British military buses were waiting on the runway to ferry privileged passengers to the officers' hotel. The officers' quarters, on the picturesque waterfront of the port of Bari, was once, and soon would become once more, the best hotel in town. But at that time, having passed from occupation by German officers to Allied officers, the hotel looked desolate. English military signs everywhere gave its depressed interior an air of lost glory.

I went for a walk in the streets of Bari, relishing the fact that I was now on newly liberated Axis territory, and I felt cheerful, although I was on the run from the British police and carrying dubious credentials as the correspondent of a kibbutz news bulletin and a Palestinian passport that was a drag-chain rather than a helpful document. With macabre humour, we used to enjoy the formal phrase on the inside cover of the passport: 'By His Majesty's High Commissioner for Palestine: These are to request and require in the Name of His Majesty all those whom it may concern to allow the bearer to pass freely without act or hindrance and to afford him every assistance and protection of which he may stand in need.'

Children were hanging about the hotel waiting for an opportunity to beg for food or perhaps receive a cigarette from a charitable foreign officer. Poorly lit buildings lined the almost empty streets, now void of echoes of fascist glory. But there was – or so I imagined – a general feeling of expectation in the air, and possibilities for completely new challenges that would draw on the untapped capabilities of the people.

Imitating the other guests in the officers' transit quarters, I went into the mess for a drink and for dinner. It was clear that I could not stay in this place for very long. The gentlemen who shared the dinner-table with me discussed the difficulties of air travel in these days of restricted space on the very few planes, and I felt my breast pocket for my A1-priority travel orders, with a warm thought for Captain Parkes.

I had no precise instructions from home and therefore had to decide for myself where to turn. Italy was firmly under the control of Yehudah Arazi's fast-growing organization. But from across the Adriatic Sea, the long coast of Yugoslavia was beckoning. The thousands of tiny inlets lured us even during our Istanbul days, when we dreamed of the time that had now come – meeting survivors of the extermination and finally being able to turn the weak rivulet of illegal immigration into a gushing stream. Lulled by the humming conversation of my British fellow-travellers in their smart uniforms, I suddenly thought of Eliahu Dobkin, the head of the Immigration Department of the Zionist Organization who discreetly supported the fledgling Mossad in the pre-war years and who believed 'where there is an outlet to the sea, where there are Jews and where there is the will, you have the ideal conditions for illegal immigration.'

I kept my ears open to what the experienced insiders had to say about the availability of seats on planes out of Bari, and from the information I gathered my logical destination was Belgrade. A British colonel indicated that he was looking forward, weather permitting, to a flight to the capital of Yugoslavia the following afternoon. It was settled.

After dinner, poor coffee and excellent French brandy, I leisurely walked over to the transport office and informed the clerk that it was my intention to proceed to Yugoslavia on the first available plane. With the courtesy that my travel papers commanded, the sergeant told me that I should be ready to be taken to the airport the next day at 3 p.m. I could not help smiling to myself. This was, I thought, an auspicious way of being brought to my destination: with full honours by exactly those against whom I was to organize illegal activities.

The winter sun was shining as I left with my small suitcase for the short flight across the Adriatic Sea to Belgrade. In Athens, when I realized that sooner or later I might have to move on, I had obtained a Yugoslav visa. I felt like a tourist on a pleasure trip as I boarded the military Dakota, flown by a grim Yugoslav pilot in the casual uniform of the partisans. After a flight through the peaceful skies of the southern Adriatic and over the rugged mountains of Montenegro and Serbia, we landed at Semun Airport in the pell-mell of partisan military personnel, with submachine-guns and red armbands. It was a blissful feeling to be in a country that had fought for its own liberation and was now on 'our' side, despite the suspicion of the communist frontier police and the dark looks of the people who had been living in hiding or on the run for years and were understandably wary of outsiders. It seemed that there were thousands of people milling around the airport terminal. With some difficulty, I obtained a seat on the ramshackle bus that shuttled passengers from the Allied plane to the centre of town. Here, my status as a civilian guest of the British Army began to lose its charm. I had to look for my own accommodation, while the victorious officers were taken to quarters prepared especially for them.

I found my way to the Hotel Majestic, which had been

mentioned by the officers in the Bari mess as the best hotel for the press corps and other privileged foreigners. I was lucky to find a pleasant room and, to my delight, there were also warm water and clean towels in the bathroom. I strolled through the lobby, looking for familiar faces from the 'old days' in Istanbul. I did meet an American reporter I knew. He was well aware of why I was in Belgrade but said nothing, except to explain how to obtain accreditation as a foreign correspondent.

At the government press office the next morning, I decided to be very careful. I knew very little about Yugoslav politics: the partisan government was friendly to the British, who had helped so much during the Nazi occupation, but also sided with the Russians, who had rarely shown Zionist sympathies during the war.

The decision to make Yugoslavia a focal point for the next phase of our activity was based mostly on instinct. Situated between Rumania (with over half a million Jewish survivors) and Hungary (with 150,000) the country had a long coast marked by numerous bays and inlets – perfect for our kind of shipping business. As it happened, three separate streams of Jews, all dedicated to the rescue of the remnants of our people from Eastern Europe, converged upon Yugoslavia within a very short time. Without any formal policy planning or orders from above, there soon arrived, singly and in groups, Palestinian detachments of the Jewish Brigade, who had somehow worked their way to Yugoslavia from Italy; Jews from Palestine, often those who originally had come from Eastern Europe; and finally, people of the Mossad who – like myself – somehow had the idea that conditions for our work were good in Yugoslavia.

At the same time, in an enormous wave of disorganized mass migration, came the Jews of Eastern Europe. Instinctively, too, they felt that if only they could somehow reach the southern shores of Europe, their chances of reaching

Palestine would be much greater. The place where most of these streams met – at first haphazardly and eventually through contacts that became an informal network – was the Belgrade office of David Alkalay, the President of the Jewish Community of Yugoslavia, who became a generous and resourceful partner in our work.

Until the proclamation of Israel's Independence, when 'illegal' immigration changed from a pressing problem to a daring chapter of Jewish history, Yugoslavia supported our efforts faithfully. Our largest ships would sail from her ports, and the greatest courtesy was extended to us and to the refugees, who were allowed to pass through Yugoslav territory freely. Officials, as well as the people of Yugoslavia, retained fresh memories of the horrors of Hitler's war. They had fought against the Nazis and paid the price of courage; they had witnessed the destruction of the Jewish community through deportation and mass execution. Better than many others, the Yugoslavs understood that the remnants of the destroyed Jewish communities refused to return to the graveyards their homes had become and regarded their support of the Jewish underground in Palestine as the logical corollary of their own struggle for national independence.

Mulia Ben Hayim, one of our activists in Eastern Europe, was among the first to establish operations in Yugoslavia. Even before the war officially ended, he arrived in Yugoslavia as an emissary of the Jewish underground in Poland. Mulia was from Vilna, had been a member of the youth movement Hashomer Hatzair and had experienced life in a ghetto, a concentration camp and the permanent expectation of death. Immediately after the liberation of Poland, together with the poet and Jewish partisan Abba Kovner, he was one of the initiators in moving Jews towards the sea as a first step towards their immigration to Palestine. It was clear to Kovner and his friends that Jewish life in the Axis and Axis-dominated countries of Europe had come to an end. Jews could not resume their lives among people who had actively liquidated or passively allowed the extermination of their families and communities. Vague rumours had reached Poland about the Jewish Brigade and other Jewish contingents fighting within the British Army, and Kovner selected Mulia and seven other youngsters to go to Yugoslavia and search out military units from Palestine.

Mulia arrived in Belgrade on 24 April 1945. He immediately sent one of his men on to the Adriatic port of Split. Pinhas Zeitag, better known as 'Pinie the Yellow' (because of his blond hair), was a swashbuckling partisan from Lithuania. Working out of Split, Zeitag succeeded in establishing contact with the Jewish Brigade stationed in the Italian town of Tarvisio, just across the Yugoslav border.

A few days later, during the week following VE day, when the whole world was enveloped in the euphoria of all men at long last being brethren, Mulia was busy establishing contact with the remnants of the Jewish community of Yugoslavia. Through David Alkalay he obtained official Yugoslav understanding for the urgent need to help East European Jews to proceed to the Mediterranean coast. Alkalay put Mulia in touch with the Yugoslav Repatriation Office, a department already involved in the transit of Jews through Yugoslavia. Armed with home-made Rumanian Red Cross documents presenting them as citizens of West European countries on their way home, Jews from Rumania made their way through Yugoslavia to Italy.

At the same time that Mulia's group was setting up its operation in Yugoslavia, another leader of the Jewish partisans in Poland, Mordechai Rosemann, had found his way to Hungary and had begun to organize the movement of refugees through the Hungarian frontier town of Szeged into the Yugoslav towns of Subotica and Novi Sad, where they were aided by the Yugoslav repatriation authorities. In Budapest, Rosemann found the escape organization that had operated under the Nazis fully intact. Yoel Palgi, a parachutist from Palestine, still headed the umbrella organization of all Jewish groups in Hungary. In most cases they were the same people who had helped Hungarian Jews escape to Slovakia and Rumania during the last year of the war.

The leadership of the partisans, who had set up posts in Budapest, Bucharest and Belgrade, was about to move from Bucharest westwards. Just at that time a delegation of four Palestinian soldiers from the Jewish Brigade arrived in Bucharest. They had learned of the activities of the partisan command and had already met some of the refugees who, thanks to the partisans' initiative, had arrived in Italy. The delegation from the Jewish Brigade, all members of Haganah, came to Bucharest to establish personal contact with the partisan high command. It was the partisans in their will to renew life after liberation, rather than 'Zionist propaganda' – as the British later suggested – who created what was to become a mass movement of Jews from Eastern Europe to Central and Southern Europe. Among their own survivors, they found the leadership and the force to organize the first step of their surge to Palestine.

In the winter of 1944/5, Leibl Abramovsky, a man firmly rooted in the kibbutz way of life, but nonetheless still tied to the community of Polish Jews from which he had originated, made the long voyage back. He was to become typical of a new kind of Mossad operative.

A member of a kibbutz in the vicinity of Haifa, he had lived the hard life of a stevedore in Haifa port; but his heart and mind were with his friends in Nazi-occupied Poland. He had left a crowded training farm in Poland prior to the outbreak of the war and before the fate of Poland's Jews had been sealed. He felt that he could not be satisfied with hard physical labour alone; he was doing it because this was the one way he knew to build the land for more Jews to live in

freedom. But his most fervent desire was to rescue the besieged he had left behind when he went to Palestine.

Leibl decided to join the British Army and fight against
the Nazis, but his kibbutz decided otherwise: he was sent, in
the cadres of the Mossad, to Baghdad to aid in the escape of
Iraqi Jews to Palestine. He was also entrusted with the task
of trying to establish contact with Polish refugees who had
reached central and eastern Russia during the war and to
create facilities for their movement over the wide expanses of
desert and hostile territory to Palestine.

Illness forced Leibl to return to Palestine for medical care.
When he had recovered (temporarily, as it turned out), he
persuaded the senior members of the Mossad to send him to
Europe to join up with his charges, working his way towards
them from recently liberated countries in Eastern Europe.

Leibl was detailed by the Mossad to travel to Europe with
forged papers identifying him as a British soldier on his way
back to his unit. Just a week before his departure, three of
our people had been apprehended; but despite rumours about
their fate, he did not change his plan. In December 1945 he
left by train for Port Said and there, in the uniform of a
British Army private, boarded the first available troop transport. He offered to carry the heavy bags of the more senior –
and unsuspecting – personnel up the rope-ladder, thereby
getting around the necessary check of his papers. Then he
volunteered to serve on guard duty over the German prisoners of war who were located below, so that he could keep
out of sight while learning to imitate the smart behaviour of a
trained soldier.

Having worked his way to Italy in this manner, he proceeded at once to Milan, using military transport with the self-
confidence of a seasoned warrior. There, one of the first
people he encountered was Tuvia Arazi, Yehudah Arazi's
brother, who had been a Mossad agent in Beirut and in
Baghdad. Tuvia knew of Leibl's work in Iraq and arranged

for his brother to offer Leibl a place in his organization. This was a great compliment for Leibl, as Yehudah Arazi was not always generous towards people who had won their spurs in the Mossad and was critical of the Mossad's complete obedience to the prudent leadership of the Jewish Agency and its consequent cautiousness in undertaking unorthodox coups.

Once inside Yugoslavia, Leibl hit upon a snag and found himself arrested by the Yugoslav Secret Police. But forty-eight hours later he was released and a partisan vehicle took him to the railway station. There he saw his chance when he came by a train transporting wounded soldiers to Belgrade. Speaking Russian freely and with gusto, he was respectfully admitted to the train, although he could show no papers crediting him with the right to travel in Yugoslavia. It was a time when a Russian accent was hard currency in Yugoslavia.

In Belgrade, he found the local Union of Jewish Communities, where he was met with some suspicion: the President was just in the midst of discussing what to do about people like him – refugees who came through Belgrade on their turbulent errands and endangered the stability the Union wanted to restore to the decimated community. Even so, he was given hot tea and crumbled corn bread and was allowed to squat in the remodelled waiting-room.

Leibl was kept waiting there for hours. From time to time he fell asleep in the warm room, stretched out in a soft chair that had seen better days. It occurred to him that he might just as well tell the President who he really was so as to be admitted to the talk going on and on behind the closed door. They were most probably discussing the very topic that had made him take his long and frightful voyage. Then again, it might be premature to take them into his confidence; he might need his disguise in case the functionaries of the official Union of Jewish Communities turned a deaf ear on him. In the midst of these thoughts, the door suddenly opened.

David Alkalay preceded me out of the office and turned to the awkward figure in the stuffed arm chair. But before he could utter a word, Leibl and I played out our scene. We had last seen each other in the Mossad's roof-top office in Tel Aviv. Alkalay stood there wonderingly as we embraced and rejoiced in having found one another in the maze of post-war Europe.

I was by now an established correspondent in the foreign press corps of Belgrade. My journalistic experience in Athens helped; but while it was more difficult to obtain interviews with cabinet personalities in Yugoslavia than it had been in the fluid Greek situation, it was also less necessary to keep up the appearances of a journalist. Leibl was given the official identity card of a Polish refugee issued by the Union of Jewish Communities, and each under his own cover, we were ready to start operations.

Leibl decided to contact the Jewish partisans who had established posts on the borders between Yugoslavia and her neighbours. One day in the winter of 1945, he took off for the Hungarian border town of Szeged, finding it easy, as a Polish refugee who spoke Russian, to cross from one communist country to the other. But in Szeged he was warned by a Russian officer not to proceed to Budapest on his own. The road was dangerous, and refugees were often arrested on suspicion of black-market dealings and other nefarious activities. He thanked his benefactor with a bottle of slivovitz, wisely carried from Belgrade in the large pocket of his German greatcoat, and telephoned Yonah Rosen, another parachutist leader of the Jewish underground in Budapest. Yonah, happy to hear that another Mossad emissary was on his way, sent a car with a reliable driver to bring Leibl to Budapest. They had just started to move when their car was hit by a huge Russian lorry and completely smashed. To the amazed surprise of both Leibl and his driver, they emerged from the wreck with less than a few scratches. Philosophically, Leibl and his carless driver stood on the roadside, waiting for a passing car to stop and take them to Budapest. A Russian officer on a motorcycle with a side-car stopped for them and most obligingly brought them right to the centre of Budapest. That very night Leibl began making contacts.

My 'journalistic' work brought me into contact with the officials of the Yugoslav Government Press Office. Not surprisingly, I met a few who had a sincere respect for our struggle in Palestine, about which they received quite one-sided reports from British sources. But after the war they regarded their former British Allies as having reverted to the stance of imperialist suppressors, and they felt the partisans' affinity for a small people fighting against a superior enemy.

In consultation with Alkalay, I decided to ask for an interview with Moshe Piade, the Speaker of the Federal Parliament and one of the chiefs of the Communist Party. Piade was a Jew, and Alkalay had been in touch with him on matters concerning the revival of Jewish communal life after the war. Alkalay had found him friendly and sympathetic, although he hardly regarded himself as a member of the Jewish community about to be re-established. When I was finally told that Piade was ready to receive me, he asked that I come to see him informally at his home.

A stoutly built man with the face of a scholar and intellectual, Piade opened the door for me himself when I arrived at his villa for our talk. Completely dispensing with formality, he brought me into his drawing-room.

'Here you can speak absolutely freely. I have switched off all the microphones and we are alone,' he said with a sarcastic reference to rumours, then current in Belgrade, that even top leaders of the Communist Party were closely watched by the Secret Service.

As we settled down for a long talk, Piade told me of his curiosity about everything concerning the 'Zionist effort in Palestine'.

'I am, as you may know, of Jewish descent,' he said, 'but I regard myself as a Yugoslav communist and nothing else. This is my country and my people; among them I have grown up and fought my political battles. Till recently I was with them in the mountains fighting against the Nazis. But I want to hear from a primary source about your work, your ideas, you life.'

Moshe Piade's manner made me think he might well be called 'Tito's Berl Katznelson.' He listened with sympathy, interrupting with keen questions as I tried to explain our way of life and our thinking. The organization of the kibbutz – a collective 'from below', as he defined it – interested him most. It was obvious that he pondered the possibilities of a similar movement in the new social reality of the 'People's Democracy'. At the end of the long and stimulating evening I knew we had won a friend.

'You will hear from me again, both directly and indirectly,' Piade said as we parted, and I knew by his tone that I would receive an affirmative reply to my request for permission to organize illegal immigration to Palestine from the shores of the Adriatic.

Leibl returned from his exploration of the Hungarian track full of hopes and more than pleased when he heard that on the diplomatic level things looked good too. But he was not satisfied with one link: he knew, and he had been told once again in Budapest, that many Jews from Poland had moved to Rumania. So he decided to 'open the border' between Rumania and Yugoslavia too. At the frontier post of Kikinda, again by speaking Russian and showing his Polish refugee card, he received assurances from the Rumanian frontier guard that any Jewish refugees wanting to cross into Yugoslavia would be helped.

A few days after my talk with Piade, Slavko Radej, the head of the emaciated Jewish community of Zagreb, came to meet with me. He had survived the war with his vigour and optimism fully intact and had visions of streams of Jewish refugees from Hungary and Rumania on their way to the Dalmatian coast. Slavko was glad to discover the existence of the Mossad. He had already hoarded food, blankets and boots and had made arrangements for transit quarters on the outskirts of Zagreb. His contacts with the Yugoslav communist administration had been forged while he lived with many of the new leaders as partisans in the mountains, and these friendships facilitated his new task as host to the expected refugees from beyond the Yugoslav borders. As we ate breakfast together in the dining-room of the Majestic, he told me about the arrangements he had made with Leibl for transient refugees from Rumania.

Suddenly the hall-porter came up to me with a telegram. It was from Paris and it read: 'Chief Editor needs you for urgent discussion at once. Ruth'. I turned the telegram over in my hand. There was absolutely no indication of what it was all about, and Slavko shared my curiosity. I explained to him that it could mean that Ben Gurion – who I knew was in Paris – wanted to see me urgently. Or was I imagining things? The quiet atmosphere of our talk suddenly vanished. Slavko suggested that I try to telephone Paris and find out for sure before I made any decisions.

This time the telephone connection worked reasonably fast. I was able to distinguish Ruth's voice faintly over the line, and she confirmed my interpretation of the message. I left with Slavko on the train to Zagreb, after having taken leave of Leibl and of Alkalay.

After a short stop in Zagreb for a visit to Slavko's home and to take up food supplies, I continued on to Vienna. From Zagreb through the snow-covered mountains of Slovenia, as far as I could make out I was the only passenger on the unlit train. It moved with great effort up the steep ascents, and I wondered how long I would be stuck in the bitter cold of the unheated carriage. Passport formalities on the frontier were purely perfunctory, and my provisions helped to lighten the atmosphere. On the Austrian side of the border, a noisy group of peasants with baskets, bundles and a varied assortment of possessions boarded the train, and the voyage through the night became more human and real.

Large, watery snowflakes descended upon the badly mutilated terminal as the train slowly moved into Vienna's Süd-Ost-Bahnhof. I was unprepared for my arrival at this point – the substitute for the regular station, which had been destroyed completely in the final battle for the liberation of Vienna – for it happened to be located near what used to be the 'Jewish' district. My return to my native city began where the club of our youth movement once had been, where in later years I used to meet Hanna and where – was it really only six years ago? – both of us had been beaten up by Nazi storm-troopers.

The heavy layer of new snow had turned everything into a deceiving white; but underneath, the open wounds from the punishment Vienna had received remained unhealed. At first I attributed the silence around me to the shock of finding myself in Vienna again. Then I realized that the tram was not functioning – because of the lack of electric current and the dislocation of large stretches of rail as a result of the bombing – and there were no motor cars.

As I stood in front of the damaged terminal, a horse-drawn cart moved slowly towards me. The coachman took my suitcase and put it under his seat. Without shaking off the snow and slush that had settled on his blanket, he helped me climb up on his cart. As the emaciated horse carefully put one foot before the other on the slippery street, I realized that we were re-crossing the circuits of my youth, travelling through streets I knew so well. Such a macabre home-coming, I thought to myself. Only – I thought, spotting the name of the new owner – only the Jews are not here anymore.

My destination was Frankgasse 2. If Israel had already

been a sovereign state, the office located at this address would have been our Embassy. The head of the office was destined to become one of the outstanding ambassadors of the country he helped to establish. Asher Ben-Natan was born in Vienna. In 1938 he went to Palestine, joined a kibbutz and became a member the Haganah. He had returned to Vienna as an emissary of the Mossad a few months before we met. He presented himself as a newspaperman, and he was known to all as Arthur Pier. His good looks and self-assurance facilitated his work. In Four-Power-controlled Austria of 1945, he soon acquired the epithet of 'the Fifth Power': moving among the diplomats and secret agents, he struck everyone as a likeable fellow, phrasing his arguments in the mildest of tones.

The interior of Frankgasse 2 bore no resemblance to an Embassy. The high-ceilinged apartment had once belonged to a wealthy Jewish family that had perished during the Nazi occupation. The flat had become a transit camp for refugees from the east on their way to the sea. From there Arthur supervised the ever-growing network of border-crossing stations into Austria and through the intricate regional borders dividing one zone of occupation from another.

I asked Arthur's advice about how to best continue on to Paris, and at his suggestion I took the A1-priority travel orders, issued when Captain Parkes expelled me from Greece, to the American Air Transport Command. This organization, which later became part of Trans World Airlines, ran the only more or less regular flight to Paris. Pier believed they would act quickly for official-looking travel documents, and they did. I received accommodation on a flight that was to leave early the next morning.

A snowstorm forced the American Dakota to set down unexpectedly in Nuremberg and made it impossible to continue. This had been the 'Capital of the Movement', so named by the Nazis when they still celebrated their tumultuous Party conventions with tens of thousands of iron-fisted SS men marching through the streets of the medieval town towards the enormous stadium built to provide their *Fuehrer* with the over-sized platform he required. The name of this picturesque little town had been attached to the race-laws promulgated by the triumphant Nazi government in the early days of the 'thousand-year-Reich', laws that condemned Jews under Hitler's rule to degradation and to death. At present, however, all authority in the 'Capital of the Movement' seemed to have passed into the hands of an American Sergeant-Major in charge of the local garrison. Politely, and with the profuse apologies of the Air Transport Command, the privileged passengers from the incapacitated plane were transferred to a luxurious train known as the 'American Officers' Leave Train'; it was the most elegant conveyance at the time. Brandishing my travel orders from Athens so that the words 'A1-priority' were clearly visible, I joined the high brass as they were boarding and arrived early in the morning in liberated Paris.

(19)

New Headquarters

RUTH ALIAV was waiting for me at Claridge's, the only large hotel not taken over by either the Allied armies or the newly reconstituted French authorities. Like the rest of us, she had spent the war years thinking about what could have been accomplished on the eve of war if only we had worked more efficiently, with greater vision, with more money, with the experience and maturity that we accumulated only as the tragedy unfolded. Like the rest of us, she had taken a silent oath not to repeat mistakes we had made, not to compromise, not to relent.

Ruth had greatly enhanced her status in the Mossad. She had reached Paris (with the help of one of the central figures in de Gaulle's immediate entourage) as soon as the city was liberated and while the war was still being fought on French soil. Without delay she had applied herself to the most urgent task: to recover Jewish children who had been placed by their parents in monasteries or in the homes of sympathetic Christians. One by one, she brought these children – often the only surviving member of an entire family – to centres established with the help of the Jewish community of France. The Jewish Maquis, under the leadership of Avra-

ham Polonsky, also put itself at Ruth's disposal. As one
concentration camp after another was liberated and the
losses suffered by individual families became manifest, Ruth
and the young men and women of the Maquis worked
together in mute sorrow.

While Ruth described her activities to me, I felt some of
the all-pervading optimism that was in the air of the lovely
city. There were intimations of endless possibilities, hints of
hidden opportunities, calls for bravery of unheard-of proportions. Ruth had established contact with SHAEF, the Supreme Allied Headquarters under General Eisenhower. She
had made friends with the officer in charge of 'Displaced Persons' and Eisenhower's advisor on refugees. The magnani-
mous Americans, as yet quite unaware of the political
implications their British Allies attached to the rescue operations, agreed to let Ruth have a large troopship. She
planned to transport several thousand of her children to
Palestine. In fact, 2,600 people sailed on the *Ascania* in the
autumn of 1945. They were not all children: as news of the
American troopship spread through the DP camps, men and
women of all ages rushed to Marseilles, and no power in the
world could have stopped them from boarding a ship intended to carry 900 children but large enough to accommodate nearly three times as many people determined to leave
Europe.

The arrival of the *Ascania* in Palestine caused frantic
embarrassment: the mandatory authorities were at a loss
how to treat an American troopship bringing Jewish refugees
without immigration permits, a ship commanded by American naval personnel and released for that purpose by the
Supreme Allied Commander. They decided to let the refugees
come ashore but deducted a landing certificate for each of
the *Ascania*'s passengers from the quota at the disposal of
the Jewish Agency. They also admonished the Americans not
to repeat their generosity.

But Ruth was able to organize one more departure of the American troop carrier before the Americans had to adjust their humanitarian attitude to the strict limitations of the hostile White Paper policies. Her philosophy was clear: 'We must take advantage of the chaos while it still exists.'

Ben Gurion, who was in Paris on his way back to Palestine from an extensive visit to the United States – his first since the end of the war – saw me that afternoon. After inquiring keenly about my experiences in Greece and particularly in Yugoslavia (it was clear that the stubborn fight put up by Tito's partisans was much to his liking), he brought me up to date on the political problems that concerned him most:

I have asked you to come here in a hurry because we shall have to work fast – and on a large front. We must bring tens of thousands of survivors to Palestine. We must create new kibbutzim in the desert and on the frontiers, and we need the people to build them. The survivors of the Holocaust are the ones who will be happy to join us. We must train them in the use of arms even before they reach Palestine. It will be easier to do this here in Europe than at home, where the mandatory government is so hostile. And we shall bring the arms we need to defend ourselves when the inevitable showdown comes. These are the tasks. The remnants of Europe's Jewry are with us.

I want you to join Ruth and a member of the High Command in being responsible for the co-ordination of the Jewish Resistance in Europe. The time has come for great battles and for great decisions. It will be the responsibility of the three of you, with all the help you need and all the support you can use, to put this plan into effect. Are you prepared to undertake the responsibility?

Ben Gurion's question was, as usual, solely rhetorical. The interview was over. He did not intend to go into organizational details or to answer requests for further illumination on the subject.

The man from Haganah High Command, Nahum Kraemer (formerly the Commander of the Haganah in Jerusalem) had recently arrived in Paris, also at the express command of Ben Gurion. He was to supervise the activities of all Jewish soldiers in the British Army. These soldiers had had an unofficial Haganah commander ever since they had joined up. But as the British were not generous about elevating Jewish soldiers to officers, and as not all those who made the grade were, in the eyes of the Haganah, the most reliable commanders, in some cases the Haganah commander was quite low ranking – perhaps even a private.

Now that the war was over and soldiers were being demobilized, officers and men could take advantage of the general relaxation of army discipline to advance the interests of the Haganah. The High Command therefore decided to send a generally respected person from Palestine to take command over all members of the Haganah in Europe, whatever their position or assignment.

Nahum Kraemer enjoyed the trust and confidence of us all and was the natural leader of the group of three Ben Gurion had appointed. It was under his chairmanship that we met the next morning in Ruth's office for our first discussion.

As soon as the meeting ended, I went to see Chanan Eynor, the Mossad's chief representative in Paris. Although we had never met before, Chanan received me warmly, more, I suspected, because of my credentials as a member of the Istanbul team than as a result of my recent appointment by Ben Gurion. As the Mossad was truly an organization that lacked a hierarchy, one gained the respect of his colleagues not by virtue of senior rank but because of his achievements in practical operations. Chanan was able to give me a clear picture of the local situation: France was not an occupied country but a free one with a government that sympathized with us. Public opinion was on the side of justice for survivors of the Holocaust.

'We shall have great support in France,' he said, 'but we must organize our work so that the French won't become embroiled with the British over the issue of illegal immigration. They have troubles enough of their own with their neighbours and Allies. We must carry out our work as unobtrusively as possible. That means that we must disguise transports of illegal immigrants as authentic emigration overseas. We must obtain genuine travel documents whenever possible and not sacrifice the appearance of legality for shortcuts.'

It was hard to contest Chanan's opinions. What he proposed was difficult to implement, but it was a surer way to better results.

Walking back to my hotel through the unfamiliar city, I found myself contemplating how we were going to carry out the programme Chanan had described. There must be people in Paris itching to work with us: some out of purely humanitarian instincts, to rescue the survivors and give them a new chance; some for materialistic purposes, to take advantage of a desperate situation in order to sell their services; some out of a spirit of adventure; some because of a dislike for the British; or some simply because they liked Jews. My problem was to locate these people in this maze of a city – and soon.

The lobby of Claridge's at lunch hour was a strange assortment of characters, for it was one of the few hotels in which French civilians mingled with foreigners. Glad to have reached the relative warmth of the congested lobby, I tried to make my way into the hotel bar. Just then, a rather tall fellow approached me from behind, put his hand on my shoulder, and I heard a vaguely familiar voice ask in Viennese German: 'Your name is Ehud, isn't it?' There was no time for my confirmation. The man drew me to his chest and kissed me; and it took quite a while before he released me long enough for me to get a look at my attacker. I recognized him at once as Joszi Friedmann, the red-headed renegade I had last seen in my office in Vienna in the autumn of 1938. He was eager to tell me all that had happened since our last meeting and I was equally interested to hear his story – how he had survived and what he was presently up to.

With the permit I had helped him get in 1938, Joszi had gone to Holland. Thanks to the kindness of the Dutch family that adopted him, he was one of the very few who was able to bring his entire family after him. When Holland was over-run by the Nazis, Joszi and his family moved to the south of 'unoccupied' France, and from there he helped his parents cross the frontier into Switzerland. He continued to travel between France and Switzerland, helping people to cross the border and smuggling watches to support himself and his friends. This occupation, as he somewhat shamefacedly ad-mitted, he maintained up until the present. It was as profit-able now – perhaps even more so – than it had been during the war. But a few weeks before, as he was hitch-hiking his way from Aix-les-Bains with a suitcase full of watches, he picked up a ride in a rather elegant car. Somewhere along the road they stopped at a roadside inn for a drink. The driver sent Joszi in to find a table while he parked the car, but Joszi never saw the man, car, or his watches again. He had lost all he owned.

Penniless as he was, he could not move in on his girl-friend in Paris. He had to make some money first. So he took a room at Claridge's, confident that the money to pay the bill would turn up somehow. It did. Joszi bought himself a red-and-blue Buick, paid his hotel bill and was in business again. To crown it all, on this lucky day he ran into me in Clar-idge's bar.

Joszi admitted to me later that he had assumed that I, too, was in Paris on some sort of shady business. But he was not greatly surprised when I told him the real purpose of my presence in Paris. His old sense of rebellion against injustice was aroused, his boyhood Zionist education re-emerged, and he volunteered to put any of his contacts at my disposal. During the war he had been in close touch with the Maquis, of which Madame Bidault had been a member; and through a friend who was in the same Resistance cell as she, he could approach the wife of the present French Foreign Minister.

I pointed out to Joszi that of all the Frenchmen who might be inclined to help us, those in the Foreign Office were the least likely. He agreed that he should start with someone from a different stratum. What about a White Russian who was working for a foreign government and who therefore might have access to visas for exotic places? That sounded more like a man we wanted. I indicated that I would be glad to pay for the services we required, information that was well received by Joszi.

'What sort of numbers are you interested in?' he asked.

'Let's start with 3,000 visas at one dollar each.'

Joszi whistled. He was impressed.

Early the next morning, he telephoned to ask if I had a black suit. I said that I did, and he told me to expect him at Claridge's at about ten p.m. He would brief me on our meeting with the mysterious White Russian and give me a chance to get out of it if I did not agree to the terms. He arrived promptly at ten in a midnight-blue tuxedo, wearing the elegant suit with a perfectly natural air.

'The man you are going to meet is a Russian nobleman, a prince in fact, but he modestly calls himself Wladimir Kiewski. He is a personal friend of "the Ruler". (For reasons concerning current diplomacy, I must refer to his realm as "X".) He performed many favours for "the Ruler" while the latter was in exile. Now that the war is over, "the Ruler" has been reinstated in his country, which is on the threshold of great economic and social development. Kiewski came up with a brilliant idea: he wants to enlist artisans and craftsmen from among the displaced persons and promises them excellent conditions if they come to "X" and help to rebuild her.'

'All this sounds fine,' I said. 'But where do I come in? I'm

sure that Kiewski takes his duties seriously, and much as I
admire "the Ruler" and his great land, I want those people to
build up another country.'

'That's the problem,' said Joszi. 'To tell you the truth, I
don't have a definite plan at the moment. But during the
evening things may develop.'

We took the lift to the lobby, where I met Gisi Vega,
Joszi's elegant girl-friend. She was as tall as he and had long,
beautiful auburn hair, and an air of royalty. In the presence
of this glamourous couple I felt quite out of place in my old,
worn-out black suit. Gisi was completely in the picture and
had caught on to the nature of our enterprise. In Joszi's
Buick, as we were speeding to the famous night-club 'Monseigneur', Gisi leaned over and whispered in a conspiratorial
tone, 'Don't worry for a moment! You are sure to get what
you need from our friend.'

While most Parisians lived on insufficient rations, a small
but exceedingly luxurious black market flourished in various
eating-places and night-spots. Monseigneur was at that particular moment the 'in place'. Almost everybody was in
evening dress. Perhaps twenty violinists moved through the
room, never standing still, never congregating in one place as
ordinary orchestras do. They played and played, and the
place echoed the delightful mood. The head waiter received
Gisi and Joszi like old and highly respected *habitués*. We
were led to a corner table, and there we met the gentleman
whom we had come to see.

Wladimir Kiewski may not have been his real name but he
certainly looked like my vision of a Russian prince – tall,
sunburnt, with a shock of completely white hair over his high
forehead – and his brown eyes looked youthful and reliable.
Remembering Joszi's description of the man's activities and
vision, I looked at him and thought to myself: How shall we
ever lead him on our devious ways?

Joszi explained to Kiewski that we were celebrating a

reunion. I was the European representative of an influential American organization that was helping refugees (a brilliant idea Joszi had evidently just invented, since we had ignored the pertinent detail of my identity on our way to the meeting), and surely he and I would have many interests in common.

I cannot remember ever having attended a more elegant and sophisticated dinner-party before. Joszi had become a man of the world. He knew how to create the impression that he was a man involved in a great and important enterprise, but who still could take time to relax and spare an evening for good friends engaged in more sublime and humanitarian pursuits. Gisi, who honestly wanted to help, played her role as the lady of the evening with great *aplomb*. As a result, Kiewski felt secure in our company and began to complain about his lack of success in enlisting experts for distant land 'X'. Joszi patiently listened to his problems. Suddenly, as if bursting with an idea that had occurred to her on the spur of the moment, Gisi turned to me: wouldn't I, with my enormous connections and with the might of the American Army behind me, help our friend Kiewski? Joszi, more than delighted by his girl-friend's initiative, promised Kiewski that on the very next day we would explore ways in which I could turn his mission into a success.

When Kiewski asked Gisi for a dance, and Joszi and I remained alone, he said: 'In what way do you need the visas? Stamped in individual passports, as I hope you won't, or will a covering letter from the Consulate of "X" attached to a collective passport be sufficient?'

As we were not planning on obtaining individual passports for the DP's, I thought that the collective visa would be the answer to our needs. I told Joszi as much just as Gisi returned on Kiewski's arm.

The next day passed without a sign from Joszi. I began to wonder whom he had fobbed – Kiewski or me? I accused myself of having fallen for Joszi's facile optimism, but least I still had the 3,000 dollars I had promised Joszi for the 3,000 visas.

The following day, as my anger was turning to despair, Joszi entered my room without even knocking. He was full of apologies for keeping me waiting an entire day and profusely asked my forgiveness. He had had to handle Kiewski gently; he could not make this man of noble birth deviate from his sacred honesty and lofty principles. Also, he could not give himself away by suggesting to Kiewski something that was not utterly above-board and in line with the most correct procedures. Therefore it had taken an entire day to transact our business.

Naturally, I supposed that all this was only an explanation of why Joszi had failed to bring the documents he had so light-heartedly promised me two days before. Then he drew out a bulky manila envelope from his elegant, black brief-case and carefully and with great delicacy placed its contents on the coffee-table: 300 pages of stationery with the insignia of the ruler of 'X' on them.

'Each of those will serve as a covering letter for a list of 100 names,' Joszi announced. And in three green, flat boxes there were three rubber stamps carrying the lawful authority of the country of destination.

I literally gaped at the treasures in disbelief. But scrutinizing them, it became evident that everything was in perfect order. Kiewski had given us all the implements he considered necessary for us to help *him* do *his* job. I was about to explain how badly I felt for having misled such a fine man as Kiewski must be, but Joszi cut me short.

'Think nothing of it,' he said, 'You are doing your duty, and he is doing his.' And with this pronouncement, he pocketed the envelope in which I discreetly had placed thirty 100-dollar bills in payment for the superlative service rendered.

Some twenty-five years later, Joszi told me he had a confession to make: he had given only 1,000 dollars of our money to Kiewski, as a charitable contribution to his work. With the rest he had bought Gisi a diamond ring. I consoled him by agreeing that it was a gift she richly deserved for her part in the plot – and in general.

With Joszi's help, we now began to see a possible solution to our problem. I decided to turn Joszi's fictitious description of me into a reality. He had explained my function as that of the European representative of an American organization helping the survivors of the Holocaust; I decided to be just that.

At the time, it seemed that all high-powered organizations were known just by the capital letters abbreviating their title. We therefore decided to reduce the incredibly intricate organization and task of moving DP's out of Europe to a short and appropriate abbreviation. The name we needed was to imply that the organization had an American base, because questions were never asked when American authority and prestige came into play; it had to be clear that it was a non-profit humanitarian organization out to do good in a world so much in need of help; and obviously, the name had to indicate that we were servicing Jewish survivors of the Holocaust.

After much thought we came up with what sounded both dignified and impressive: The Jewish Refugees Welfare Society, Washington D.C. We decided then and there to write to Dani Shind in New York and ask him to register the society legally and to print stationery for us bearing, as was the style in the US, the names of the distinguished people who made up the board of directors. The fact is, however, that we never got around to doing so. Each time we were on the point of writing to Dani, asking him to make the necessary arrangements, we shrank from it. There was a faint feeling of the ridiculous in asking Dani, who had so much on his hands, to trouble himself with such details. Also, we could not face the idea of the tedious elderly ladies and gentlemen whose well-known names would adorn the stationery of our organization. After all, the purpose of the exercise was just to create a façade, a tool for the appearance of legality. In short, we simply went to a printer in Paris and ordered the stationery on the spot. We made up a list of respectable-sounding 'American' names in alphabetical order, and having promised the printers an extra bonus for speed, we became on that very same day the proud representatives of the Jewish Refugees Welfare Society, Washington D.C. – JRWS for short – and the representatives of the Consulate General of a generous and humanitarian state, which proved to be no less valuable.

To broaden my exploration of conditions in France, I decided to visit Marseilles, where the Mossad was well represented. The head of the team there was Shmariah Zamereth, who throughout his life in Palestine and thoughout the war had retained his American passport, rather than exchange it for one of mandatory Palestine. On the strength of this invaluable document he had worked for the Mossad in Europe even before America joined the Allied effort. Now an experienced operative, he was one of the first to be dispatched from Palestine back to Europe at the end of the war. In Marseilles he chose to live under the cover of a repatriated refugee from the camps. With the help of the reviving Jewish community there he obtained the necessary personal documents; his broken French, with the slight American accent, was explained by the fact that he had spent most of his youth in refugee camps, rather than in school. He told such a persuasive story that he was never asked for credentials or further proof of any kind.

Shmariah – now known as Rudi in Marseilles – had rented a small furnished flat overlooking the port. In the winding streets leading to his quarters, few, if any, foreigners were ever seen, and Shmariah felt that in this neighbourhood he was safe from surveillance by British agents.

His reaction to the news that the Mossad had decided to establish a European headquarters in Paris was ambivalent. France, he argued, was too obviously the ideal country for our work: the French mood was anti-British; the public and government were on our side and were ready, with much practical assistance, to alleviate the suffering of the survivors, whose fate they had shared. To establish a central office in Paris was to attract attention to our activities there and risk embarrassing the French by drawing British pressure on them. Nonetheless, he agreed that we had to have a European centre somewhere, and it would make little sense to establish it in the midst of less friendly surroundings. In the end, he accepted the fact that Paris was to be the headquarters of our future clandestine work.

Shmariah was reassured – and perhaps even a little impressed – when I reported on the visas to 'X' and the invention of the JRWS. He agreed that we now had two out of the four assets we needed, which changed the picture considerably. The two missing assets were transit visas to the friendly shores of France, and, above all, ships to finally transport the refugees to Palestine. Since his arrival, Shmariah had explored around the Côte d'Azur for large estates to rent and had found two or three places marvellously suited for what he had in mind: transit camps where the refugees could wait in relative seclusion until their departure.

After talking most of the night, we drove to one of the dream *châteaux* Shmariah had acquired on the coast near Marseilles. The estate encompassed a lovely little bay admirably suited for a boat to slip in, take on passengers and leave without attracting undue attention. A huge park around the main building sheltered it from the main road and surrounding estates. The owner of the property had been a wealthy French country squire unavoidably absent, as he was in jail for collaboration with the Nazis. The main building could temporarily house at least 200 refugees – and many more, as it turned out. Shmariah had obtained this wonderful estate from the regional *commissaire,* a young Gaullist activist to whom he had disclosed his true identity and aim. The rent, he told me quite contentedly, was less than for his two-room flat in Marseilles.

On the evening of my second day in Marseilles, Shmariah brought two associates to a meeting. Chanan Geismar (now known as Fernand in Marseilles) was born in France, had gone to Palestine and joined a kibbutz long before the war and had returned to Marseilles to work with Shmariah as an emissary of the Mossad. He was a practical man with, as he put it, the business sense of an Alsatian horse. He could be stingy and obnoxious in bargaining – useful talents, as his main responsibility was to be the fitting of ships. He had to order the work, supervise it and bargain for speed and prices within our means. Chanan possessed genuine French documents and needed no forged papers or imaginary identity. No one suspected him of being anything but a hard-working, hard-driving, French *entrepreneur.*

Shmariah's other companion, Willi Katz, also spoke excellent French, which was acquired in a Protestant high school in his native Bucharest before he left for Palestine. Like Shmariah and Chanan, he had joined a kibbutz but had retained the manners and wisdom of a diplomat of the old school. His task in Marseilles was to maintain contact with the official world and with other sources that might be helpful to our work.

At the meeting, first Willi reported on his trip to Belgium, arranged by the Mossad because the Jewish Brigade was stationed there. Its presence had attracted large numbers of refugees from Germany and Holland, and the Brigade established camps for them and began to organize their life in a civilized manner, providing them with schools, medical centres and so on.

Then we took a number of decisions: as soon as we had arranged for French transit visas, we would bring a ship to

Marseilles and fit her for transport. We resolved to order the *Asia,* the one boat left in Istanbul from the period of Lord Cranborne's letter, and registered her in the name of our old friend D'Andria. We also decided to send Willi back to Belgium in order to organize, with the help of the Brigade, some of the refugees there for departure on the *Asia.* We wanted to show our Belgian friends that there was some movement of refugees out of their country, for at present all they saw was a seemingly endless stream waiting for admission; and we wanted to give the refugees there some hope by releasing at least a small group from the dreary camps. Since we were establishing our centre in Paris, Marseilles was no longer as essential, and Willi became available for the opening of a new Mossad station in Brussels.

I returned to Paris for a decisive talk with Marcel Pages, Secretary-General of the Security Services in the Ministry of Interior. Ariel, the representative of the IZL in Paris, who had worked with us in Bucharest during the war, had cultivated Pages' trust and support and was prepared to introduce me to this key figure in the organization of a reliable operation to transport illegal refugees through France. It was with some foreboding and anguish that I faced this meeting with Pages, but I was fortunate to have been briefed by one who knew both Pages and France well.

Marc Jarblum, already an elderly man with the sadly smiling eyes of a *chassid,* was the head of the Zionist Organization of France. A socialist activist, he was the peer and close friend of many socialist leaders in France and other countries of Western Europe. He had spent the war in France and had suffered together with Blum and other leading socialists, and a bond of eternal friendship developed between him and them. Jarblum's flat was in the Latin Quarter, but there was nothing French about it. It had been the quarters of a Russian scholar and had come equipped with countless books on socialist theory and philosophy and a samovar that produced real tea. It was Jarblum who gave me the courage to see Pages the next day.

I found Marcel Pages, stern and full of authority, sitting at a large desk covered with dossiers and official documents, waiting for me to present my case. As I had rehearsed with Jarblum, I explained that the JRWS was anxious to move as many Jewish refugees as possible out of Europe. It was at present making arrangements to transport them to countries in Latin America and Africa and was in the process of renting and buying ships for this purpose. But, as Pages knew, ships were very hard to come by, and lack of space would limit the speed of our operation. The JRWS would, therefore, be grateful if it could, in case of need, keep some of the refugees on French soil until the arrival of the boat destined for their departure. It would guarantee departure in every case.

Pages listened to my request without interruption. His face was inscrutable. But when I finished he said, 'Monsieur, I served with the Free French Forces during this last war. I have seen the British "liberating" former French territories from Lebanon and Syria to Morocco. Believe me, I am prepared to do all I can to help the JRWS in the direction of Latin America and Africa.'

No clearer indication was ever given that a leading official of the French Government knew the destination of the refugees who would pass through French territory with official visas. No clearer indication was needed. A simple and efficient procedure was established: we would bring the Visa Department of the Ministry of Interior lists of the names of refugees from German camps, accompanied by a covering letter from the consulate of the country of destination certifying that the refugees would be admitted into that country. The Visa Department would stamp the list of names, thereby issuing the collective French transit visa necessary for the voyage through France from the German border to the port.

There was one condition: refugees could be brought into France from Displaced Persons camps in Germany only.

D'Andria arrived in Marseilles in February 1946, ahead of his ship, and settled down to work as if he had always lived there. He understood perfectly well that Chanan Geismar was now his boss and immediately established a smooth relationship with him. The *Asia* was registered in D'Andria's name, but he never pretended that she was anything but our property, destined to carry as many refugees as she possibly could.

'We used to take one passenger per ton,' D'Andria told Chanan when he arrived. 'Now, with more passengers available, how about taking ten times as many?'

The time had come to start worrying about the arrival of passengers for the *Asia*. The dockyard was working feverishly. The cubicles typical of our clandestine boats were built into the empty holds. These narrow cells obviously could serve no purpose other than the transport of people, but the workmen were at ease. They realized that they were engaged in an illegal operation, but they knew their government was firmly behind it at both the national and local level. What's more, the workmen received a bonus for their extra-curricular activity, although they had the vague feeling, often expressed in gruff remarks, that they were doing something for the benefit of the most pitiful victims of a common enemy.

Nahum Kraemer convened our co-ordinating committee, and I reported on progress in Marseilles. He suggested that we evacuate the refugees who had reached Belgium. As the overall Commander of the Haganah in Europe, Nahum wanted a clear division of risk: Belgium was the main hunting-ground for the tight and highly secretive operation 'Rechesh' – the procurement of arms for the Haganah from British arms stores and other sources. Munya Mardor was in charge of this branch. He and his men had established a transport unit, using British Army lorries, to move their goods. Their work was vital, and everything had to be done to avoid the risk of discovery. The presence in Belgium of Jewish refugees clamouring for emigration might attract British suspicions. Furthermore, British influence in Belgium was strong, and the presence of British Army units in the process of demobilization made it easy for the British to move around freely and stick their noses into other people's business. Nahum wanted Belgium for 'Rechesh'.

He agreed, however, that Mardor's transport command should be used to ferry refugees from Belgium to Marseilles. They were familiar with this stretch of roads as they had used them for the transport of arms, and we saw no other way of getting the refugees from Belgium through France, for the transit visas Pages had granted us were exclusively for transients from Germany.

When I reported this to Shmariah, he showed just a hint of glee: let the smart officers do a real job for once! These privileged ones were accustomed to moving mute boxes and pieces of metal. Let them try their hand, for once, with human beings, who talk and laugh and moan . . .

Munya Mardor's men worked well. With speed and quiet efficiency they requisitioned enough petrol from army petrol stations, first-aid kits from the infirmary and rations from army stores to service 500 people on a trip through the whole length of France. All of this was done on orders produced and signed by Mardor's expert forgers. Barely forty-eight hours after Nahum Kraemer had issued his instructions, Mardor was able to report that the convoy was ready for departure.

Captain Memi de Shalit of the Jewish Brigade (and a member of Haganah) was the only authentic officer of His Majesty's Forces to come along on this occasion. Accompanied only by his driver, he rode in front of the long convoy in a shining jeep. There were only thirty passengers to each truck, as Mardor wanted them to enjoy maximum comfort and keep them from reliving memories of other trips in military vehicles to very different destinations. Mobile kitchens and ambulances were attached. It had been easier to obtain the latter than Mardor had expected. He asked a British Major, Leon Shalit, to lend him two ambulances. Shalit, a Jew but not an officer of the Brigade, categorically refused this demand: the good name of the unit he commanded was at stake, and it should be at stake for more than two ambulances. Mardor raised his demands, and they were duly authorized.

When the convoy moved out, the civilian passengers and their belongings were carefully hidden from dubious eyes. Only the smart officers in their British uniforms were visible from afar. The convoy crossed into France with no questions asked – military convoys were a common sight – and the trip went by without incident.

On the outskirts of Marseilles, which the convoy reached at nightfall, it was met by Shmariah and Chanan. At this point the Mossad took charge and, in a battered French Ford directing the British lead-jeep, Shmariah conducted the convoy to the remote corner of the harbour where the *Asia* waited for her passengers. When the refugees boarded the ship that was to bring them to their new life, she was renamed the *Tel Hai*.

The tension and excitement of launching a boat filled with Jewish refugees destined for Palestine was not new to us. But somehow, no matter how many times this drama had been played out before, we never became *blasé*. And this sailing was, after all, a novel one: the first clandestinely organized large Mossad boat to sail from a West European country in peacetime. It appeared as if we were finally on our way to the top: the operation had gone without a single hitch – so far – and our optimism left little room for thoughts of failure. Unfortunately, optimism alone is not the key to success. The *Tel Hai* was caught by a British patrol off the coast of Palestine on 27 March 1946, and its passengers were interned in the Athlit detention camp.

At about the same time, my brother, Chagai, who had been assigned to Marseilles by the Mossad at the close of 1945, received an urgent summons from Shmariah. When he arrived at the office, to his surprise he found Shmariah cleaning a revolver. He told Chagai that just before he had been called, Hubert, one of his French associates, had phoned the office on the unlisted line. Shmariah was greatly stunned by the fact that Hubert knew this number. What was worse, Hubert informed him that a most urgent matter had compelled him to use the secret line and phone in direct contradiction to Shmariah's conspiratorial instructions.

The urgent matter was that a very handsome, tall, quietly moving and well-mannered 'Palestinian' had come to Hubert's house, and both Hubert and Shmariah sized the fellow up as a British spy! Hubert volunteered to liquidate him if Shmariah so ordered. But Shmariah was a prudent man. He decided to have Chagai investigate before he decided how to deal with the mysterious intruder. He finished fiddling with the revolver and pushed it over to where Chagai sat, but Chagai refused it. Shmariah just shrugged and asked Chagai to give him a ring in case he survived the interrogation of the suspect.

When Chagai met with him, the Palestinian told him the following story. He was from Tel Aviv and had joined the merchant marine; he was neither in the Palmach nor any other paramilitary organization. When his ship was docked in Alexandria, he attended a thanksgiving service in the local synagogue on the occasion of the British victory at El Alamein, and there he met a fellow-Palestinian by the name of Barpal. In the enthusiasm of meeting a fellow-countryman on such a felicitous occasion, Barpal disclosed his position as one of the heads of the Mossad. He also promised the young sailor that he would explore whether or not his maritime experience could be put at the disposal of illegal immigration.

The young man stayed on in Alexandria, and when weeks passed without a word, he began to assume that Barpal must have forgotten his promise or lost his address. It was about that time that he learned from a Norwegian sailor that somebody called Rudi (Shmariah) was involved in some Jewish maritime business in Marseilles. The Norwegian invited him to come along as a stowaway on his ship to Marseilles, and he readily took up the offer. When he arrived in Marseilles, he tried to contact fellow-Jews where they were most likely to be found – in the synagogue. It was there that he met Hubert, and here he was.

Chagai was instantly convinced that the story was true. A contrived story would have contained fewer elements that would be easy to check. He phoned Shmariah and reported that the man was genuine. Shmariah told him to bring the stranger over. The Mossad now had in its ranks a future Admiral of the Israel Navy, Mordechai Limon (Mokka, for short) – who would become famous for his successful command of the mission to spirit away Israeli gunboats under French embargo from the harbour of Cherbourg in January 1970.

Mokka's flair for handling the unexpected with verve and dash became known during his first important Mossad mission. Shortly after his recruitment, he was put in command of a large ship that Dani had sent from America, and which had been fitted at Bayonne in the southwest of France. Mokka was taking her to Bulgaria, where she was to pick up a transport from Rumania and Hungary.

But a few days before Mokka's ship left Bayonne, something jarring occurred in Haifa, at one of the links of the Mossad network. A Palyam sailor suspected by the British was searched by the Customs Police at Haifa port. He was asked to undress, his clothes were inspected at their seams, his pockets turned inside out – and the result of it all was that a tiny slip of paper fell into the hands of His Majesty's Customs authorities. On this tiny slip of paper was written the line from the Bible which was the basis for coded telegrams to and from illegal ships. The British gleefully advised their branches that supervised illegal immigration that there had been a major breakthrough: the Haganah code was in their hands.

But they had not reckoned with the Haganah Chief of Communications. He had foreseen exactly such a mishap for some time now and had prepared a new, infinitely more sophisticated code system according to the lights of the day – practically unbreakable. The new system had been distributed to all wireless posts. Even if our man had not been caught, in a week or two all posts would have received the flash sign from Gideon: 'By the three hundred men that lapped will I save you' (Judges 7:7). This was the last message in the old code. It was the instruction to change over to the new one.

As soon as Haganah headquarters learned what had happened, the central transmitting station in Tel Aviv flashed the message long held in readiness. Within an hour of the search at Haifa, radio-operators of our far-flung network from Stockholm to New York, from the high seas to the Tel Aviv flat of Golda Meir, all switched over to the new code.

As it happened, Mokka was playing a game of backgammon on deck when the radio-operator came up from below excitedly waving an incoming message. It was astonishing: 'Return to Palestine at once without approaching the Yugoslav coast and without taking refugees from any other port.' It was in Hebrew, and was signed 'The Mossad'. It sounded peculiar: the Mossad would never have given such a drastic instruction to the commander of one of its main ships without a single word of explanation. And that was the first cable the radio-operator had ever handled which was expressly signed 'The Mossad'. But the give-away was that the message had been transmitted in the discarded code that the British had intercepted a few days earlier.

Mokka gave a low whistle, took a pencil from his pocket and jotted his reply on the form for cables: 'Admiralty, Mediterranean Command: Save it, you lappers,' paraphrasing the Lord's reply to Gideon. Then he turned back to his game of backgammon, as his ship continued steadily towards her destination.

Four months had passed since I had arrived in Paris to accept my new assignment from Ben Gurion, and the grim winter had turned into a spring of unusual promise. The young men and women of the Mossad all over Europe were blossoming in the atmosphere of cloak-and-dagger operations, as untapped sources of imagination and ingenuity brought about visionary feats: whole convoys were smuggled across borders, boats from America were refitted clandestinely and made their way out of Mediterranean ports, documents were culled from exotic sources. Being stationed at the hub of all these operations could well make one's head spin. But for all the tension and excitement of that spring, one small event – not the kind written up in history or woven into legend – overshadows all else in my memory: the arrival of Zivia Lubetkin.

Towards the end of April, word spread like wildfire through the Haganah community in Paris that Zivia Lubetkin, one of the few surviving leaders of the 1943 Warsaw Ghetto uprising, was on her way from Warsaw, via London and Paris, to Palestine. This young woman, whom we had never met, commanded our awe, and her coming had about it the aura of the arrival of an empress. She symbolized to us the ultimate in personal courage and heroism, and we awaited her in a mood of anticipation tinged with anguish, because we also felt the magnitude of the tragedy that had befallen European Jewry. Venya, who had been so close to the struggle in Poland during our stay in Istanbul, had recently arrived in Paris, and he and I admitted to each other a fear that she might accuse us of having done too little.

As the time of Zivia's arrival drew near, we tried to learn from people who had seen her what this woman was actually like. The atmosphere was a throw-back to a time before the age of modern communications, when word-of-mouth notices passed among the people that some regal personage was on the way. Finally it was Venya and I who went to the station to meet her.

Zivia Lubetkin was dressed exactly like the partisans in newsreels: she wore breeches, boots and a cap. Though her expression was serious, it expressed no bitterness, but her lips were set in a grim, determined line. I noted that one corner of her mouth was pulled down, as though she were looking at us with great scorn. But this was more my imagination than her intent, as we realized when we began talking. And aside from her clothing and the look of sadness in her eyes, she seemed like a perfectly ordinary woman – not at all like the extraordinary creature we had made her.

We began our long-awaited talk as if we were taking up the thread of a conversation that had been interrupted. Zivia was eager to hear about our current work, and we described our participation in what had been done during the war as well. Used to hearing reports from men under her command, she interrupted only once: 'Never say "We did *everything* necessary," ' she corrected me at one point. 'Say, "We tried, as best we could." '

Thinking back on that short interlude with Zivia Lubetkin, it is somehow easier to understand why her coming and her presence had such an indelible impact upon us in that eager, wild spring of 1946: she gave us a sense of perspective on ourselves.

(20)

La Spezia

FOR THE SURVIVORS of the Holocaust, the Jews of Palestine and their emissaries in Europe, the month of April 1946 was marked by a series of headline events that were to crystallize our policy for the immediate future. On the eighteenth of the month, the League of Nations in Geneva voted itself out of existence and turned its physical assets over to the United Nations. A week later, on the twenty-fifth, the Big Four foreign ministers opened their conference in Paris to settle on peace terms with Hitler's five satellite countries.

On that very same day, a tragedy occurred in Tel Aviv that further escalated the struggle between the Jews of Palestine and the British. During the spring in which the rest of the world was turning towards the business of peace, in Palestine the Freedom Fighters for Israel (Stern Gang) raided a British military installation and killed seven soldiers. The Zionist Organization dissociated itself from such practices, but Ben Gurion explained to the British that the continuation of the White Paper policy on immigration made cooperation between the Jewish Agency and the mandatory government impossible. The Jews of Palestine were not at war with the mandatory administration; and while a clear-cut answer to our demand for the admission of 100,000 refugees was delayed, ever-harsher police measures were employed to keep the refugees out and suppress the activities of what the British came to call 'private armies'.

Five days after the incident, the Anglo-American Inquiry Commission issued its long-awaited report. Based on its finding that the partition of Palestine was impractical, it recommended the establishment of a bi-national state in Palestine. On the question of immigration, however, the committee reached the unanimous conclusion that 100,000 survivors of the Holocaust should be admitted to Palestine.

Clement Attlee, the British Prime Minister, was so taken aback by the recommendation on immigration that he reneged on the promise he had made to Richard Crossmann, one of the members of the Commission, that if the Anglo-American Inquiry Commission reached unanimous decisions, they would be implemented by the British without question. President Truman, on the other hand, came out in full support of admitting 100,000 refugees to Palestine. This move had become a matter of primary humanitarian importance to him. And although he was bitterly accused of succumbing to the pressure of the 'Jewish vote', the fact of the matter is that he supported only the recommendation regarding the refugees; the other, he felt, was a question of long-range policy and international law that demanded long and careful study.

British wrath against the American President was heightened by the unpleasant fact that at the same time they had to defend Palestine against the survivors of the Holocaust, it was necessary to ask the United States for a loan to bridge them over the financial difficulties that had begun to beset Britain's declining imperial power. In this light, British reaction against their senior partner was understandable. England had not yet adjusted to the role of client-state, and the visions and postures of its great imperial past died hard.

With all these sensitive nerves exposed, Attlee decided to

strike back in the most vulnerable direction. On 1 May he stated in the House of Commons that there was no question of admitting 100,000 Jews into Palestine as long as the Jews had not disbanded their 'private armies' and surrendered their arms to the mandatory government. Insistent in its belief that there was no differentiation between the military arm of the Jewish Agency (the Haganah) and the smaller dissident groups (the IZL and Freedom Fighters for Israel), the British Government did much to unite Jewish public opinion in Palestine. Barely eighteen months after the victory over Nazi Germany, His Majesty's Government decided that decisive and energetic action must be taken against the entire Jewish community in Palestine. If the cancellation of the Balfour Declaration was not to be achieved with the consent of the Jewish Agency, the dissolution of the Jewish National Home in Palestine would have to be achieved by force.

Attlee's attitude was not only an open threat to our cause in the widest sense of the word, it caused attitudes to harden on both sides of the dispute between the British and the Jews of Palestine. Yet for the first time, we began to sense that public opinion among the other Allied nations, especially the United States, was clearly in our favour; and at least one member of the Mossad decided to put this change in atmosphere to good use.

Yehudah Arazi was a dare-devil virtuoso with the imaginative flair that made him the Haganah's star performer in Europe until 1948. My contact with him that spring was largely on the telephone, for he was operating in Italy while I was at the Paris headquarters. Yehudah had arrived in Europe in August 1945 in the uniform of an officer of the Free Polish Forces. After changing it for the more convenient uniform of a British sergeant, he quickly used his magnetic personality, cool analytical mind and indelible experience as an inspector of the Jerusalem CID (where he worked as a double agent) to organize a small Haganah empire within the 462nd Royal

Army Special Service Corps. Vehicles and supplies were made available to him by Haganah men within the celebrated unit who accepted his overall command without question. Refugees were transported, fed and assembled in specially created camps – all facilities supplied by His Majesty's forces or by black-market supplies purchased by Yehudah's men with their liquor rations. For one case of whiskey, Arazi bartered from the Italian Navy a detailed map of all the minefields in Italian territorial waters.

Yehudah's way of working precluded his being a member of a team. On close personal terms with his superiors, he regarded Eliahu Golomb, the leader of the Haganah, as his peer. He had little time for the 'kibbutznik idealists' of the Mossad and had an ambivalent attitude towards its Chief. Being the more colourful of the two, he objected to Shaul Avigur's notorious prudence, even when he knew that it was well advised. As the Chief's adjutant, I became Arazi's channel of communication whenever he needed the Chief's approval, without wishing to accept his authority.

Yehudah's organization continued to grow. Uniformed soldiers transported refugees in trucks released for that purpose with the consent of loyal officers, and on the strength of dispatch orders prepared by the specially skilled personnel on Arazi's staff. Palmach escorts arrived in Italy to assist in the management of transit camps, to prepare the immigrants for the strenuous trip on the tiny boats, and to accompany them on their voyage to Palestine. Radio-operators came to man the expanding network of posts in Italy, as elsewhere in Europe.

Every one of the small boats Arazi sent from Italy, starting with the *Dalin* and its thirty-five passengers, eluded detection by the British. Their size enabled Arazi to conduct his operation in complete secrecy, but that same characteristic was an unsatisfactory solution for the ever-growing number of refugees from displaced persons camps arriving in Italy and pressing for emigration to Palestine.

Arazi would never have admitted that he was impressed by the much larger number of people who departed from Marseilles in the spring of 1946. But having carefully solved the problems of clandestine departures, he decided, after the voyage of the *Tel Hai*, to obtain a larger boat – into which about 1,000 people could be crammed (by our standards) – to bring her into a regular port and to fit her there properly. The ship he acquired was the *Fede,* and he secured the whole-hearted cooperation of the port authorities of La Spezia on the Italian Riviera to fit it and have the transport ready to move.

Under the command of the scholarly and introverted Sergeant Shalhevet Freier and the self-confident and lively Sergeant Yisrael Libertovsky, the first large transport converged on the La Spezia area from two directions. It was an unlucky day. At the pre-arranged meeting point, troops appeared unexpectedly. There was Arazi's motorcar, which the two sergeants knew so well, but there with it, pushing him on, were two Italian police vehicles filled with *carabinieri* armed to the teeth, ready for action. The Italian police had got wind of the movement of people. The British vehicles did not fool them; there was a trick somewhere – of this they were certain. They were equally convinced that Arazi was the mastermind behind some political scandal. All during the confused argument between the 'British' officers and the Italian police, the refugees sat bundled in their canvas-covered lorries, aware that something had gone totally wrong.

As the convoy of passengers was stopped by the police, a thorough search took place on the ship in port. Captain Moshe Rabinowitz, the Palyam man in charge of the boat, was placed under arrest in his cabin. The searchers told him that the police were convinced they were engaged in smuggling Polish fascists out of the country into Franco's Spain.

Arazi decided on a desperate measure to get out of the situation: he told the suspicious Italians the truth. A few of

the refugees were called out of the trucks and asked to roll
up their sleeves to show the abashed Italians the concentra-
tion-camp numbers tatooed into their forearms. Some of the
carabinieri were overcome with sympathy. The two sergeants
convinced them to let the refugees board the waiting ship. It
was imperative to return the lorries to their bases before their
absence was discovered by the Military Police and some new
calamity developed.

In the confusion, Arazi changed into clothes more suitable
for a refugee and joined the sombre procession. Once on
board he took full command of the new situation. Now the
British came upon the scene: a gunboat placed itself squarely
in front of the *Fede* and closed the harbour.

Arazi was now to show his real capacity. His well-laid
plans had gone wrong; and though the British themselves did
not yet realize that the head of the Mossad in Italy was at
last in their hands, he was in effect a prisoner on the boat he
had intended to be his triumph. With doggedness and insight,
he proceeded to turn this apparently stunning defeat into an
outstanding victory for the Mossad and the campaign it was
fighting.

The British surrounded the *Fede* and addressed a curt
order to her commander: disembark immediately or we shall
take you off by force. Arazi, in his new role as the representative of the refugees, gave the British the first intimation
of what they were up against. Orders had been issued, he
announced, for the ship to be blown up with everybody on
board the moment a British soldier laid hands on an immigrant with the intention of forcing him back to the hated
European mainland. The refugees were desperate. Unless the
British troops were withdrawn from the port immediately, he
could not answer for their safety. The British, in doubt about
the seriousness of the threat, retreated to ponder their next
move. The port area, however, remained sealed off by tanks
and a British warship anchored alongside the *Fede*.

Arazi exploited this opportunity. Carried away by the unusual absence of censorship or the need for further secrecy, he sent telegrams over the *Fede*'s radio to the leaders of the Big Powers – Attlee, Truman and Stalin: 1,000 survivors of Hitler's death camps were crowded into a small ship in an Allied port and were besieged by a huge force of British tanks, warships and infantry.

Thousands of Italians crowded the port daily to watch the unfolding drama. Their sympathy was clearly on the side of the victims. Arazi, happy in his new element, fanned Italian feelings by daily speeches from the port gates. He explained the plight of the immigrants cooped up in the old ship, their hatred for Europe and bitter memories of torture and death and their one wish to build their lives in Palestine. As the siege continued, the British moved their troops farther away from the *Fede,* but unrest in the city grew: demonstrations were held demanding the release of the *Fede;* and the British Army commander's house was attacked and all its windows smashed. Army reinforcements moved into La Spezia and added tension to the ugly temper. Reporters converged on the port city from all over the West. Our struggle for free immigration had never been better covered or advertised more vociferously.

Arazi went one step further: with the acquiescence of the municipality, a sign appeared over the port gates bearing the inscription 'The Gate of Zion', and Italian and blue-and-white Zionist flags adorned the quay. He held daily press conferences on board, showed the curious journalists 'immigration certificates' of his own creation and quoted liberally from the Bible, the League of Nations Mandate for Palestine and the Balfour Declaration in order to assert the right of the Jews to return to their homeland.

The country most affected by the events in La Spezia was, of course, Palestine. Public opinion expected the Jewish Agency to take an open stand in defence of the prisoners of the *Fede*. Demonstrations and expressions of solidarity took place on every level. The Political Department of the Jewish Agency was in constant touch with the office of the High Commissioner. The mandatory government counted on the wisdom of the Political Department to dissociate itself from the rousing buccaneer on board the illegal ship. The Jewish Agency had never taken a stand against illegal immigration, but neither had it *openly* identified itself with the 'breach of law' committed by the organizers of unlicensed immigration and the immigrants themselves.

The head of the Political Department, Moshe Sharett, and the Chief of the Mossad, were in touch with Paris by phone and cable. Shaul Avigur had realized that no force on earth could restrain Yehudah Arazi once he had been crossed by the British. He decided to back Yehudah without compromise, although his very nature rebelled against the open admission of our clandestine activity. But now that the battle was on, and the commander on the spot had set the course of events, Avigur had to support him unflinchingly. Tactfully but unperturbed, the Chief rejected Sharett's exhortations for restraint and prudence. He refused to accept the premise that larger issues were at stake and would suffer if we continued the shrill conflict surrounding the *Fede*. I, in turn, would call La Spezia every evening and reassure Arazi's contact that there was nothing to worry about – the Chief was behind his grandiose spectacle.

Encouraged by his public-relations success, Arazi prepared the next step in his campaign: a hunger strike. Crowds gathered around the port gates, where a new board had been hung next to 'The Gate of Zion'. It had two numbers on it: one denoting the number of hours of the hunger strike, and another the number of refugees who had lost consciousness from lack of food. As the two figures steadily mounted, the crowds outside the port swelled into a threatening demonstration that the British tanks held in check with difficulty.

Strikes flared up in the city. In nearby Genoa, port workers went on strike in sympathy. The situation was becoming grave.

By the sixty-third hour of the hunger strike, the deck of the *Fede* was covered with unconscious refugees. Those who fainted were offered food by the Palyam men, but the majority refused to touch it. Not a sound came from the ship tied to the quayside. No moans, no cries: it was by now too much of an effort for the refugees to cry out. But to the crowd of spectators watching the refugees fainting on the deck, the silence which pervaded the ship seemed more ominous than any cries could have been.

That day Arazi held another press conference. He told the assembled newspapermen that because of their previously weak condition, some of the refugees' lives were in danger, but they refused to break the hunger strike. He stated that he would issue no more press *communiqués* until the boat was released. He refused to see representatives of the British Embassy who wished to talk to him and told the Palmach guards at the gates not to let them in. At the same time he sent a cable to Clement Attlee warning that he would be held personally responsible for any loss of life on the ship, as it was in Attlee's hands to let the ship go.

Weakened, yet obstinate, the refugees carried on their strike. For them this was no political game. They had come a long and hard way – through the ghettos of Eastern Europe, through 'selection-actions' by the extermination commandos of the Nazi machine, through concentration camps. Now they again faced starvation, but they refused to surrender. Better starving than remaining in Europe; better death itself than return to the hated camps.

Overcome by the hunger strike on board the *Fede* and the realization that there was no hope for a humanitarian gesture on the part of the British Government, the hard-liners in Jerusalem, led by Golda Meir, won the day. In solidarity with the prisoners of the *Fede,* the leaders of the Jewish Agency went on a hunger strike that was to last until the release of the ship and the arrival of her passengers.

In La Spezia, Arazi received messages of sympathy from such people as Italy's first post-war Premier, Alcide de Gasperi; from the Admiral commanding the Italian Fleet; and from many an ordinary citizen outraged by the suffering on board the imprisoned ship. He also had the benefit of the excellent work of the Mossad representative Ada Sereni, the widow of the Labour leader and philosopher, Enzo Sereni, who had died behind enemy lines when he was caught by the Nazis after parachuting into occupied Italy. With the resurgence of Italian democracy, Ada Sereni – herself of a distinguished Italian family and a born diplomat – had established a network of political connections that were able to move mountains in a country most sympathetic to the victims of Nazism and Fascism.

In the seventy-fifth hour of the hunger strike, two British Embassy cars drove up outside the port gates. The group that emerged included high-ranking army officers, a representative of the British Embassy in Rome, and Harold Laski, the Chairman of Britain's governing Labour Party. Laski was on his way to a Socialist Conference in Florence when the venerable leader of Italy's Jewish community, Raphaele Cantoni, interceded with him on behalf of the refugees in La Spezia.

Arazi turned down Laski's proposal that the refugees return to the camps established by the British in Italy and await their turn for immigration to Palestine. Patiently he explained to Laski the refugees' determination to fight for their right to go to Palestine now. To the utter shock of the British party leader, Arazi then proceeded to announce that the refugees had decided to die for their demands: unless they were allowed to sail, ten refugees would commit suicide on the deck in public every day, until only a coffin-ship of bodies would be left in La Spezia port. The British could then dispose of the refugees as they saw fit. The first ten, Arazi told Harold Laski, had volunteered. The 'operation' would begin the morning after their talk.

Laski reported to his colleagues in London that a lunatic was leading a group of 1,000 desperate men. They were ready to go to the bitter end. What had begun as a calamity was turning into catastrophe. To Arazi he explained that he was not in a position to make decisions. But if Arazi agreed to call off the hunger strike and all ensuing action, he would faithfully present the case of the *Fede* to Britain's Prime Minister and to the Foreign Secretary, Ernest Bevin.

Arazi accepted this offer, but attached three conditions to it: neither British nor Italian police would enter the port while the reply from London was being awaited; the Italian police officer who had openly shown his sympathy with the Jews and had been arrested by the British must be released and reinstated immediately; and a time limit was fixed for Laski's endeavours. Laski accepted all three conditions and the truce came into immediate effect.

The truce was agreed upon just before Passover, the Jewish holiday commemorating the Exodus from Egypt. Arazi decided to celebrate Passover eve in the port of La Spezia in a fashion suitable to the occasion. The entire port was decorated and illuminated with soft lights. Long tables laden with delicacies sent over by the Jewish community of Italy delighted the hundreds of invited guests, among them the local authorities and representatives of the citizens of the town that had adopted the unfortunate refugees with moving emotion. An artist prepared special medals and ribbons commemorating their feat and these were presented to the police officer who had been arrested for his show of solidarity with the refugees, as well as to those refugees who had refused to break their fast, thereby endangering their lives.

Addressing the assembled guests and the refugees around the festive tables, Arazi declared that the *Fede* was prepared to repatriate the Italian prisoners of war from the Middle

East as a token of gratitude to the Italian people, once she was allowed to sail. Since the British had repeatedly declared that repatriation of prisoners was delayed by a lack of shipping, the ceremony and Arazi's offer was the sensation of the entire Italian press. The Mossad was the hero of Europe's public opinion.

Laski kept his word. Although he needed more time than he had asked for, he finally was able to communicate that the British Government was ready to compromise: 679 certificates would be allocated to the passengers of the *Fede* out of the monthly allocation of 1,500 certificates. The remainder would proceed to Palestine as soon as more certificates became available. Arazi, encouraged by the waves of sympathy that surrounded his struggle in the European press and in Palestine, refused to accept half-measures. The ominous threats of the still imprisoned refugees were fresh in everybody's mind.

Thirty-three days after they had captured the boat, on 8 May 1946, the British surrendered. All the immigrants could go to Palestine at once. Arazi was on the threshold of total victory.

Now that the transport had been legalized and there was no further danger that the ship would be impounded by the British, Arazi arranged a second boat for the comfort of the passengers who had already suffered so much and divided them between the two. They were re-named *Eliahu Golomb* and *Dov Hos,* after two leaders of the Haganah who had died not long before.

The passengers, who more than six weeks earlier had attempted to depart furtively, were given a rousing fanfare as the Italian pilot guided them out of the port and into the open sea that led to their freedom. Arazi turned the command back to Moshe Rabinowitz, gracefully descended the rope-ladder into the pilot's motor-boat and returned to the mainland. His victory was complete.

(21)

'Black Saturday'

THE SHOWDOWN in Palestine came on 29 June 1946. Twelve days after Palmach units had destroyed every bridge connecting Palestine with the surrounding countries, the British launched a counter-offensive. The huge army they had amassed, together with the Palestine Police, implemented an operation that had been in preparation for some time. It was directed against the entire Jewish community, but its primary target was the structure of the Haganah.

Before dawn, a large number of villages – mostly kibbutzim – were surrounded by British units. At the same time the main building of the Jewish Agency in Jerusalem was occupied by British troops and searched; and the Central Committee Offices of the Histadrut in Tel Aviv were invaded and their files torn apart for evidence of a connection between the Histadrut and the Haganah, which was known to use the Histadrut building as a meeting-place. It was Saturday, the day of rest.

Curfew was imposed on all the larger towns and a meticulous search was begun throughout the country. Slowly the troops unfolded collapsible iron cages secured with barbed wire. In full view of the encircled population, the soldiers prepared the kennel into which they were soon to cram thousands of prisoners for identification and later detention.

The targets of these preparations flexed their muscles. To cover up for the suspect members of the Haganah, specifically activists and soldiers of the Palmach, it was tacitly understood that everyone would refuse to give his name. The laconic answer of each person interrogated was, 'I am a Jew from the Land of Israel.'

The soldiers gave vent to their pent-up fury. They had suffered from disobedience, provocation, scorn and terror long enough; now their moment had come. About 3,000 men and women were taken from the villages. As they had refused to identify themselves, the British brought them to detention camps in Sinai, where they would be given time to crack and change their minds. In a few places, hidden arms caches were found and sequestered. In others, lists of names were confiscated in the hope that one or another would be the list of members of the Palmach. The main purpose of the exercise was to break the spirit of the Jewish community, frighten the people and their leaders and induce them to submit to British decree.

Ben Gurion was with us in Paris the day these violent clashes occurred. He was on his way home from an extended trip to the United States, where he had sought the consolidation of Jewish opinion in favour of the struggle for the 100,000 certificates and mobilized support for the idea of a Jewish State in Palestine. He was booked to leave France on 2 July. Much as we pleaded with him to be careful and not to let himself fall into the hands of the British waiting to catch him and put him out of action, he would not listen to such caution. Perhaps it made him even more determined not to show any sign of regard for his own person.

The Mossad's secret radio picked up the first indication of the coming showdown on Saturday, 29 June: Yagur, a kibbutz near Haifa, was surrounded by the units of the 6th British Paratroop Division. Minutes after the first flash, we heard that about a dozen other kibbutzim, known as strongholds of the Haganah and bases of the Palmach, found themselves surrounded as they awoke to the hot summer day of rest. It was clear from the urgently transmitted messages that we were confronted not with an isolated attack, but with a synchronized assault on a network of defence establishments throughout the country.

I phoned Shaul Avigur and gave him a brief survey of the incoming news. Then I called Ruth, but she had just received a résumé of much the same baffling details over the phone from London. Finally, I went to the Royal Monceau, where Ben Gurion was staying, to report. As I entered his room, he was listening with a grim face to Ruth's telephoned report. Avigur came in too. A bit later, Ruth appeared in person, accompanied by two of the emissaries of Hehalutz, both members of kibbutzim that were at that very minute surrounded by the Red Berets.

Gradually more and more members of the Haganah team in Paris arrived in Ben Gurion's room. They had heard about what was happening at home on the French radio and from private sources. Nobody bothered to ask questions. Furtive glances stole from time to time at the 'Old Man' sitting on the couch, deep in thought. His face expressed no emotion. He did not utter a sound. He was visibly absorbed by his own thoughts. Nobody dared to interfere with them by asking the questions that were on all our lips.

At intervals, a runner from the secret radio station appeared with announcements of details. The news grew worse. In several places British soldiers behaved with uncommon cruelty, dragging their victims into the cages, often by their hair, in order to break their resistance to the interrogation. Floors and walls were ripped open with bayonets to reveal hidden arms caches. Much damage was caused to the property of the kibbutz members, who were imprisoned in the iron cages while their houses were torn apart.

Then came the news we had feared the most: police, supported by army personnel, descended upon the members of the Jewish Agency Executive and arrested whomever they were able to find. In callous disregard for Orthodox sensitivities, they carried away the venerable Rabbi Fishman on the Sabbath. The members of the Executive, together with other 'political prisoners' – the heads of the Histadrut and the Jewish municipalities – were brought to the Latrun detention camp at the foot of the Judean Hills.

Each time the runner from the radio station opened the door and made his way through the crowded room, Ben Gurion would read the message and hand it to the Chief. After brief scrutiny of the text, Avigur would read it out in his toneless voice to the rest of us. All barriers of secrecy seemed to have disappeared. We were like people shipwrecked on an island in a hostile ocean, feeling great warmth towards one another and a rage of fury because we were so far away in a secure place while our comrades – as well as our wives and children – were exposed to an immensely superior enemy.

Shortly after eleven p.m., a call came through from the radio station: no further transmission would take place before the next morning and there was no substantial change in the situation.

'I am going for a walk,' Ben Gurion announced, as everybody stood up to end the long day pressed together in the near-silent room.

Instinctively, we formed an aisle to let the 'Old Man' pass towards the door. Each one of us represented a branch of vital Haganah activity: the men of the Mossad, people who procured arms, one or two radio-operators and maritime escorts for our boats, emissaries of the youth movements who were in Europe to train youngsters for kibbutz life. Ben Gurion turned to each as he passed. 'What do you think we ought to do now?' he asked as he stared unblinkingly into each pair of eyes. And each one replied according to his mission: we must buy more arms, as the final showdown is at hand; we must organize more youth for the battles of the near future; we must increase the speed of our work. Ben Gurion was not satisfied with any of these answers. I was standing next to the door, and he spared me the question. Instead he said, 'Take your car. We are going for a little drive.'

I drove into the warm summer night, criss-crossed the Bois de Boulogne and continued up the Avenue Foch. At the Arc de Triomphe, I glanced at my passenger for a sign to turn towards his hotel. But although he was sitting next to me, Ben Gurion was worlds away. I could feel his mind at work like a calculating machine dissecting details, conjuring up alternatives and gradually constructing a coherent scheme. His face was expressionless. His sad eyes looked into an infinite distance. I think he was so absorbed in his inner self that he was not aware of my presence or of the fact that we were driving through the 'City of Lights'. I must have driven the length and width of Paris several times. On the horizon, the first signs of the new day appeared and the birds began to chirp.

We were at the Arc de Triomphe again, and I peered at my silent passenger. Luckily for me, he made a slight sign in the direction of the Royal Monceau. As I stopped the car and hurried to his side to help him alight, he had already opened the door. He stopped for a split second to turn to me. 'I'll tell you what we must do,' he continued the interrogation of several hours before. 'We must establish a Jewish State.' Then I was alone. Ben Gurion had already disappeared into the hotel.

I went directly to the office and found Shaul Avigur at his desk. 'I believe I have witnessed the thought process that led to the decision on the proclamation of Independence,' I told him. He made me repeat the story again and again and warned me to remember the exact words Ben Gurion had used.

Before I had time to change or get some breakfast, Ben Gurion appeared at the office and told Avigur to get all our emissaries together. 'We shall hold a council of war. We must make plans quickly.' Ben Gurion was now in full control. The emissaries gathered without wasting a moment, grateful for the invitation. On a day like this, we wanted company and the opportunity to exchange news and thoughts. Ben Gurion presided over the meeting. He demanded more and bigger ships. There was to be an arrival of an illegal boat at least once every week. We had to prove that our spirit was unbroken, that resistance continued, that we would not cease our activities until we reached our goal. 'We are on the way to statehood,' he proclaimed as he closed our deliberations several hours later.

Three days after that 'Black Saturday', on 2 July, I went to Greece to discuss with Benyamin, the man in charge of our operations there, ways of implementing Ben Gurion's call for larger ships and more frequent sailings. I travelled via Marseilles to spend time with Shmariah and hear his views on the Greek situation. He was familiar with it, and I wanted to ask him whether the facilities Greece offered could be exploited particularly for the fitting of boats. Marseilles had been worked too intensively during the past few months, and British interference there might become too strong for our French friends and allies.

Increasing British pressure on the Greek Government had made the movement of 'illegal' refugees more difficult there too. British agents followed Greek sailors connected with us, interfered with their normal work patterns and spoke threateningly to them about involvement in illegal immigration. 'The Goose' and other friends were worried that Greece would go so far as to close her hospitable door to us, just as she had done on the eve of the war. Shmariah warned against the precipitate evacuation of Greece: he counselled caution, but opposed the total abandonment of the useful base, despite the growing pressure there.

On the same day as I arrived in Marseilles, a daring action was being carried out a day's sailing distance off the coast of Palestine. For a long time we had dreamt of developing a ruse to save our expensive ships from confiscation by the British at each intercepted arrival. Now that Dani was able to buy relatively new vessels in America, compared with the junk available on the European market, we were even more anxious to develop a method by which the ships could be used for more than one trip. I never found out who was the father of the simple yet daring idea we applied – perhaps it was Stefano D'Andria, our faithful friend since the days of Istanbul. In any case, without him and his old boats we could not have instituted the new trick.

D'Andria owned a Turkish boat called the *Akbel*. It must have been older than the ship on which the Turks took Istanbul in the fifteenth century: moaning and groaning, she had slowly made her way from Izmir to Marseilles. No one honoured her with a glance once Dani's much better ships, the *Bilboa* and the *Wedgewood,* two World War Two corvettes, arrived from America. The *Wedgewood* was at Yehudah Arazi's disposal; the *Bilboa* was to depart from France.

D'Andria proposed that the *Bilboa* and the *Akbel* rendezvous beyond Palestinian territorial waters. Even if the British spotted the *Bilboa,* they would not dare sequester her on the high seas, for this would clearly be an act of piracy. The illegal passengers then could be transferred from the *Bilboa* to the *Akbel*. They would be extremely uncomfortable in the wretched old boat, but only for twenty-four hours: the British Navy would dutifully relieve them as soon as they entered the territorial waters of Palestine. And the British would be stuck with the *Akbel,* not with the *Bilboa* which would by that time be on her way to a European port to fetch another group of refugees. The same operation could be performed repeatedly, using another ship of the same category, age and value as the *Akbel*.

Yehoshua Ben Nun, a hefty man from Kibbutz Ginnosar on Lake Kinneret, where he had worked as a fisherman, had joined us in Marseilles at that time. He had won his laurels in the Mossad in the dangerous Baghdad operation, where he worked together with Leibl Abramovsky. Enterprising, reliable as a rock and unaware of the existence of 'danger', he was so enthusiastic about the plan that it became clear he would be the first commander to implement it. Yehoshua took command of the *Akbel* (the Haganah ship *Biria,* as we renamed the *Bilboa,* was the easier job) and, a few days after 'Black Saturday', met the *Biria* at the pre-arranged place.

Trouble started as soon as the trans-shipment was about to begin. The Turkish captain of the *Akbel* had been promised by D'Andria an extra £1,000 for his short trip. He now demanded 1,000 British gold coins (sovereigns) instead of paper money and refused to take on the refugees from the *Biria* before he was paid. During the protracted negotiations – hampered by the fact that the captain of the *Akbel* spoke only Turkish – the sea was particularly rough and it was difficult to keep the *Biria* at anchor for an extended time. Although larger than the *Akbel,* she was still a Mossad boat, and that meant she was dangerously overcrowded.

Yehoshua explained in sign language that he was going to ask Marseilles for instructions over the *Biria*'s radio. In fact he boarded the larger ship only in order to select a number of tough men from among the refugees. He returned with them to the *Akbel* and overpowered the captain and one or two of the crew who remained loyal to him.

The transfer of passengers proved more difficult than we had anticipated when we had visualized the scene in Marseilles. Because of the rough sea, the two ships were unable to come alongside each other long enough for a plank to be thrown across for the passengers. They had to climb down a rope-ladder from the *Biria,* jump into a small lifeboat and climb a rope-ladder from there up to the *Akbel.* It was a perilous operation that did not end even when the last man had reached the deck of the *Akbel.* Yehoshua was obliged to transfer the poor bundles, all the refugees' remaining possessions, before the *Akbel* could sail. As this was going on, the outline of a battleship became visible in the distance.

Yehoshua's heart sank: after all their troubles were they to be caught red-handed by a British destroyer? He ordered the *Biria* to start up her engines and sail away. The *Akbel* lifted her anchor and sped in the opposite direction. Confuse the enemy, Yehoshua thought, as he observed the battleship faltering with indecision about which of the two to pursue. She went for the *Biria.* Only then, as she came closer, was she identified as a French warship, anxious to be of help. Yehoshua signalled back a grateful acknowledgment of the kind offer, but no help was needed. On 2 July, the *Akbel* was on her way to Palestine.

Less than twenty-four hours after the transfer to the small, derelict boat, the hardship ended. As soon as the mountains of the Haifa coast came into sight, the inevitable British escort appeared. The *Akbel* surrendered her 1,350 passengers without resistance and they were taken into detention.

On the day I left Marseilles for Greece, the only plane available was a Lebanese Airlines Dakota, fitted with flimsy military seats on aluminium pipes. Crossing the Mediterranean in this plane was one of the worst flights I can remember, and it is an understatement to say I was relieved when I finally saw the Greek coast and Athens airport again. This time I entered with an ordinary Greek visa. The British had handed over their administration to the local authorities, and I was not worried about my expulsion from occupied Greece eighteen months earlier.

Benyamin and his senior colleague, Yani Avidov, analysed the situation and reached exactly the same solution Shmariah had suggested: save Greece for the preparation of boats and for the supply of fuel to ships departing from other, nearby ports.

At Gaganis's, we talked until the small hours about what had become of the Mossad since the renewal of its activities at the end of the war. Benyamin was satisfied with what I was able to tell him but he was extremely critical of the professional level of our maritime activities. True to his character, he was taking a correspondence course on ship-building. 'We are dealing with people who have gone through every hell, and we must make every possible effort to make their voyage to a new life as comfortable as humanly possible,' he said. Few of us had a better chance to translate our fervent conviction into practice than this young captain.

We were in full accord about the future of our work in Greece. The British had discovered our connections, the improvised dockyard where we fitted ships and our mode of operation in Greece. We could deceive them without losing what had been built up over the years only if we discontinued departures of people and confined our work to supply and liaison.

The first instance of implementing our new policy was to follow immediately. The *Biria* sent a coded message to the secret transmitter hidden in Nikos Kirinakis' barn: Yehoshua had transferred his passengers to the *Akbel* and was on his way to Yugoslavia. He was also running out of fuel near the island of Milos and was in a hurry to reach Backa, the hidden bay in northern Yugoslavia, where he was long overdue.

Just as we were discussing how help could be arranged, I received a coded message from Belgrade: Yanek, our new man there, wanted me to come and help him with a number of complications. We were in the midst of preparing our departures: Benyamin, equipped with seaman's papers identifying him as 'Captain Pedro', rolled several huge barrels of fuel onto a small boat he had in store for just such an emergency. Within hours after the receipt of Yehoshua's request, he was on his way to Milos. Fuel was put on board the *Biria,* and Benyamin helped Yehoshua to supply her with provisions for the next trip from Backa. And I was on my way by Greek Dakota from Athens to Salonika, where I would continue by bus to the Yugoslav border.

After about a two-hour ride in a battered bus to the border and a multi-language interlude with the communist border guards, I boarded the train to Belgrade. Yanek was waiting for me at the railway terminal. I was not able to go to the Majestic and indulge in old memories from the great days in the friendly capital of Yugoslavia; we took a train straight to Zagreb. Yanek gave me a quick review of the developments. The *Biria* had been late in arriving at Backa. Meanwhile, more than double the number of people she was scheduled to transport had arrived from Hungary and Rumania, and the transit camp near Zagreb was dangerously overcrowded. Discipline in the camp was difficult to maintain. We had promised the Yugoslav authorities that the refugees would be kept inside the old castle that served as a transit camp, but the overflow of people made it impossible to keep them from leaving the building for a stroll in the surrounding forests. Yanek was angry at Leibl for not understanding the danger in angering the Yugoslav authorities. Maybe, Yanek admitted, Leibl was more concerned for the suffering refugees than for the Belgrade authorities, but we had to impose stricter discipline if we wanted to continue our friendly collaboration. As far as the increased number of potential passengers, I continued to count on Yehoshua: somehow he would find a way to take more people on the *Biria* than had been planned.

We arrived in Backa just a day after the *Biria*. Yehoshua

was beaming. His complicated trans-shipment had worked, and he had saved the ship. 'The problem' had been solved, in fact, before Yanek and I reached the scene. Leibl was overjoyed by his meeting with Yehoshua, whom he had not seen since Baghdad, and implored his old friend to install 'another thousand berths' on the *Biria*. But Yehoshua brushed that fantastic demand aside: 'The *Biria* has already been spotted by British planes. This time we won't be able to evade the blockade, and she'll be picked up by a British escort as soon as she enters the Mediterranean. It's summer – let's take all comers and have them sleep on deck. They won't be any more uncomfortable than in the narrow berths below.'

To our delight, we found Leibl in a mellow mood. Yehoshua had not only solved the problems for Yanek and for the Yugoslav authorities, he had avoided a potential clash between our two men in Yugoslavia and was able to organize the largest transport so far on a Mossad boat: 2,670 men, women and children. (She eventually arrived at her destination with 2,672 – two babies were born during the voyage.) We cabled a coded report over the *Biria*'s radio to the Chief in Paris. He was delighted and expressed his satisfaction in his own unique way: the *Biria* would be renamed; it would bear the most coveted name the Mossad could possibly bestow upon a boat – *Haganah*.

(22)

Jewish Resistance

THIS TIME, the odyssey of a boat that was to take our people from the ruins of Europe to the shores of Palestine began in New York. Soon after I began working out of Paris, Dani Shind, the alternate candidate for my job, was sent to the United States to join a team of Haganah men. The Haganah's activities in America had blossomed following Ben Gurion's visit in June 1945 to mobilize Jewish initiative in our struggle. He called on Henry Montor, whose boundless drive had moved the United Jewish Appeal to unprecedented achievements, and Montor organized a meeting of thirty-five outstanding community leaders at the home of Rudolf Sonnenborn. Ben Gurion confronted the assembly with his urgent demand for arms, machinery for arms production and funds, and from then on the Sonnenborn Institute – as the distinguished gathering came to be known – supervised the growing activities of the Haganah in America.

Dani took up residence in the Hotel 14, a beehive of Haganah emissaries and ardent American volunteers, and was soon joined by Joe Boxenbaum – whose expertise in commerce was invaluable – and his wife, Pearl – who supplied the legal front for Dani's illegal schemes. This was a turning point for the Mossad. Not only were we to buy bigger and more seaworthy ships than ever before, but with Dani's arrival in the United States the Mossad had truly become a world-wide organization.

Dani sent word to Greece to expect a huge American ship, the *Anna,* flying the Panamanian flag, in Piraeus. In order to obscure the real purpose of her transoceanic voyage, the *Anna* had brought regular cargo to Greece, and a shipping agent (one of Gaganis' acquaintances) handled the routine unloading job. Benyamin could not restrain his curiosity to look the new ship over. As hold after hold was emptied of cargo and the immense space, unobstructed by partitions and divisions, became visible, he practically danced with joy – the 2,000-ton ship was a dream. He raced back to the office and cabled Tel Aviv, 'On this one we shall bring 6,000.'

The crew observed Benyamin's joy with mixed feelings. The professional sailors thought he was mad – a ship with such large holds was hard enough to handle for general cargo. The Mossad in Tel Aviv also took a cool view of Benyamin's enthusiasm. 'Have you by any chance gone mad?' was the radio-operator's laconic observation in response to the announcement of a capacity of 6,000. But the Jewish volunteer sailors from the United States shared Benyamin's delight.

The Palyam escorts, led by Yossi Harel, arrived at Piraeus and reinforced the forebodings of some of the *Anna*'s Greek crew. It suddenly dawned on the Greeks that the owner's joy was not because of the large cargo shipments, but because the ship was destined to carry illegal refugees. After difficult negotiations, Benyamin promised to transport the crew back to land once they had taken on their passengers. The Greeks were satisfied; it pleased them to participate in this kind of mercy action, as long as the security of their own families was not jeopardized.

Even as these talks were going on, the British journalist

Jon Kimche appeared at Benyamin's with bad news: British agents had identified the *Anna* as a Mossad boat and were pressuring to have the Greeks sequester her right then and there, in the port of Piraeus. Benyamin decided to move out at once. The fitting could continue during the trip to Yugoslavia; all the necessary material for the job was already on board.

Leibl was waiting there to greet the two ships, along with the dignitaries of the port and town, the Communist Party Chief of the area and a number of gifts for the 'Officers of the Jewish Underground in Palestine' who brought the boats. Tito and Ben Gurion were toasted at a gay party on board the *Anna*. But Leibl's spirits sank when he realized that the ship really was not ready for departure and that in the hurry of the escape from Greece no provisions were taken on; there was nothing on board except the dry food carried from the United States. Sheyke Dan, a Haganah parachutist during the war and now on hand, solved the problem. He spoke bluntly of our predicament to the celebrating Yugoslavs, and the representatives of the loyal – if somewhat penurious – friendly government undertook to supply our every need.

While the fitting of the *Anna* was in full swing at Backa, Sheyke Dan suggested to Agami to send the *Agia Anastasia,* code-named *The Saintly One,* to Backa too. For months *The Saintly One* had been idle in some forgotten corner in the Rumanian harbour of Constantsa, out of bounds for our work since the Soviet Navy had taken full control of the area. When she arrived after a strenuous trip from Rumania through the Black Sea and up the Adriatic coast, we had the largest convoy the Mossad had ever assembled in one port. Under the friendly guard of the Yugoslav People's Republic, the Mossad prepared the departure of about 4,000 illegal immigrants, about half of them pregnant women, children and old people.

Yitzhak Artzi, one of the immigrant leaders of this huge

convoy, kept a diary of the trip from his vantage point on the
Anna. He started his notes on 5 November 1946, the day
they took to sea.

We are on our way, with *The Saintly One* behind us. Amnon
is the commander of the entire transport, and Mati is the radio-
operator. As we move into the calm sea, the 3,500 illegals on
the *Anna* join the 500 on *The Saintly One* in an enthusiastic
outburst of 'Hatikva', the national anthem. Many people weep
as our convoy moves solemnly on its way towards Palestine.

8 November 1946: *The Saintly One* has had her new name
painted on her bow: she's called *Abba Berditchev* to honour
the memory of one of the Haganah parachutists who was dropped
behind enemy lines in Rumania and killed by the Nazis.

9 November 1946, 2:00 p.m.: We could see that the *Abba
Berditchev* was not responding to her captain's wheel. She was
at the mercy of the waves. Mati and Amnon were as white as
ghosts. They ordered the passengers of the *Abba Berditchev* to
clear the deck. The ship was moving helplessly fast in the direction of some rocks. A few minutes more and she would have
foundered on the rocks like a box of matches. But she was suddenly carried into a calm current. Her speed diminished and
somehow it looked as if her engines had started to work again.
Then a gigantic wave pushed her onto a rock, but the clash was
softened thanks to the reduced speed of the ship. We could
not approach her to help because the water was too shallow.
From afar we saw how the passengers jumped from the sinking
ship onto the rock. We lowered one of our lifeboats with five
selected rescuers in it. They rowed towards the scene of the
accident and as soon as they arrived they signalled us the good
news: all are safe, though most of the baggage was lost. We
quickly prepared to welcome another 500 passengers on our ship.

18 November 1946: Only tonight Amnon explained to me
why he had been so worried during these last few days. We had
just passed through an uncharted minefield.

24 November 1946: A siren shattered the quiet morning,
and the few people on duty on deck disappeared below. Within
seconds an airplane appeared above our ship. It dived down,
nearly touched our masts. I stayed on deck and could see the
pilot's face clearly. The plane circled above our ship, ascended
and disappeared. Five minutes later another plane appeared.

The deck was practically empty, and the few sailors continued their routine duties undisturbed. But below, in the holds, 4,000 Jews, bathed in sweat, waited anxiously for the outcome. Mati received a signal from the plane: 'Identify yourself.' He answered: 'Our ship is *Anna* under the Panamanian flag. We carry 2,000 tons of cargo and a crew of sixteen'.

'Where to?'

'Port Said.'

The British pilot disappeared. But did he believe us?

As soon as night fell, the crowd poured onto the deck: they had waited through the long, hot day for a bit of fresh air. There was only one topic of discussion: the plane. Have they found out that this is an illegal immigrant ship bound for Palestine? From time to time an airplane seemed to be flying overhead. The blinking lights made it look like a falling star. Suddenly the darkness turned to blinding light: searchlights pierced the night from all directions, engulfing the multitude in the merciless glare. A British cruiser drew near enough for us to read L-75 on its bow. Panic broke out on deck. But the orderlies blew their whistles and everybody instinctively began to follow directives. Everyone wanted to disappear from the deck, but it was clear that camouflage was no longer needed. The British Navy had discovered us. In a little while we were surrounded by British warships on all sides. Someone intoned the 'Hatikva'. The national anthem was picked up by the 4,000 people who understood that from that moment on, our voyage had turned into a battle. And if battle were to be our fate, we decided to respond to the British challenge by renaming our ship *Jewish Resistance*.

The battleships stayed on our heels, searchlights flashing on and off, but two hours passed before the command ship signalled to us:

'Identify yourself.'

'The Haganah ship *Jewish Resistance*.'

'Where to?'

'Home. Palestine.'

Hours passed and we continued on our way. After midnight, the British commander sent a message: 'I am asking you for your understanding. There is absolutely no chance of your reaching Tel Aviv. As soon as you enter territorial waters, we shall board your ship and arrest you. Then we shall transfer your passengers to other ships and deport you to Cyprus. Your troubles could be over tomorrow if you agree to turn directly towards Famagusta.'

After a short while our signal lights replied: 'We come from German concentration camps in Europe. We don't intend to exchange them for British concentration camps. Do you seriously believe that we are out on a picnic? Four thousand men, women and children are crowded into this ship under conditions difficult to describe. Can you imagine the sufferings of the women who have given birth on this ship? Are we delinquents or murderers? Why do you hunt us like wild animals? Can you imagine that a free man voluntarily chooses to go to a concentration camp, even a British concentration camp? No, we shall fight for our right to live. We shall fight on the shore, in the streets and on the deck of this ship!'

We were a bit embarrassed as we formulated this message, an imitation of Churchill's rhetoric. But in fact, it truthfully expressed our feelings. Would the British open their hearts to us and remember what they went through in their hour of desperation? The answer to our questions came about four hours later: 'Our advice is unchanged. Please refrain from all action that stems from the fanaticism of your passengers. We have taken note of your protest, but I must warn you that any opposition to arrest will be futile. Out of fairness to your passengers you must make this abundantly clear to them. I am asking you to make it possible for me to address myself directly to your passengers.'

25 November 1946: At 7:00 a.m. we conveyed our agreement that the cruiser might approach us. The L-75 drew up alongside our ship. This time its captain did not speak to an anonymous commander of our ship, but to the 'people'. He repeated his friendly suggestion that we go directly to Famagusta. Our people listened attentively, and their answer was swift in coming. It consisted of one word repeated rhythmically: 'Palestine, Palestine!' The die was cast. We would not be known as the Haganah ship that surrendered to the British and went to Cyprus voluntarily.

It was decided to resist with force any attempt to board our ship. Mati was in constant radio contact with the shore and received instructions to alter the name of our ship to *Knesset Yisrael*. Amnon told us that in Jerusalem urgent negotiations are going on concerning our future. This explains the moderation which expresses itself in the change of name. Headquarters insists on the less provocative name *Knesset Yisrael*.

An alarm was sounded at 3:00 a.m. and I rushed to the command room. One of our passengers, a teacher from Hungary, had jumped overboard, determined to reach the coast of Palestine. One of his friends told us that he had tied a plastic bag filled with food and water to his body. He was a champion swimmer, but as we were still 30 kilometres off the coast, we felt his life was in acute danger, that he would never make it. We decided to inform the British Navy. The searchlight flashed on again and swept across the surface of the sea. One of our three escorts turned around. At 4:00 a.m. the British sent us a brief message: 'Your man is in our infirmary. All is well.' We relaxed a little. At dawn we caught sight of the coast of Haifa. We were by now completely surrounded by cruisers, patrol boats and speedboats of the Coastal Police, and airplanes hovered overhead.

26 November 1946: Amnon informed us that the attorney of the Jewish Agency, Dov Yosef, has filed a writ of habeas corpus on our behalf. As we continued full-speed towards Haifa, we received new instructions: 'There will be no resistance to any British boarding-party, but we should vigorously resist transfer to the deportation boats.' We entered territorial waters with our naval escort now only centimetres away from either side of our ship. Strong and healthy-looking sailors with lifebelts around their chests lined up along the rail of their ship. Facing them were 4,042 civilians: among them 2,100 men, many of them elderly but some of them just as strong and healthy as the British sailors; 1,487 women and 455 children, including ten babies born on board during the voyage. All were dressed in torn and dirty clothes; they hadn't tasted cooked food for over a month; and their eyes were inflamed from lack of sleep. The sailors crossed energetically from their decks to ours and took up strategic positions. The commander's first move was to the communications room.

Haifa was there in front of us, so close we could almost touch it. From the rooftops crowds of friendly people were waving to us. Our ship suddenly became tiny and shabby as she was encircled by the gigantic warships. Soldiers swarmed about the pier, separating us from our land and our people. Right next to us a huge ship lay at anchor, full of soldiers. Was there also a representative of the Jewish Agency somewhere around? We had no time to get excited over the way the country received its returning sons after our arduous 24-day trip.

Everything happened quickly. We had only just reached the pier when a voice over a loud speaker asked us to prepare for the transfer. That was the signal. A hailstorm of tin cans, chips of wood and iron bars came down on the heads of the unsuspecting soldiers and policemen. Three soldiers, who had remained on our deck, were thrown into the water. The battle had begun.

Suddenly a shot pierced the air. Berele, the son of the Rabbi of Nodvorna, in his long black coat, long sidelocks curling down his youthful cheeks, fell down in a pool of blood. He died even before the stretcher-bearers could reach him. The clatter of the machine-guns continued, while the stretcher-bearers moved swiftly from one casualty to another.

We had not yet recovered from the shock of the shooting when a new rain came down on us. This time it was tear gas. The air was stifling and people scattered in all directions looking for shelter. The British took advantage of the panic, jumping aboard and beating hard to the left and right with rubber clubs. Then they opened fire without warning. Our only weapons were empty sardine tins, bits of wood and iron bars; they fought us with rifles, machine-guns and tear gas bombs. Two of our people were killed.

The British had already begun to drag people from our ship to theirs. They started with the elderly and the weak; after that the mothers with their children. The first deportation ship was already moving away from the pier. It was a short journey on the sacred soil of the Holy Land from the *Knesset Yisrael* to the *Empire Rival,* the deportation boat.

As I descended the gangplank of the *Empire Rival,* a British officer greeted me with a package of biscuits and the blow of a rifle butt. We were imprisoned in the holds, surrounded by sentries. The vibration of the ship told us we were moving. Destination: Cyprus. A few hours ago we were on our way towards Haifa. Now we are moving away from it. Our struggle would make a headline, perhaps, but it would soon be overshadowed by other events, an episode to be forgotten. But 4,000 anonymous witnesses would never forget the scene in Haifa port.

About a month after the *Knesset Yisrael* docked at Haifa, the Twenty-second Zionist Congress opened in Basle, where nearly fifty years earlier the First Zionist Congress had convened under the leadership of Theodor Herzl. It was a significant gathering, the first congress since the end of the war, taking place against the background of growing conflict with the mandatory power. Trust in the possibility of reaching an understanding with Britain was waning. The pressure for an activist policy was increasing. Even the more moderate elements within the Zionist movement realized that we were near the moment of truth: a clash with Britain seemed unavoidable.

All the members of the Mossad who were able to leave their posts for a few days and who were in possession of documents that enabled them to travel congregated in Basle, where the Chief had called a general meeting.

It was a warm gathering of comrades devoted to a common goal and sharing a crucial mission on behalf of the Jewish people. When one would ask another for a service, one's first obligation was to fulfil the request and ask for the reason later. Together with the other emissaries of the Haganah and the daring maritime escorts and radio-operators, we were a large unit of fighting men and women. Trust and mutual friendship, as well as the common language we had developed in the course of duty, were not the product of orders from above, but the result of our desire to create facts, to serve, to find strength in unity.

Yet we were not a docile herd of pious sheep. At one point during the few days we spent together in Basle, there was a moment when we seemed very near a rebellion against authority – both of the Chief and of the Jewish Agency. Comparing notes, we found that infinitely more could be done if we had more freedom from political considerations, from the ups and downs (there were hardly any ups lately) in the relationship between the Zionist movement and the

British Government. We criticized the Jewish Agency for hindering the full display of our capabilities. The restrictive role the Political Department of the Jewish Agency had played in the La Spezia incident was still fresh in our memory. We accused the Chief of procrastination over unimportant details and of more caution than most of us found necessary.

As many of my colleagues considered me the man closest to the Chief at that time, I was the recipient of much of the adverse comment and had to move carefully. I could not adequately defend decisions that I myself considered out of tune with the speed and vigour of our work; but neither could I acquiesce to the mood of resentment that might endanger the unity of our organization. Yet, as it was less awkward for my colleagues to talk to me rather than to the Chief directly, I bore the brunt of their discontent at Basle.

This atmosphere of uneasiness passed as soon as we met with Ben Gurion. Avigur had asked me to go over to the Congress Hall and bring Ben Gurion to our meeting. When I arrived back with him, Ben Gurion took over the meeting at once, asking for concise reports, country by country. In questions shot at the speakers, he revealed a surprising knowledge of precise detail, and his familiarity with our every problem encouraged us immensely. It was a clear sign that the Jewish Agency was taking our work more seriously than we had suspected in our grumblings before this meeting.

His reaction added further to our morale because he was obviously discontented with even the most daring plans we put forward. Neither the total volume of our work nor the amount of money budgeted was sufficient for his liking.

'We are entering upon the decisive phase in our struggle for independence,' he said time and time again as he discarded the plans we had elaborated. He again demanded more departures from more ports and in larger boats. He asked for stiff resistance against British boarding-parties once the boats were – inevitably – caught. He shoved aside our apprehension concerning money for ships and the additional men needed for enlarged operations. 'Do your share in this,' Ben Gurion assured us, 'and we in the Agency shall do ours.' When the meeting was over, we again were a united group of fighting men and women working in the anonymity of the Mossad.

One of the members of the Mossad had come to Basle on his own initiative, without an invitation from the Chief. He was Shlomo Zimmerman, our 'man for all seasons' from Haifa. Shlomo had come to Basle at his own expense because he had devised a plan. He wanted to canvass members of the Mossad, and he hoped to convince the Chief of the value of his idea.

Babies had died on our overcrowded boats; pregnant women had been beaten up by British soldiers during fights against detention of illegal arrivals; several real hardship cases of survivors of German death camps had arrived in a state of complete exhaustion because of the miserable conditions of Mossad boats. Tormented by such memories, Shlomo had to find a better way to bring special people to Palestine. He knew there must be a method as yet undiscovered for getting around immigration restrictions without exposing people to risks.

Suddenly an idea took shape. Legal immigration, on the basis of visas and entry permits, had been reduced to a mere trickle, but it was nevertheless going on. So why not forge 'legal' entry permits!

As so often in the past, Davidka Nameri, the creator of our landing teams, was the first person to whom Shlomo turned with his inspiration: Nameri would comprehend that it was basically wrong to leave so important an avenue for clandestine immigration untapped, and, indeed, the Palmach commander was immediately taken by Shlomo's logic. The two of them had long talks with a Jewish official of the mandatory Immigration Department who was a member of the Haganah. Meticulously, they examined official procedure and found that it was truly not very complicated to penetrate the official routine of returning residents. A more difficult problem was the supply of consular stamps on visitors' visas, which had to be forged and stamped into foreign passports.

Shlomo was not a theoretician: he was not satisfied with merely an abstract analysis of British procedures. With Davidka's expert assistance, late one afternoon he let himself into the Central Immigration Office in Jerusalem. In the quiet of the deserted building, well guarded by red-bereted British sentries, he had the entire night to study the archives and files of the office he was preparing to supplement with material of his own production.

Shlomo decided to deal with consular stamps later. On his way to Basle, he stopped in Paris, where – accompanied by a secretary from our office – he simply walked to the British Embassy's Consular Department to study the issue of British visas in foreign passports. While the British passport official was kept busy by Shlomo's companion, Shlomo helped himself to a bunch of British Consular Stamps out of a wooden box on the official's desk. In Haifa he had found an engraver, also a member of the Haganah, who had testified that he was able (and willing) to produce any stamp or any other implement for Shlomo's scheme that would be useful for clandestine immigration. Now he felt fully equipped for his talk with the Chief.

Avigur listened carefully to Shlomo's explanation. He did not like what he heard. 'Soon you will find yourself printing Sterling,' Avigur said without a trace of humour. 'Money, too, is in very short supply.' But encouraged by some of us to whom he had revealed his plan, Shlomo went to Avigur a second time.

'Even if we succeeded in getting a few people past British controls, the scheme is bound to explode in our face,' Shaul insisted.

Unable to control himself any longer, Shlomo banged his fist on the table. 'All right,' he shouted. 'But let me work until it explodes.' His utter confidence finally won the Chief over.

Shlomo's scheme (known as 'Scheme D') came into existence, but it never exploded. It did bring over 15,000 persons into Palestine.

(23)

Masquerades

GILLEL STORCH found the Mossad office in Paris on his own initiative. Storch, originally from Riga, was a successful businessman in post-war Stockholm. He had been on a business trip to Sweden on the day war broke out, and instead of returning home, he brought his family to Stockholm. More fortunate than most, and a man of considerable business ability, he soon became a prosperous merchant. He also soon found himself deeply involved in matters concerning refugees in Sweden. His contacts with people of consequence in Swedish politics enabled him not only to help refugees with money, but also to pull strings where an identity card or the prolongation of a residence permit was needed.

On one of his business trips to Paris early in 1946, Storch arrived in our office with a letter from Günther Cohen, a German refugee who had found a temporary home in Sweden and who was known to us. Günther recommended Storch as trustworthy and asked us to listen to his story of 700 women who had survived the Ravensbrück concentration camp. They had been welcomed in Sweden, but wished to go to Palestine.

We were familiar with the general background. Shortly before the end of the war, the Swedish Government had given refuge to several hundred women from the notorious concentration camp of Ravensbrück. Their release from Germany and transfer to Sweden was one of the achievements of the negotiations conducted between Heinrich Himmler and Count Bernadotte, head of the Swedish Red Cross and a member of the royal family. When Himmler realized that Germany was losing the war, he sought some cover for his crimes. Bernadotte took advantage of this situation by demanding the release of Scandinavian prisoners and a number of Jews as tokens of Himmler's intentions, while he pretended to mediate between the Nazi leader and the Allied command.

The women of Ravensbrück were most kindly received in Sweden. Many were adopted by farm families and practically became members of their households; others were employed in the cities in various industrial jobs. Some married and stayed in the country that had saved them. But the majority of the Jewish girls from Ravensbrück wanted neither to stay in Sweden nor to return to their native countries. They wanted to go to Palestine.

The Zionist Organization of Sweden had promised the young women that it would use its influence to obtain immigration certificates for them as soon as the political situation made their transfer from Sweden to Palestine possible. Storch now promised us his help with the Swedish authorities.

If we could provide a ship and somehow create the impression that the trip of these 700 women was in fact immigration to an overseas country, rather than a plain, illegal convoy, Storch would see to it that everything went smoothly. We were delighted. We needed to diversify our work even further and disperse our activities in order to evade British agents who were becoming more numerous and efficient all the time. If we could save the 700 young women and establish working contacts with a base hitherto outside our orbit, all the better.

I informed Shmariah of the new opportunity. At that time,

he was negotiating with a Greek shipowner for three ships. They were not exactly what we wanted, as they were river-boats rather than ocean liners, and older than Shmariah and his whole team combined, but they were on the market and could go to Sweden almost at once. We decided to make their owner a final offer, which he – surprised that we had made any offer at all – accepted without much ado. We realized that we had bought no great bargains, but the Greek crews on at least two out of three ships were magnificent, honest people ready to cooperate with us fully.

I travelled to Stockholm as the European representative of the Jewish Refugees Welfare Society of Washington. The Swedish Consulate General in Paris stamped my Palestinian passport with a courtesy visa. When I inquired how I had received such favourable treatment (not really surprising from a civilized country like Sweden), I found that the consular official who handled my passport was herself a Jewish refugee. I was to get ample proof of her humanitarian broadmindedness when I met her again many years later, this time as the wife of the celebrated violinist Isaac Stern.

The only problems we encountered in the splendid dock-yards of Stockholm harbour were the cold weather and the shortness of the days: the carpenters who were reinforcing our three ships and building the berths could begin work only at dawn, meaning at about nine a.m.; when they departed at about two p.m. the street lamps were already burning and night had fallen.

Storch also felt that the lengthy stay of our ships in Stock-holm's peaceful harbour might attract the attention of the British Embassy. And while the Swedes were neutral, faithful to high moral standards and not easily impressed by diplomatic pressure on matters about which they felt strongly, in Storch's opinion, the sooner we sailed, the better.

Günther Cohen agreed to act as the representative of the Mossad in Stockholm, helping to select the candidates for the voyage and explaining to them that the destination of their trip was supposed to be Cuba. He asked them to be discreet and not to discuss any particulars with strangers.

Back in Paris, one icy Sunday morning in January 1947, I received an unexpected call from Günther in Stockholm: 'You must come here at once. Storm clouds are gathering. The Embassy of you-know-who seems to have found out about us, and the whole operation is in the balance.' I knew Günther was not easily shaken, and he confirmed my assumption that he had thoroughly discussed the situation with Storch before he put through his alarming call. I left for Stockholm on the first available plane.

We spent the evening examining the signs Günther had poetically called storm clouds. There were persistent rumours that the British had repeatedly intervened with the Swedish Foreign Office. They had warned that our three ships were not banana boats, offering internal evidence that these ships were being fitted for illegal immigration. Counting upon the well-known Scandinavian rectitude, the British made much of the fact that neutral Sweden was being misused by a band of mischievous foreigners to prepare for an operation that was against the law. The Swedes, it was true, procrastinated in the best tradition of diplomatic evasion; but British pressure on them persisted.

The Deputy Director of the Special Police Branch dealing with foreigners had paid two visits to Günther during the last few days. He had also gone to the hostels where the women from Ravensbrück were staying and interviewed many of them. Then he had come to see Günther, asking awkward questions and dropping hints. That was when Günther alerted me. He was sure that something threatening was afoot and did not want to bear responsibility alone and perhaps make a last-minute mistake that would spoil our scheme.

'Let's take the bull by its horns,' I said. 'Let's meet with Dr S., the Deputy Head of the Special Police Branch.'

The elegant dining-room was half dark. Candles were burning on each table. Well-dressed, decorous ladies and gentlemen were having lunch in an atmosphere of carefree serenity. Dr S. arrived punctually and reacted warmly when Günther introduced us. I was on my guard to detect even the faintest hint. It would have been impolite to discuss anything serious during lunch, so our guest talked freely and gaily in excellent English. There was absolutely no reference to the dismal topics we had met to debate until the meal was finished with a glass of brandy and a cup of strong coffee.

Dr S. hesitated and seemed to stammer slightly as he braced himself for the painful talk that was now about to begin. He apologized profusely for having inconvenienced me and explained that he understood some thoughts he had shared with Günther about our forthcoming expedition had caused me to make this trip to the extreme north in this ghastly weather. I encouraged S. to speak up and to tell me frankly what was on his mind. By now I was quite prepared to hear him say that the show was off, that we could never depart from a Swedish port with the flimsy camouflage we were using for the improper and illegal activities in which we were engaged.

Ill at ease, he took a deep breath and plunged into the unpleasant task. 'You see,' he said, 'I have had many talks with your representative here and I find him an exceptionally honourable man. You will permit me to compliment you. I was greatly honoured to meet you personally, and I believe that you too are quite incapable of doing anything that is not strictly in the spirit of morality and law.'

My heart sank. I began to realize that Günther's prediction was correct.

'You will forgive me if I am being completely frank with you, although I have some very harsh things to say.' His circumlocution was purely politic. He was now in full command of himself, and there was no longer anything awkward or shy about this man of authority.

'I have taken time out to visit the hostels in which the young women you are sending to Cuba are staying. I spoke to most of them openly and quite seriously. And do you know what I found out?'

At that point I no longer bothered to play the game, and with a weak nod I indicated that I could well imagine what it was he had found out. Günther was nervously stamping on my foot under the table.

'I'll tell you exactly what I found out.' Dr S. now had begun to thunder in a subdued voice, as befitted the utter silence that prevailed in the elegant dining-room. 'I found that none of these young women whom you are forcing to leave Sweden for Cuba wants to go there. They spoke to me with utmost frankness when they learned that I had made a few investigations concerning their trip. They want to go to Palestine, not to be white slaves in Cuba.'

He had said it all. Günther was as dumbfounded as I. I needed time to gather my wits about me. Was this the ruse to end all ruses, or was the Deputy Head truly so naïve? I searched his eyes, not to impress him with the solemnity of the promise I was going to make but to scrutinize the sincerity of his emotions.

'One thing I can honestly promise you, Dr S. We shall transfer these young women to Palestine as soon as our organization can obtain the necessary entry permits for them. There will be no question of expenses. They will be in Palestine as soon as we can manage to get them there.'

We shook hands on this. S.'s conscience was visibly relieved; Günther's was not. Neither was mine. 'Why do we have to behave like skunks,' I said to Günther when we were alone, 'with decent chaps like this?'

'Worry not,' Günther said bravely. ' "*Navigare necesse est. Vivere non est necesse.*" '

I returned to Paris, where Willi Katz, our man in Brussels, had arrived at our headquarters to discuss the deteriorating situation in Belgium. Willi had first moved from Paris to

Brussels on Mossad business in the spring of 1945 when
Belgium was newly liberated and the Belgians warm-
heartedly opened their frontiers to refugees from German
concentration camps and from Eastern Europe on the march
towards the sea – and Palestine. Soon after his arrival he met
Professor Pearlman and his wife Fella, who adopted him and
his work without qualification. Professor Pearlman, a teacher
of logic and an experienced underground fighter, was close to
people who had fought in the ranks of the anti-Nazi resistance and were now in key positions. With their help Willi
made it possible to legalize our work. The 'Jewish Refugees
Welfare Society' soon opened a 'branch office' in Brussels.
While the parent organization existed only on hastily printed
stationery, Willi's branch was a genuine humanitarian body,
and some of the outstanding intellectuals and resistance
heroes of the Belgian underground joined the representative
committee. The Belgian Foreign Office gladly cooperated
with such a distinguished group, and the Belgian Government
went so far as to grant financial aid to the refugees through
the JRWS, for it was understood that most, if not all, of the
refugees would sooner or later leave the country.

Through her own connections with the Cuban Consul in
Antwerp, Fella Pearlman obtained the necessary visas for the
transport of 500 refugees. Again, the alleged destination was
Cuba. On a quiet night in July 1946, a Panamanian freighter,
renamed *Jewish Soldier,* slipped stealthily into the busy port
of Antwerp and took on 500 illegal refugees right under the
nose of the British Navy and without arousing the slightest
notice.

No one in Belgium ever spoke to Willi or to Professor
Pearlman and his wife about the illegal departure. The ship
had left, 500 refugees had been removed from Belgium's
strained economy and the chapter was closed. But suddenly
there was increased supervision and controls were tightened.
Imperceptibly at first, more and more open as time went by,

the British intervened in all matters concerning Jewish refugees. The officers and men of the Jewish Brigade were sternly
warned not to engage in illegal activities. Roadblocks were
set up to check British army transports for illegal refugees.
The Foreign Office received urgent requests from their
chief ally not to abet any further adventures concerning the
clandestine departure of refugees under the guise of emigration to Latin America.

In Paris, Willi discussed his predicament with us. It was
now out of the question to transfer the remainder of the
refugees out of Belgium in the same way the first transport
had been moved. It was also impossible to bring them overland to France, for the visas we had been granted by Marcel
Pages were restricted to refugees from occupied Germany
only. We examined every possible solution and discarded one
after another. Finally the Chief reached a decision.

'If there are no transit visas,' he concluded, 'we shall have
to transport the people without visas.'

Fortunately, Benyamin had just arrived in Paris for a new
assignment, and when Avigur instructed me to plan the
Belgian adventure, he was my immediate choice for a partner. The scheme we worked out was as logical as it was
risky. Willi prepared the refugees for departure while we
readied a large boat in the southern French port of Sète.

At Benyamin's request, one of Willi's aides went to the
central railway station to reserve coaches for the transport
from Belgium. We planned the departure for a Sunday, and
as we had rented the entire train, we insisted that it cross into
France at a remote station, rather than at one of the more
generally frequented border crossings. Then Benyamin and
his two assistants drove to the chosen station to reconnoitre
conditions there and to strike up a friendship with the
officials in charge.

Benyamin invited the station-master for drinks in the
canteen. He was soon joined by all the other officials at the

crossing: the customs inspector, police officer, health inspector. Benyamin explained his presence in the God-forsaken place by saying that on the following day some of his relatives would be coming through on their way to Cuba, and he wished to be on hand to help his rather large family with border formalities. In the course of his entertaining conversation with the men, he was careful to drop a few important names – among them Marcel Pages. In fact, Benyamin claimed he was one of Marcel Pages' best friends: they had been through the war together and even now, with Pages back in his elevated position, his war-time pal kept in close touch. Actually, he had seen him that very morning, just before setting out on this trip to welcome his family.

Enchanted by the stranger's magnetic personality and proud to rub shoulders with one who had such marvellous connections with people in high places, the station-master invited Benyamin to spend the night at his modest place. The police officer and the customs inspector divided Benyamin's *entourage* between them.

The train was due shortly after nine a.m. the following morning. Benyamin and his assistants, suave and gay, had breakfast with their new friends. 'Champagne must be served,' Benyamin announced, 'in honour of the arrival of my family!' Then the special train puffed into the station, and the smiling faces of the French frontier guards dropped in bafflement as Benyamin revealed that all of the passengers – 1,500 of them – were 'his relatives'. The bafflement turned to outright consternation when it became evident that not a single person in Benyamin's 'family' had a visa. The only documents they were able to produce was a list of their names in alphabetical order and a letter on the stationery of the (non-existent) Agence Maritime Internationale, stating that the refugees were bound for Cuba.

The amiable atmosphere of the previous night gave way to irritation. The dutiful officials of the frontier police were appalled that they had become involved in a law-defying action of such unprecedented scope.

So far, all had gone according to plan. Now came the real test.

Four people were gathered in Joszi Friedmann's Paris apartment. He had just moved to a luxurious bachelor's flat on the Champs Élysées. Venya, Joszi, Gisi and I were waiting for a phone call, as Benyamin had succeeded in persuading the station-master to phone 'Monsieur Pages' and to obtain approval for the transit of the 1,500 passengers. Venya, remembering Agami's prescription from Istanbul days, was reading Psalms. The rest of us were busy pretending not to be nervous.

When the telephone finally rang, Joszi let it go on for quite a while. He had agreed to play Pages' part in this deception, as he was the only one of us whose French accent was appropriate. 'Pages,' he announced as he lifted the receiver.

The prolonged silence on the other end could mean that the station-master was impressed by the authoritative tone of his 'boss's' voice. Or had he somehow recognized that it was not the voice belonging to his master? Joszi glanced at us as he strained his ears to catch any further comments from the other end.

After what seemed like an eternity, the station-master came on again. He asked Monsieur Pages' pardon for disturbing him so early on a Sunday morning, but such and such had happened. Monsieur La Ferge-Benoit, as Benyamin had chosen to call himself, had promised the station-master that Monsieur Pages would not take it amiss if he were called at his good friend's behest.

'But haven't you seen the letter of the Agence Maritime Internationale?' Joszi barked in a voice as gruff as he could feign. 'It clearly indicates that a ship is waiting for this transport of emigrants in the harbour of Sète. The ship is scheduled to leave tonight. The train has barely time to reach its destination. Do you really want to burden France with these 1,500 refugees? If they miss the boat to Cuba because of your petty procrastination I shall personally dismiss you first thing tomorrow morning.'

The ruse had worked – so far. The train was still going to be on French territory for the better part of the following twelve hours. We had to stay in Joszi's flat for the whole day, for if anything happened to the train, Benyamin would try to get in touch with us there. Gisi served us refreshments with her easy charm, and we sat around listening to good music. Once or twice during the day the telephone brought us all to our feet with a start. But there was nothing to it: they were private calls for our host. Then, late at night, the phone rang once more.

'La Ferge-Benoit here,' Benyamin's booming voice could be heard clearly across the room. 'You will not dismiss the station-master after all, Marcel,' he said and hung up. The 1,500 were on their way to Palestine. And, as it turned out, so was I.

When I left Palestine shortly after the birth of my first daughter, I had reckoned on an absence of a few months. Now over two years had passed, though the satisfaction of participating in the Mossad's work at its centre in Paris was partial reward for the loneliness of separation from my family and my kibbutz. Dates for my return had been set, only to be postponed as new emergencies made departure feel like desertion in the midst of battle. What's more, I was still blacklisted by the British in Palestine for 'subversive activities'.

At the time that Captain Parkes had issued me top-priority travel orders to get me out of Greece, he warned me of the danger of arrest by the mandatory police were I to return to Palestine. My idea of returning on an illegal ship was discarded by the Chief: if I were recognized by the police, punishment would be even tougher.

When Venya and Yoel Palgi arrived at Paris headquarters in 1946, I could start thinking seriously about using the services of 'The Studio' at Les Grands Arenas.

'The Studio' was a reliable outfit that had acquired a special standing in our small world of conspiracy. The workshop near Marseilles had reached a high level of proficiency. The two women in charge were now assisted by experts and resources in every aspect of forging documents: there was a printer from Haifa who had been brought over to make rubber stamps; a young painter who knew how to imitate calligraphy; a huge selection of passports from various countries that could be used by anyone merely by changing the photograph; and a variety of inks that would pass the more common tests for authenticity. Once one became a 'patient', 'nurses' took complete charge, and as in a hospital, all distinctions of rank or privilege vanished. The greatest operator in his field became the passive object of quiet efficiency; he had to live by their instructions and forget his private tricks and past achievements.

A few days after my request for transformation was put through to 'The Studio', one of the 'nurses' called to inform me that I would become a British industrialist from Manchester going to Palestine to investigate business possibilities 'in an ever-expanding world market'. I was given the customary round of farewell meetings, at which there was much sentimental talk about the past and rather melancholy prognoses concerning the future. I had long working sessions with Venya and Palgi, during which we went through a thorough briefing of contacts, names and various bits of information concerning my work, which could be used after my departure. A colleague arrived in Paris to introduce me to the world of British business, provide me with enough gossip so that I could drop the right names, and familiarize me sufficiently with English affairs to be able to pass as a young Manchester executive in case I met a real one on my trip.

I was happy to hear that my friend Chanan Geismar would be travelling on the same boat, disguised as a returning Palestinian who had left the country before the war. The two of us were given a stern lecture by one of the 'nurses': never talk to strangers on your trip, never leave the ship in port, avoid chance meetings with acquaintances, never get involved in arguments, and generally be as inconspicuous as possible.

It was a long voyage on an old Greek passenger vessel with about 300 passengers. We surveyed the ship and concluded that had we used it for illegal immigration it could easily have held 3,000 by our more than spartan standards. On the way from Marseilles, the ship called at every conceivable port to refuel and to take on provisions. We dutifully obeyed our instructions not to be sociable and not to go ashore while in port. But when we reached Alexandria after almost ten days, the luscious sight of the Mediterranean harbour was too much for us, and we decided to have a look around.

Passengers who wished to disembark queued up in front of the purser's office early in the morning to get their passports. Just as I was given mine, a tall man three or four persons behind me in the line put his large hand on my shoulder and said, 'I say! Another Englishman!' with joy in his deep voice.

So this was it: I was going to perish in an Alexandrian jail or in the obscurity of a British police cell just for having disregarded 'The Studio's' orders. Actually I did pay dearly for my irresponsibility: my fellow-Englishman turned out to be a jolly good chap who had been away from home long enough to be thrilled by my well-learned stories about Manchester. But even more, he was interested in having gallons of beer in the nearest pub, and so I spent most of the day with him trapped by counterfeit bonds of common nationality.

The last call before we reached Haifa was Beirut. Chanan

and I, having had enough of sightseeing, decided to sit it out in the ship's bar, where tea was served. Looking out through the porthole we found our ship tied up in the immediate vicinity of that great British battleship the *Ajax,* notorious for her action against illegal immigration in the blockade of the shores of Palestine. Soon thereafter we were joined for tea by one of those English gentlemen who look like a retired colonel and arouse immediate suspicion in the minds of sinners. He pointed the *Ajax* out to us and held forth against the cruelty of his great country towards the innocent victims of absurd policies. Convinced that he was an *agent provocateur,* we found ourselves explaining the need 'to understand the other side'. This made our English friend quite angry. He mumbled something about people with absolutely no feeling for their fellow men and who were only interested in doing business. He left us quite abruptly after that, and we began to prepare for our arrival in Haifa and for the final test of our forged identities.

At dawn the next morning, we drew nearer to the familiar coast of Haifa. The harbour was strewn with battered parts of immigrant ships that had fought their way into the port. Our own boat was soon surrounded by small police patrol-boats and assiduous, unfriendly officials. Just before my turn to present my papers, a Haganah officer (who was acting as the head stevedore) nudged me and whispered encouragement. I could hardly contain my annoyance at his gesture of goodwill, considering the fact that under the scrutiny of so many hostile eyes his very contact with me could have destroyed my meticulously constructed and jealously preserved cover.

The passport officer was not inherently suspicious, but training and experience had turned him into a professional at his task, and he knew that a glance at a passport was not enough; one also had to examine its bearer. I tried to meet his eyes with a look of total boredom for a procedure that I frequently had to put up with in my travels as an established businessman. When I noted that his eyes moved downwards to assess my clothing and my hands (which might, indeed, have borne traces of manual labour on the kibbutz), I began to wonder whether I was suspect or his behaviour was truly no more than routine. It was then that I considered a smile of fellowship might be in order. We were, after all, two Englishmen far from home and in hostile territory. But before I could weigh the pros and cons of changing my approach, the mini-drama was over.

'Thank you, sir. Have a good stay.'

I dared not speak for fear of ruining it all. The bored Manchester businessman placed his passport back in his breast pocket and proceeded towards the gangway. I had passed.

(24)

A New Mission

I HAVE ALWAYS BLAMED the White Paper and Britain's policies for the friction between my eldest daughter and myself during the first year of our life together. When I finally returned home to the kibbutz, Dinah – born a few weeks before my departure nearly two years earlier – welcomed me warily. At first, she agreed to play with me a bit as I awkwardly tried to win her friendship, but when she realized that I was staying and infringing on her monopoly on her mother, she was not as sympathetic to the intruder, and it took time to overcome the tension between us.

The return to kibbutz life was far easier. After a few short de-briefings at headquarters, I once again settled down to the serene life of the Galilee, with my pair of mules, a cart and a scythe. My assignment was cutting alfalfa, which was used for fodder for our small herd of cows, Hanna's charges.

This bucolic work contrasted sharply, to say the least, with my recent activities in Europe. It is one of the basic tenets of the kibbutz that one should be available for all sorts of work, manual as well as political, skilled jobs or a 'stopper' – in kibbutz lingo, the not very desirable function of filling odd vacancies.

Barely one month after my return, the Mossad despatched the *Exodus* from France. The operation was carried out under Venya's brilliant leadership, and it was the largest boat ever. It was also the operation that opened the final chapter of the Mossad's struggle with the British.

The French port of Sète was chosen as the port of departure for the *Exodus*. Over 4,500 refugees from German camps had been assembled in villas along the picturesque coast and 200 lorries moved in orderly fashion toward the big ship. Aided by Mossad workers brought to France for this special occasion, the embarkation proceeded in perfect order.

The first incident occurred as embarkation was almost completed: strict orders from the French Foreign Office, conveyed through the Prefect of Marseilles, prohibited the ship's departure. British agents had worked as hard to prevent the sailing as the Mossad crew had laboured to get the ship away. Intervention through the overtaxed channels of the Mossad in Paris bore no fruit: the Quai d'Orsay was adamant.

So was the Mossad. Ike (Yitzchak Eran), the young captain of the huge ship, decided to weigh anchor and slip out of the port of Sète not only without official permission, but without the assistance of the pilot. He nearly missed his chance as he brushed the quay and the ship seemed to settle on a reef. But with the determination that distinguished the *Exodus* operation from beginning to end, Ike floated his ship and emerged into the open sea. There he was met by a most unwelcome reception committee: five British destroyers, led by the indefatigable *Ajax*, escorted the *Exodus* towards Palestine. A permanent accompaniment of Lancaster bombers flew overhead. For the British, this was to be a total effort to prevent the *Exodus* from reaching Palestine.

The Palmach commanders had prepared the stiffest possible resistance against British attempts to board the ship.

Nevertheless, when the British attacked 22 miles off the coast of Palestine, well outside territorial waters, the passengers were taken by surprise. In an unprecedented three-hour battle, in which the British used machine-guns and tear-gas freely, three immigrants were killed and many injured. But so were many of the British sailors who attempted to board the *Exodus*. Finally, the order to cease all opposition was given by Yossi Harel, the senior Haganah officer on board, when he realized that the warships had made holes in the wooden structure of the *Exodus*.

Exhausted and embittered, the ship's 4,500 passengers were tugged into Haifa harbour. All Jewish Palestine was in a state of uproar: everybody had been listening to the running reports about the battle on the clandestine Haganah radio network. By early next morning, the refugees were again at sea: this time in the infamous deportation cages of the navy vessels that shuttled new arrivals from the shores of Palestine to the detention camps on Cyprus. But suddenly it dawned on the prisoners that they were not being taken to the island. Now that the war against Hitler was over, the British Government had returned to its pre-war policy of sending the illegals back to their ports of departure. The Haganah, as well as the other two underground organizations, answered this act with a week of organized attacks on British targets.

Then, as the deportation ships arrived in French territorial waters, the British Labour Government realized – belatedly and with consternation – that their French neighbours wanted no part in this new policy: only those refugees who disembarked on French soil of their own free will would be allowed to do so. The exhortation of the Palmach commanders on board was hardly necessary: only three immigrants chose French hospitality.

But the height of British vengeance was yet to come. On 21 August the Labour Government announced that the passengers of the *Exodus* would be disembarked in Germany. A further announcement, which almost went unobserved in the midst of the uproar against the British and in support of the refugees, stated that the British soldiers would be armed only with truncheons (not with rifles) when they pushed the refugees out of the detention cages, and they were *not* being sent to the area of the Bergen-Belsen concentration camp. As the refugees descended from the British ships onto the German prison trains they remembered so well, Ernest Bevin, Britain's Foreign Secretary, cabled his victorious troops 'an expression of . . . personal appreciation'.

His was a pyrrhic victory. By his act Bevin had insured Zionist determination to fight to the end. Such changes do not take place overnight, and, indeed, it took almost five months after the uproar over the *Exodus* for the leadership to formulate a solid policy and give direction to the struggle.

I spent those five months in the fields of my kibbutz. But one November afternoon I was suddenly summoned to Ben Gurion's office. Three hours after receiving the urgent message on my alfalfa cart, I was standing opposite his desk in Jerusalem. Ben Gurion looked up from his notes and spoke with a gravity I had never before recognized in his voice.

'In a few days the United Nations will decide on the partition of Palestine. If the vote is favourable, there is bound to be war. The Arab members of the United Nations obstinately oppose the establishment of our state. Their armies will invade. If the United Nations comes to a negative decision, there will also be war: the Arabs will be emboldened by the anti-Zionist decision and attempt to push us into the Mediterranean.

'Much as I regret to tear you away from your family and your kibbutz so soon after your return, you must go to Europe again. On a short mission this time – to buy arms.'

He took a meticulously folded piece of paper out of his breast pocket and handed it to me. It contained, in six typewritten lines, one of the best-guarded secrets of the Haganah:

the list of arms we needed. Ben Gurion instructed the Haganah emissaries obtaining arms in Europe to collaborate with me. We were to change our methods: rather than continue to stuff a few rifles into agricultural machinery and send them to Palestine, we now had no time to lose and had to assume great risks. The arms had to come quickly and in the right quantities.

Ben Gurion's assistants arranged a flight for me on Swissair leaving the next morning. I went to spend the evening with Dani Shind, who was at the American Hotel in Tel Aviv, and phoned Hanna to tell her of my immediate departure. I was hardly dressed for a European business trip, but Dani lent me one of his shirts and an overcoat. Fortunately I had my passport, the Bible Hanna gave me when we were married and the copy of *Faust* I always take on trips.

The evening after my talk with Ben Gurion, I was already in Geneva meeting with Munya Mardor, head of the 'Rechesh' team – the Haganah unit responsible for arms acquisition. He received me graciously and, although he could not have been overjoyed by my arrival, he accepted my mission with the discipline that had become second nature for this Haganah officer and extended the facilities of his operation to me. I assured him that although I was given extraordinary authority and a million dollars waited for me in a Zurich bank, I was not planning to set up a parallel organization, but that I regarded myself as a member of his team.

From Geneva I went to Paris, for the one hard lead I had was that a leader of the Revisionist Party had informed Ben Gurion that a French friend of his had an offer of arms. I checked in at the Hotel California, next door to the Mossad office I knew so well, and contacted the French businessman. He turned out to be a disappointment: he simply had heard of someone who knew a man who might be able to put us in contact with someone who, in turn, could procure arms from a certain South American country.

Next, with the help of my Mossad colleagues, I lined up

several arms dealers and spoke to each in turn in my hotel
room. The results were nil. I listened more or less patiently
to many fascinating schemes, all based on the obvious fact
that we certainly needed arms for the coming showdown and
were probably ready and able to pay fabulous prices. The
intermediaries, fixers and *commissionaires* I met were all
prepared to take an advance of several thousand dollars –
and then try hard to find a suitable proposal. Ben Gurion's
grave voice droned in my ears throughout these futile meetings. I had no time to lose, and I was not getting anywhere.

When I shared my discouragement with my colleagues,
Yosef Ilan made a suggestion. Somewhat timidly, he proposed that I see just one more arms salesman: a Jew from
Rumania who worked for the reputable export-import firm of
Joseph Nash, and who claimed to know about arms. I was
not particularly impressed with these credentials. After some
of my prompting, Ilan revealed that this man, Robert Adam
by name, was his fixed supplier of tickets to the Ballet des
Champs-Élysées, of which Serge Lifar was at that time the
shining star. He had promised Adam that he would put me in
touch with him in return for the tickets he so kindly provided. As I was well aware that Ilan was an ardent balleto-
mane, I at least had to do him the small favour of wasting a
quarter of an hour on another *fata morgana*.

As soon as Robert Adam entered my room at the California, I sensed that the ballet tickets were not the only
difference between him and the others. My visitor put his
briefcase on the low table between us and took out two
catalogues of armaments produced by the famous Czech
arms factory at Brno. Without any preliminaries, Robert
Adam pointed out to me the rifles and machine-guns he
thought we would need. And in the self-assured tone of an
expert, he quoted prices and delivery dates that sounded like
hard facts and not the sweet and expensive tales I had heard
before.

Finding it hard to believe that these arms, the very items on the short list Ben Gurion had given me forty-eight hours before, were within reach, I asked Adam: 'What is the next step?'

From his inner pocket he drew two Air France tickets. 'I expected you to be interested. So I took the liberty of purchasing the tickets for our flight to Prague tomorrow morning.'

Now I was really impressed. 'Tell me where the hitch is, or is there really no problem in buying 10,000 rifles and millions of rounds of ammunition?'

'There is a major restriction on the purchase of those arms,' he replied as my heart sank. 'Arms can be bought only with the permission of the government that sells to another sovereign government. Private individuals cannot make arms deals of such magnitude. Since the Haganah is not such an official body, you will have to get official credentials from some sovereign nation.'

I phoned Ilan, who was waiting for my call at the Mossad office next door. 'Your man can get the items we need,' I told him, 'provided you have not messed up the remainder of poor Kiewski's stationery. Eight sheets should be in the right-side bottom drawer of my old desk in the office.' While I was holding on breathlessly, Ilan searched. We had the final link: the official stationery of country 'X'.

On the flight to Prague Robert Adam told me his story. Before the war he had been a young businessman in his native Rumania. Among other firms he represented there was the Czech armsworks at Brno. During the war he and his wife and a few friends bought a small yacht and sailed to Palestine. They were stopped by a British patrol boat, arrested and detained on Cyprus for the duration of the war. In 1945 Adam and his wife, Lili, settled in Tel Aviv. He tried to adapt himself to the new country, but, accustomed as he was to a more comfortable life, to more elegance, to thoroughbred horses and to the company of glamorous women, he found Tel Aviv too drab and the whole country too austere for his tastes. He had had enough of war; while Palestine was preparing for the showdown with the British and the Arabs, he wanted to resume his luxurious life. He left both his wife and Palestine.

'Had I been of stronger character, Ben Gurion would have sent me, an experienced arms salesman, on this mission rather than a greenhorn like you.'

Robert Adam and Joseph Nash, at that time business partners, never accepted a penny or even the smallest gift in return for the services they rendered to the Haganah. It was their way of expressing their feeling of responsibility for the fate of Jewish Palestine.

The representative of the Czech armsworks was at the airport to meet us. So was my friend Felix Doron, the Haganah man in Prague, who came with us in the black, official-looking limousine to the head office of Adam's business friends.

'Have we emerged from the underground?' Doron whispered to me in the car.

'I hope we have,' I replied. 'Otherwise we shall be wiped off the ground altogether.'

Less than an hour after we entered the offices of the Zbrojovka, Brno – permeated with an air of solid authority and reliable politeness – we had concluded the deal. Adam was at home in these offices; and the younger of the two Czech directors had been at school with Felix Doron, who was born in Prague and had left for Palestine just before the invasion of Czechoslovakia. The two sides in the negotiation understood each other perfectly.

Suddenly, two questions arose that seemed capable of snatching from us this unbelievable achievement: who was to buy the arms and how were they to be packed and identified? According to international procedure, the government purchasing arms was to import them in special crates bearing the likeness of a black serpent, the accepted identification of arms and explosives.

I produced the stationery that had been preserved in the Mossad office in Paris. Our Czech partners were delighted: just a couple of weeks ago they had sent a delegation to the capital of the same country to demonstrate their products. They had not yet received even the first report from their men. 'And here you are, flattering us with a huge order for our goods. Could there be a more auspicious indication of the quality of our production?' said the senior director whimsically.

The snake problem, too, found its solution. Our hosts, as eager to sell as we were to buy, agreed to Doron's suggestion that we place the original boxes into specially built crates. The serpent would be on the inner boxes for the sake of good order, yet it would not give away the contents by advertising itself to the British soldiers who might search the boat on which these crates would arrive in Palestine.

Doron and I rushed to the Czech Foreign Office with a letter of introduction to Jan Masaryk, the son of the founder of the Czech republic and then Czech Foreign Minister, as well as a warm friend of Zionism. When I telephoned his office from the armsworks, he agreed to see me at once. I explained the situation to Masaryk, who was visibly delighted that his country could help us and pleased that we were able to overcome 'technical difficulties'. He was certain that his communist deputy, Vlado Clementis, would likewise favour assisting our war effort. 'For me, it is enough that you defend yourself against your enemies. But Clementis will be happy to know that by fighting for your life you undermine British imperialism in the Middle East.'

Masaryk agreed to help us overcome the most immediate obstacle: we had the blank stationery of 'X's' Paris Embassy, but we did not know how to compose a proper letter of credentials. With obvious glee, Masaryk dictated the letter to his secretary, in the name of the ruler of 'X'. After she typed it, he signed it with a remarkably impressive signature that, on close inspection, turned out to be his own!

(25)

From Rescue Boats
to Gunboats

AS MY ARRIVAL in Prague was shrouded in secrecy, and I was
not allowed to tell anyone exactly why I had come, rumours
were bound to start. It was whispered among my Mossad
colleagues that I had been sent by Shaul Avigur with top-
secret orders to prepare for the disbanding of the Mossad's
clandestine immigration apparatus. As the United Nations
was scheduled to vote on the partitioning of Palestine into a
Jewish state and an Arab state in a few months' time, if the
vote decided in favour of this proposal, the British Mandate
over Palestine would end and Jewish immigration would be
free and open. Rather than deny these rumours, I found them
to be a valuable cover for my real activities. If British agents
became aware of my presence, they would think that I was
engaged in efforts conducive to their own interests. I found it
quite entertaining that my identity as a member of the
Mossad could be used as a cover for activities even more
'wicked' than straightforward 'illegal' immigration.

This long-established operation – the transport of immigrants – was now reaching unprecedented proportions. Even before the *Exodus* had met its fate, plans had begun for the shipment of no less than 15,000 persons. They were to be carried on what we proudly called our 'big ships' – the *Pan York* and the *Pan Crescent,* two transports bought in America.

Although my immediate assignment was arms smuggling, I naturally followed closely all developments surrounding our 'big ships' and, at certain points, I was even drawn into the operations. My own involvement was largely at the political level, for this was a time when repercussions of our activities on the high seas were resounding in the corridors of the UN. But while I was on the telephone to our diplomatic emissaries in connection with our 'big ships', my own tactical problems had more to do with a small ship called the *Nora,* which had nothing to do with immigration. But this was very much a period of parallel plans of persuasion and intrigue.

Both in order to foster the impression that I was here to disband the Mossad, as well as for reasons of simple nostalgia, I phoned Agami in Bucharest shortly after my arrival. He knew the real purpose of my presence in Prague and sounded happy to renew our telephone conversations, which had by then been going on – except for a few interruptions – for nearly ten years. Agami implored me to use my present activities as a pretext to phone Moshe Shertok in New York. Surely there was something I had to discuss with the head of the Political Department. Indeed there was. 'I have to keep in touch with him about the American embargo on arms to the Middle East and the danger that the United Nations might enlarge this embargo to include all member states,' I reassured Agami. The embargo would hit us rather than the Arabs, as they had regular, well-equipped armies with which to attack us.

Agami's need to communicate with Shertok had a different motive: the American Government was exerting heavy pressure on the Political Department to stop our 'big ships'. Agami knew that the British had alerted the Americans. Secretary of State Marshall had summoned Shertok, who was in the United States for the feverish negotiations at the United Nations. (He was working with a large team of Zionist diplomats and with the leaders of American Jewry to win over a majority of the member nations – a total of 57 at that time – and assure the two-thirds majority necessary for an affirmative vote on the partition proposal.) Secretary Marshall implored Shertok to hold up the huge transport from Rumania, which the British, and indeed the whole world, would interpret as Zionist provocation. In face of the strong British opposition, Marshall regarded the departures of the *Pan York* and the *Pan Crescent* as so grave an act of defiance that, he told Shertok, it was endangering the emergence of an independent Jewish state, as a majority of UN members would be so irritated by our massive provocation that they would undoubtedly vote against the partition proposal.

The American Embassy in Bucharest took the matter up with the Rumanian Foreign Minister, Anna Pauker, a communist in the coalition government prior to the complete communist take-over. A Jewess herself, Anna Pauker was nonetheless a virulent anti-Zionist. Her hostility against the Jewish struggle for national liberation was equalled only by her hatred for 'American imperialism'. Eager as she was to demonstrate that her loyalty to the Communist Party preceded her Jewish affinities, she was nonetheless outraged by the American intervention. Joseph Klarmann, Agami's colleague and a man whose diplomatic skill had faithfully served the Mossad ever since he arrived with Agami in newly liberated Rumania, provided Anna Pauker with a solution. He offered her an ingenious line, typically 'dialectic', that left her animosity against our Zionist aspirations intact and yet enabled her to decline the American invitation to cooperate with them against us. After her talk with Klarmann, Madame Pauker told the American Ambassador that there was no point in his intervention. The departure of Rumanian citizens was an internal affair, and there was nothing 'illegal' about it, as the American Ambassador had intimated. These people were returning to what they considered their homeland. Rebuffed by the Rumanian Government, the Americans continued to try their hand with our own representatives, and Shertok remained under growing pressure in the form of a latent threat that the sailing of the *Pan York* and *Pan Crescent* might bring about the retracting of American support for partition and consequently the establishment of the Jewish State.

Agami was obviously worried by the increasingly urgent appeals from Shertok to stop the ships. The Chief needed only a moment to make up his mind. He gave Agami his full support and tried as best he could to convince Shertok that he was understandably, yet hopelessly, demanding the impossible. The Mossad could under no circumstances stop the momentum of over 15,000 men, women and children on their way towards the ships. Still, Agami wanted me to put in a word and help halt the flow of warnings and of stern messages he was receiving.

I listened to Agami's outburst and understood his consternation. Finally I had a chance to put in a word. 'I'm in a similar mess for quite different reasons. My problem is that I have the merchandise but I have no tent [the old code word for ship] to put it into. What chapter of the Bible do you read in a case like this?'

'I admit that I haven't worried about your troubles,' Agami replied. 'But I am reading Isaiah 60, which suits my purpose perfectly. I suggest you use the same text – it may also solve your problem: "Therefore your gates shall be open continually, they shall not be shut day or night." '

The Chief was quite satisfied with reports from Bucharest.

Agami had slowly gathered a group of the most seasoned escorts, radio-operators, Palyam commanders and youth leaders. Yossi Harel was in overall command. Ike was to be the captain in charge of the two boats. With them were veterans of the largest and most daring operations the Mossad had ever organized. After all, this was to be the Mossad's crowning achievement. Who had ever thought of organizing 15,000 immigrants at one stroke? In fact the entire Mossad was in a state of full alert. Even our people in Italy were loyally supporting the tremendous effort.

The *Pan Crescent* had been fitted in Venice; and although it was discovered by British agents and sabotaged by a mine that exploded mysteriously in the engine-room, Ada Sereni's people in Venice had given Benyamin all the help he needed when he arrived there to salvage the ship and to float her. Under British pressure, the Italians refused fuel to the *Pan Crescent* when she was on her way to Rumania. With the last drop in her huge tanks, she arrived in the waters of Constantsa. The Black Sea (which actually takes its name from being 'black' to mariners and their ships) suddenly whipped up such a storm that the ship could not enter the harbour for it was infested with floating mines. With more luck than they had a right to expect, the Palyam sailors navigated the *Pan Crescent* through the minefield at night, and she joined her sister-ship, the *Pan York,* which had preceded her by a few days.

Ya'akov Salomon, a senior Palmach commander, had organized the immense operation of getting the 15,000 refugees from all over the vast territory of Rumania into special trains that arrived methodically at the port. Then the Rumanian Government suddenly changed its mind: the immigrants would be allowed to leave as agreed, but the embarkation could not take place in Rumania! Sheyke and Benyamin flew to Sofia, knowing that the Bulgarian Government had always been friendly towards our cause. They per-

mitted the unforeseen transfer of the two 'big boats' from
Constantsa to the Bulgarian port of Varna. And under the
spell of Sheyke's irresistible powers of persuasion, they even
agreed to break a sacred rule: a number of Bulgarian youths
would be allowed to join the Rumanian immigrants.

The embarkation of the two *Pans* took two and a half
days. Like clockwork the passengers came on board already
organized in groups of fifty, accompanied by a group leader,
doctors and nurses. Those who were witness to the departure
will always remember the elation that prevailed as the two
boats began to move, the *Crescent* leading. Under the cloud
of an uncertain future and the prospect of dangers ahead, the
15,000 men, women and children burst into a ringing rendi-
tion of *Hatikva*.

Under persistent pressure from governments associated
with the tense situation in the Middle East and warned of the
dire consequences of the 'provocative sailing' of the two big
boats, the Jewish Agency felt constrained to produce some
sort of a 'gesture of goodwill' towards our 'well-wishers' and,
immediately after the *Pans* had moved out of Bulgarian
territorial waters, grudgingly agreed to a British-proposed
compromise. Rather than approach the coast of Palestine
and be transferred – in a bloody confrontation – to British
deportation ships, the refugees would sail directly to Cyprus.

Much later Yossi Harel gave me the minutes of the signals
exchanged between the commander of the convoy and the
commander of a British naval escort of three destroyers and
two battle cruisers that attached themselves to the *Pan York*
and *Pan Crescent* as soon as they had passed through the
Dardanelles. It is a remarkable document: an Admiral of the
Royal Navy, commanding a considerable force of warships,
negotiating with the 'Admiral' of the largest 'Mossad fleet'
ever to take to the seas over the smooth and non-violent
change of course from the land of promise to an island of
detention. In the end, the 15,000 passengers of the two big

ships joined the thousands of refugees who had already been interned in the Cyprus camps and remained there until the abolition of the 1939 White Paper with the Declaration of the State of Israel.

While the drama of the *Pan York* and *Pan Crescent* was being played out on two continents, we had simultaneously acquired our arms with surprising speed. But the search for a suitable ship to transport them turned out to be more difficult than expected. The Mossad had none available: had there been one, it would have been turned over to us, for at that moment arms took priority over people. Shipping agents were wary of doing business with Palestine because the increasing violence in the area made war seem imminent.

As in so many difficult situations, I once again turned to Benyamin and asked him to buy a small ship immediately at any cost. Assured of the necessary funds and authority, he was optimistic at first. This time there was no need for protracted discussions with a crew in order to convince them to take illegal refugees. This time they would carry ordinary cargo, silent boxes, dead wood.

Benyamin finally found what he was looking for in the lobby of an elegant Venice hotel. A man was loudly talking Hebrew on the phone, and Benyamin could not help overhear him speaking of a consignment of thread that he wanted to ship urgently from Italy to Palestine. Benyamin put his heavy hand on the shoulder of the fellow-Palestinian, sensing that he was in the presence of one who knew how to secure items in short supply. He invited his new acquaintance to have a drink, and they soon concluded a deal. Ephraim Elin, the textile manufacturer, agreed to collaborate with Benyamin, who had not yet explained his intentions in detail.

Several weeks later, Benyamin was able to report that he had purchased a small steamship called the *Nora,* along with an agreeable crew. The original boxes bearing the serpents were packed into larger crates. From the various alternatives open to landlocked Czechoslovakia, we chose the Yugoslav route, as we were well acquainted with the Yugoslav authorities from joint exploits in illegal immigration and trusted their understanding. This was no time for experiments. I went to Belgrade for a talk with our official friends there and found them ready to do everything necessary to facilitate our task. When they learned that we were covered by a destination outside the tense Middle East, they were visibly relieved. The United Nations was debating a general embargo on the conflict area, so it was helpful that our arms were ostensibly going to 'X', in a quite different direction.

From the diplomatic point of view, things were set. But time was going by and no arms shipment had yet taken place. I was receiving urgent messages from Ben Gurion several times every day and sensed how desperate the situation was at home. So I decided to go to Venice and impress my feeling of urgency on Benyamin and Elin. But as soon as Benyamin and I arrived – in a romantic gondola – at the hotel where Ephraim Elin was waiting, I realized my trip had not been necessary.

Trade with Palestine, Benyamin reminded me, had come to nearly a complete standstill. In the early winter of 1948 there was, in fact, only one firm left doing normal business: the government-owned 'Steel Brothers'. Other activities had been suspended with the expectation of war. The problem was how to equip and load a boat, in view of the very well-known fact that only the large ships of the 'Steel Brothers' were now plying between Europe and Palestine. British agents were in every European port, particularly in Italy, where the British were more welcome than in France. The command of wisdom was to make haste slowly, Elin explained. He was the type to whom slowness was anathema, for he was bursting with energy and drive, so his analysis sounded convincing to me. But the question still remained: when would we get the *Nora* going?

Benyamin and Elin were certain they were doing the right thing. I could not move them to less cautious, faster action. They presently were loading onions on the *Nora:* a ship could not lay at harbour doing nothing at all without arousing suspicion. Besides, Benyamin planned to unload the onions in Yugoslavia and then cover the arms with them once they had been put on board. 'Let the British stick their bayonets into a mountain of onions covering the real merchandise,' Benyamin said. 'Those who don't faint outright will certainly not be able to search for hidden arms.'

When I returned to Prague a message from Ben Gurion was waiting for me: 'If you cannot send the arms you have bought by sea, send them by air. If this, too, is impossible, at least return to Palestine yourself.' In despair, I approached the Czech Government for permission to bring foreign planes to a secluded airfield, load our arms and fly them to their destination. The Czech authorities agreed, and the military airfield at Szatec, in the Sudeten region, was put at our disposal.

Although we enjoyed unqualified public support and President Truman expressed his sympathy for the survivors of the Holocaust and for the establishment of a Jewish state in part of Palestine, other, less friendly forces were at work in the United States. A strict embargo on arms and military equipment was enforced, and the State Department made tireless efforts to change the US attitude and make it more accommodating to the British Government's anti-Zionist approach. The Secretary of State even considered the proposed establishment of a Jewish state a grave mistake.

Conditions for the work of a Haganah team under Teddy Kollek in the United States were completely different from those in friendly Czechoslovakia. Yet, with the invaluable help of Jewish volunteers in every field, this team did wonders. The acquisition of aircraft under strict and hostile supervision was one of them. As soon as the Czech military authorities opened Szatec airfield to the Haganah, we asked our people in New York to send planes, pilots and mechanics to our base.

In a matter of days the first DC-4's arrived. With them came a gay and unruly crowd of adventurous, yet completely dedicated pilots who had won their laurels in the recent war. Some had returned to normal civilian life, but the call for volunteers for the Haganah brought them out of their routine and back to the dangers of air force life. In the austere atmosphere of post-war Czechoslovakia, with little food, no luxuries and political upheavals looming large, the arrival of an unself-conscious group of laughing American airmen – in mufti, of course – was a fact hard to conceal.

One of the new arrivals from Palestine was Yehudah Ben Chorin. During the war he had been the commander of a special unit consisting of tall, blond Palmach soldiers trained to work behind enemy lines in case Germany overpowered the British in the African desert and took Palestine. Most of the parachutists who had operated behind enemy lines were drawn from Yehudah's unit. Yehudah had joined us as an expert on German arms of the type the Czech armsworks were still producing. Now he was needed in an additional capacity. A born leader of men, he took upon himself the integration of the 'crazy American kids', as the volunteers modestly described themselves.

It soon became evident that the planes at our disposal could not fly non-stop with a full load from the Sudeten region to Palestine. I phoned the Mossad in Paris, and Venya obtained from our French friends permission to refuel at the airport of Ajaccio, the birthplace of Napoleon, on Corsica.

'Operation Balak' was small in volume. But the arrival of arms by air had an important psychological effect on the morale of the Haganah troops who were fighting with too few arms and rationed ammunition. It also prepared the way for the transfer of the first military aircraft to the Haganah.

Yet, the airlift of arms in limited amounts and the rise in morale were not enough to win, or even contain, the undeclared war that had broken out in Palestine even before the official proclamation of a Jewish state in May. And they would certainly not suffice if, as anticipated, the regular armies of Palestine's Arab neighbours would invade the newborn state upon its achievement of independence. More urgent cables had arrived from Palestine asking for a definite date for the arrival of the *Nora,* and bad news from the battlefronts had led to disconcerting noises at the United Nations, where the approaching end of the British Mandate created defeatism among some of our supporters. There were rumours that the United States was debating the possibility of retracting her stand in favour of partition and was going to support a proposal for a United Nations Trusteeship to replace the British Mandate.

A cold wind was attacking the windows of my room at the Esplanade in Prague as Doron and I waited anxiously for Benyamin's call from Belgrade. At long last the phone rang. It was Benyamin, all right, but he didn't 'sound right'.

'I have finished my preparations for loading here, and I must go to Venice to fetch the *Nora.* But I can't get out!' he whined in frustration. 'I am not in jail – God forbid! This is friendly territory. It's the Italians who refuse to let me return to Venice.'

In view of the forthcoming elections, the issue of Italian visas had been completely suspended to keep any undesirable foreigners out of the country on the eve of a decisive confrontation between the republican parties and the communists.

'I'll be with you shortly,' I told Benyamin. I put a few things into a bag and Doron rushed me to the airport.

The Italian Vice-Consul in Belgrade was a friend. He had often helped us with hard-to-obtain visas in the past, and we were sending food parcels to his aged mother in Calabria in return for his kindness. I decided to pick up Benyamin and see him at once. The Vice-Consul was dreadfully sorry, but this time, much as he would like to, he simply could not help. Orders were unequivocal: until election day on 18 April, there were no visas to Italy for any nationality that required them. Palestinians had been emphasized in this instruction, not in the context of supporting communist candidates at the elections, but for being involved in all sorts of 'undesirable infringements of public order' (echoes of La Spezia perhaps?). There was a loophole, though. He had spoken of 'all passports that required visas'; American and British passports were exempt. Regrettably we held neither.

Benyamin and I almost fell over each another in our hasty farewell and raced from the Vice-Consul's office directly to Belgrade airport. 'We shall arrive in Italy at least one hour before we would have reached there with the Vice-Consul's precious stamp in our passports,' I ventured as we purchased air passage via Zurich to Marseilles to pay a visit to the 'nurses' at 'The Studio'.

Remembering Phileas Fogg, we asked the polite partisan who acted as chief steward in the Yugoslav Dakota to cable Zurich airport and request that Swissair delay the departure of their Nice-bound flight sufficiently for the two of us – passengers without luggage – to catch it. The Swiss kindly promised to wait. As the Côte d'Azur appeared beneath our plane, Benyamin and I prepared for the mad rush in a hired cab to Bandole, about two hours from the airport.

Luckily we found our 'nurses' at the laboratory. Breathlessly we explained the urgent need for British passports so that we could enter Italy. Proficient as always, but without undue haste, they went calmly about their work. In less than two hours we were both properly fitted with British passports, in which only our photographs and the facsimile of Ernest Bevin's signature were genuine.

Again we hired a cab to get us to the only train crossing into Italy that night. During the short ride we discussed a serious problem: Benyamin was fluent in five languages – including Armenian – but English was not one of them. At that stage, he hardly knew the difference between 'yes' and 'no'. We decided to buy all the available English newspapers before boarding the train, to look for seats in a compartment with Latin-looking passengers and for Benyamin to keep his mouth shut as much as possible.

The train thundered into the station as the loudspeaker announced a halt of three minutes only. We ran along the train, which to our utter disgust consisted of filled sleeping-cars with only a single coach for seated passengers. As we walked through the narrow corridor, we scanned its compartments for two empty seats. The train was already moving when we discovered the compartment we had been looking for: just two elderly passengers, obviously French *rentiers*. We made our entry with all the dignity we could muster after our hurried search, and each relaxed in a corner next to the door. Benyamin, according to plan, brought out his English newspapers and buried himself in them.

Then the 'French' *rentier* turned to Benyamin with an angelic smile. 'How fortunate to find a fellow Britisher with this morning's London papers,' he chirped to his equally enchanted wife. 'I beg your pardon, sir, but may I borrow one of your papers?'

Benyamin was saved from embarrassment – and worse – by the arrival of the frontier-control guard.

'We are all British,' the elderly gentleman announced happily. The frontier guards contented themselves with a superficial look at our distinguished passports, without even bothering to open them. Then I gave all our papers, except the one Benyamin was 'reading', to our British neighbours.

We alighted at Turin and hired a cab to Milan, giving the driver the address of the hotel where the Chief used to stay. We knew that Avigur was here, co-ordinating some of Yehudah Arazi's arms purchases.

'Major Morley Morris of the CID here for you, Sir, in the

company of another gentleman, Sir,' I announced myself to the Chief in the crispest English I could command. In one of his rare moments of good humour, he at once adjusted to the situation.

'Two gentlemen altogether,' he said in his heavily accented English. 'Never mind, come straight up to my room. I'm ready for the likes of you.'

First we called the railway station. The train from Belgrade, on which we would have arrived had we had proper Italian visas, was delayed and was due in a couple of hours. The Chief enjoyed the story of our adventure. But he became his earnest self again as we began to discuss the departure of the *Nora.* He objected to 'putting all our eggs into one basket' and suggested that we break the consignment, now safely in the Yugoslav port, into several parts so we would not lose the entire arsenal if the *Nora* were caught.

I objected. My orders from Ben Gurion were to send the whole lot as soon as humanly possible. We could not waver. If a part of the weapons got by the blockade, what proof was there that the next part would also get by; and if they reached the receiving team of the Haganah, only a portion of the available armament would be in their hands. If, however, we lost even the whole shipment, all we had to do was to buy the same quantity, or more, and send them off in a ship that would likewise be exposed to British scrutiny. So it was only a question of saving some money, not of ensuring a safe way to transport arms. And my clear instructions were not to economize. If we survived the Arab onslaught, what was another million dollars? And what was another million dollars if we did not? The Chief pondered the argument and knowing that I quoted Ben Gurion's exact words, waived his restrictions.

Benyamin took leave. He was on his way to Backa once more, this time via Venice aboard the *Nora.*

The Yugoslav port authorities were alerted by the security

police, and a detachment of German prisoners of war rein-forced the team of stevedores who had been waiting for the order to load the *Nora*. So concerned was the security police with the safety of the precious cargo that the partisan officer in charge resorted to a cunning trick: he emptied one of the crates containing rifle ammunition and filled it with innocent screws. The port worker specially entrusted with the handling of this particular crate let it slip and fall on the quay, where it broke open and everybody present could see for themselves that the cargo being so urgently loaded contained nothing more than harmless metalware. Just before the *Nora* was weighing anchor, the security officer approached Benyamin with a heavy bundle on his back. He was returning the bullets he had removed to make the loading operation appear totally innocuous.

The *Nora* began her voyage with 10,000 rifles, two and a half million rounds of ammunition and 500 machine-guns. The arms were well hidden by Elin's onions from the eyes of curious inspection, and a load of planks on her deck gave the little boat the air of a peaceful expedition in a serene spring sea. Before her departure we had decided that she should keep complete radio silence until her arrival in Palestine. The radio-operator had been selected with great care. Benyamin's old friend from several voyages with illegal immigrants, Avraham Linchovsky, reluctantly accepted the order to keep his radio shut. But he was able to prove his worth in other ways.

On the third day of the trip the weather changed suddenly and one of the worst storms in Benyamin's memory broke out over the Mediterranean. The *Nora* fought valiantly against tall waves, and Benyamin saw her swallow vast quantities of fuel without progressing an inch. During a short lull in the raging storm, Benyamin decided to seek shelter in a nearby bay. Too late, he discovered the familiar silhouette of two British warships that had done exactly the same. He could not retreat without arousing suspicion, so he decided to play the game to its very end. As he slowly worked the *Nora* into the narrow bay, he aimed at the space between the two British men-of-war for her to drop anchor. Avraham reminded him of naval protocol: unblinkingly he lowered the Italian flag atop the *Nora* to comply with maritime courtesy, by which a merchant ship always salutes a battleship, whatever the nationality. As befits the brotherhood of sailors in distress, the British captains lowered the Union Jack in deference to the little Italian. Then the three of them prepared for the long watch through the stormy night.

As the storm abated, the *Nora* continued on its way in the wake of the faster battleships, which, as it turned out, were heading in the same direction, for the coast of Palestine, where they were apparently on blockade-duty.

As Benyamin steered his little ship into the port of Tel Aviv, he was surprised by the absence of the customary Haganah disembarkation team. His radio silence may have saved the *Nora* from discovery, but it had also helped to guard her secret from the Haganah, which so eagerly expected the cargo. When he finally established contact with the worried commander, who had vainly expected some signal of the *Nora*'s impending arrival, he realized that he had brought the Czech weapons just in the nick of time. They were unloaded not by the specialized team alone; the soldiers who were on their way to the decisive battle for the road to Jerusalem were brought to the harbour to speed up the operation. Their joy, as they eyed the crates, was boundless. Each man was issued a brand new rifle, and for the first time they had enough ammunition. To their consternation, though, they realized that they had nothing in which to carry their new treasures. The Palmach commander ordered his soldiers to take off their socks and fill them with cartridges.

Twenty-four hours after the *Nora* arrived, the Palmach started 'Operation Nachshon', the strike at the highway from Tel Aviv to Jerusalem.

Ayala Ironi, the wife of the Haganah's shipping expert, who offered Benyamin hospitality in her Tel Aviv flat, looked at the young captain in bafflement.

'How can it be,' she exclaimed, 'that one young man can change the total history of an entire people?'

Benyamin was given one day to visit his family on their kibbutz and then was on his way for further arms shipments out of Yugoslavia's promising coast.

Six weeks after the *Nora* landed, 14 May 1948, was a working day in Prague, like any other. But the Mossad and Haganah operators gathered in my room at the Esplanade were in a state of high tension. Was Independence to be declared today, the last day of the British Mandate? One had an acute sense of *déjà vu* thinking back to that 'Black Saturday' in June 1946, when a similar group had gathered in Ben Gurion's hotel suite in Paris and awaited incoming cables with such anxiety. The messages arriving on the familiar light-blue forms were sober and routine: the *Borea* had been released by the British; send another 450 heavy machine-guns on the first available plane; why had the Palyam escort who was supposed to take a ship from Backa not reported his safe arrival? Late in the afternoon, the operator came into the room again, this time his face beaming. He waved the light-blue form high above his head, and I grabbed it with total impatience. The message read:

David Ben Gurion proposed at a special session of the Constitutional Assembly meeting in the Hall of the Tel Aviv Museum the Declaration of Independence. By unanimous decision, a Jewish State will come into existence at midnight, when the British Mandate expires. The British White Paper of 1939 has been declared null and void. Every Jew wishing to return to his homeland is free to do so.

I asked the telephone operator of the Esplanade Hotel to connect me with Agami in Bucharest. 'Try to get him fast,' I said, and added – a bit prematurely – 'This is an official government call!'

During the ten years I had been talking to Agami on the phone, he had never answered as quickly as he did then. His voice was a little less reserved than usual. Obviously, he had just received the same message, which had been flashed to all Haganah posts abroad.

'So you didn't prevent the establishment of a Jewish state, after all, *even* with your irresponsible thrust of a multitude of "illegal" immigrants?' I teased him.

'No wonder the results were right,' he answered in the same spirit. 'I take it you recited the chapter from Isaiah that I recommended . . .'

'And how!'

Index

Abba Berditchev, the (formerly *Agia Anastasia*), 301–302
Abramovsky, Leibl, 241–245, 246–247, 294, 297–298, 301
Achdut Ha'avodah, 206
Adam, Robert, 332–334
Agami, Moshe, 17, 29–30, 31–32, 36, 64, 90, 301, 321; Austrian emigration work of, 36–38, 42–47, 51–56, 58–59, 61, 66, 70–73, 75–76, 92, 93, 100, 101–102; expulsion from Vienna, 72–74, 78; Gestapo interrogation of, 69–71; in Istanbul, 143, 158–161, 170; in liberated Bucharest, 192–193, 197, 338–339, 340, 353–354
Agence Maritime Internationale (fictitious organization), 320, 321
Agia Anastasia, the. *See Abba Berditchev, the*
Agricultural immigrants, 16, 25
"Agricultural Training Abroad," emigration channel, 16
Agricultural training camps. *See* Farm training camps
Air craft procurement, Haganah, 345–346
Air Transport Command, American, 249, 250
Ajax, H.M.S., 226–227, 325, 328
Akbel, the, 293–395
Aleppa, Syria, meeting on Eichmann "deal" at, 182, 183–185
Alexianu, Professor, 130
Aliev, Ruth, 85, 87, 93, 108, 133, 247, 251–254, 289

Alkalay, David, 239, 240, 243–244, 245, 247
Allied Control Commission, 191, 193
Allies, Western: attitude toward issue of "Final Solution," 166–167, 188–189; Eichmann "deal" for Hungarian Jews offered to, 177, 179–180, 182–188; and liberation efforts for their POW's in Germany, 114, 158; suspected by Soviets of separate deal with Nazis, 180, 186, 188; tension with Soviet Union, 204
American Federation of Labor, 19
American Joint Distribution Committee, 100
American pilots, in Haganah service, 346
American War Refugee Board, 167–168
Amnon (commander of *Knesset Yisrael*), 302–305
Anglo-American Inquiry Commission for Palestine, 276
Angriff, Der (Nazi newspaper), 66, 67
Anilewitz, Mordechai, 157
Anna, the. *See Knesset Yisrael*, the
Anschluss, 3, 8, 13, 20, 41, 162
Anti-Comintern pact, 9
Anti-Semitism, 199; in Austria, 9, 10, 14; in Hungary, 152; in Italy, 105; Nazi, 12, 14, 21, 27; in Poland, 13, 26, 32; in Rumania, 13, 130; in Yugoslavia, 68

Ehud Avriel

Ehud Avriel was born in Vienna, Austria, in 1917. Zionism was the central theme of his upbringing. He joined the ranks of the Zionist-Socialist youth movement and when Nazi Germany annexed Austria in 1938 he found himself among the organizers of escape and rescue operations. World War II had already started when he himself was able to reach Palestine. There he helped to found a kibbutz in Galilee where he and his family live to this day.

Mr. Avriel became one of the central figures in the Haganah, the Jewish resistance movement. In Europe and Turkey during the war and in liberated Europe immediately after the allied victory, he was involved in illegal immigration and the purchase of arms for Israel's War of Independence in 1948.

He became Israel's first fully fledged Ambassador (to Prague); he headed the Prime Minister's Office under David Ben Gurion, the Treasury under Levi Eshkol, and was in charge of African Affairs and International Cooperation when Golda Meir was Foreign Minister. He served his country as Ambassador in various capitals, most recently in Rome, Italy.